AF598000

Traces of Words

Art and Calligraphy from Asia

Traces of Words

Edited by FUYUBI NAKAMURA

With contributions by ALAIN GEORGE • APRIL LIU

ADHEESH SATHAYE • YUEHPING YEN

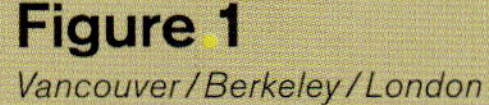

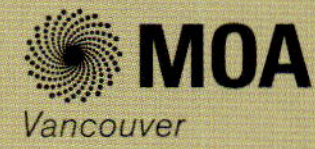

Copyright © 2017 by Museum of Anthropology at UBC
Texts copyright © 2017 by individual contributors

17 18 19 20 21 5 4 3 2 1

Published in conjunction with the exhibition *Traces of Words: Art and Calligraphy from Asia,* organized by the Museum of Anthropology at UBC and curated by Fuyubi Nakamura. Exhibition schedule: Museum of Anthropology at UBC, May 11 to October 9, 2017; satellite exhibition at the Irving K. Barber Learning Centre at UBC, May 1 to 31, 2017.

All rights reserved. No part of this book may be reproduced, stored in a retrieval system, or transmitted, in any form or by any means, without the prior written consent of the publisher or a licence from the Canadian Copyright Licensing Agency (Access Copyright). For a copyright licence, visit www.accesscopyright.ca or call toll-free to 1-800-893-5777.

Cataloguing data available from Library and Archives Canada
ISBN 978-1-927958-90-2 (hbk.)

Design by Jessica Sullivan
Typesetting by Natalie Olsen
Editing by Grace Yaginuma
Copy editing by Lesley Cameron
Proofreading by Lana Okerlund

Jacket images: Front, Kimura Tsubasa, *Outline* (detail), 2007, *Sumi* ink on faille fabric. Courtesy of the artist. See pages 100–101 for a full image. Photo: Fuyubi Nakamura. Back, Leaf from a Qur'an manuscript in Kufic script, 9th century, vellum and ink. MOA collection, 2988/1. See page 41 for more information. Photo: Kyla Bailey.

For the measurements of artworks and objects, height precedes width precedes depth.

Printed and bound in China by 1010 Printing International, Ltd.
Distributed in the U.S. by Publishers Group West
Distributed outside of North America by Prestel Publishing

Figure 1 Publishing Inc.
Vancouver BC Canada
www.figure1pub.com

Museum of Anthropology at UBC
6393 N.W. Marine Drive
Vancouver BC Canada V6T 1Z2
www.moa.ca

Contents

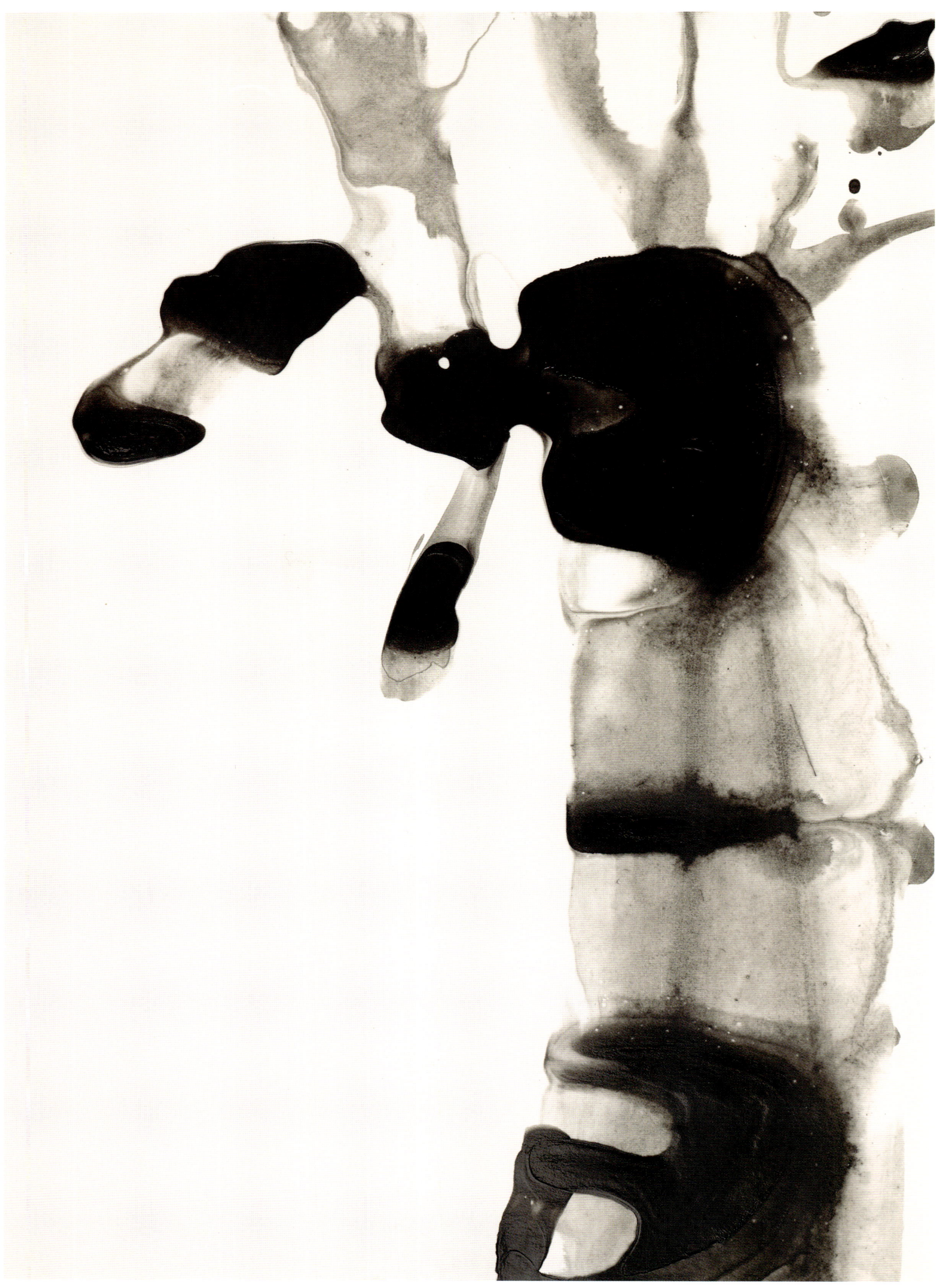

Foreword

ANTHONY ALAN SHELTON

◂ **YUGAMI HISAO**
***Se* 背 (Back)** 2008
Sumi ink on Kent paper
29.5 × 21 cm
MOA COLLECTION, 31186/1

CALLIGRAPHY CAN BE DEFINED as the art of fusing words and images using prescribed techniques and practices that are embedded in a set of cultural beliefs and values. Its uniqueness rests on its formal, social, and cultural characteristics, and despite its erasure by industrialization, globalization, and the adoption of Latin alphabets in most of Europe, it continues to be ubiquitous throughout Asia. The origins of different systems and schools of calligraphy are often closely associated with the inscription of religious beliefs and teachings. Vedic Sanskrit, Arabic, Latin, and Hebrew are all sacred languages through which divinity becomes manifest. The development of Sanskrit is entwined with the Vedas and the *Mahābhārata*; Arabic script with the Qur'an; and the Persian Avestan alphabet with the holy book of Zarathustra, the Avesta. Elsewhere, civilizations including the Sumerians and Semites attributed creation to the word of God; Egyptians believed in a god of the word; and the Greek doctrine of *logos* postulated that the essence of things resided in their names.[1] While many schools of calligraphy have close religious and metaphysical associations, their influence has also had a much broader impact on the material and visual culture of the near and far east.

Calligraphy is fundamental to Persian and Islamic architecture and, in some cases, garden design: script embellishes wooden doors, porcelain, earthenware, ceramic tiles, glass, and metalwork. Across Asia, calligraphy appears as decorative elements in carpet weaving and bookbinding. Locally, calligraphy's varied techniques, styles, and notations define an array of written media, while globally, it provides the signatures of international brands such as Al Jazeera and the Emirates airline.

Non-alphabetical writing systems have long been underestimated and undervalued in Western thought, and despite their present-day familiarity, they continue to be inadequately appreciated. The philosopher Rousseau, in his 1781 *Essai sur l'origine des langues*, divided languages into three categories, which he correlated with different stages of civilization. Notably, he distinguished oral cultures with their underdeveloped or non-existent notational systems from those cultures that had developed writing systems, which he believed were the mark of civilized society.[2] However, one must not disregard oral cultures as having been fundamental to the development of many written cultures in Asia, as discussed by Alain George (chapter 3) and Adheesh Sathaye (chapter 4). Neither oral nor written cultures can be attributed greater value than the other.

In formal terms, calligraphy is unable to privilege either its linguistic or its pictorial function. This is not to say that the relationship between meaning and form is identical in all calligraphic systems.

Calligraphy functions both linguistically as a refined notational system and potentially as an abstract composition—and in doing so, it constantly tests the limits of legibility and formal abstraction. This ambiguity gives calligraphy its poetic freedom, which more than denoting a specific state or condition, evokes and presages it, enabling it to take on a life of its own. In extreme cases calligraphy's communicative quality can even dissolve, as exemplified by the interactive digital calligraphy work by teamLab.

The indeterminacy and ambiguity generated by calligraphy provide the creative locus through which meaning is potentially transformed and propagated. This can mean experimenting with inscription's formal composition and application. Contemporary Afghan, Tibetan, Thai, Japanese, and Chinese artists—such as Shamsia Hassani, Nortse, Phaptawan Suwannakudt, Yugami Hisao, the members of teamLab, and Song Dong (discussed in this book)—have exploited this openness by combining calligraphy with sculpture, performance, installation art, and digital media. The incessant flicker between form and content, abstraction and intelligibility, and earthly existence and divinity makes calligraphy a way to generate a vision of a reality radically different from the one made up of dualisms, classificatory logic, and the logocentrism inherent to Western phonetic writing. For the philosopher Jacques Derrida, graphic forms like calligraphy can never be understood from their "intention of signification or of denotation, but of style and connotation."[3] This and the articulation of substances (inks, paints, minerals) and instruments (pens, brushes) with the fixity and sense of style are crucial in appreciating its uniqueness.

Calligraphy is also a socially embedded practice. In China and elsewhere, calligraphers follow culturally specific rules for comportment and audience engagement. Its technical procedures are strictly codified, and protocols govern the distribution, presentation, and reading of texts. Moreover, how calligraphic practices are institutionalized, whether by a religious institution or by institutions connected to art or commercial markets, further marks calligraphy's social specificity. Efficacy and agency are also factors in the bodily performance and technical manipulations of the calligrapher. A practitioner's state of consciousness and heightened awareness, the carefully modulated movement and speed of the brush strokes, the delicate changes in the pressure exerted on the flow of ink, and the handling of the instrument—sometimes considered as an extension of their body—infuse a human essence into the body of their work.

For Derrida, this type of "non-phonetic writing breaks the noun apart. It describes relations, not appellations. The noun and the word, these unities of breath and concept are effaced within pure writing."[4] To presuppose the existence of the pure word, independent of its means of inscription, endows the writing with life and lends it a transcendental reality; in the Islamic tradition, writing is conjugated with the perfection of ideograms, geometry, and algebra that allude to divinity. Derrida does not deny that pictograms can also be endowed with phonetic, sound-making qualities but agrees that such qualities never efface their pictographic references. The signifier is broken into a system of differences where the thing is part of a chain of things, while sound is inscribed into a chain of sounds. Graphic systems encourage metaphor, which, unlike Western writing, supposedly allows civilizations to grow outside of logocentrisms.[5]

Critiquing the privileged position of Western alphabetical writing, Derrida characterizes it as "the carrier of death" because it always signifies the absence of the speaker.[6] In place of the speaker is the logos, a transcendentally constituted reason derived from language; calligraphy and graphic languages escape these numbing constraints. Alphabetical writing opens the field of history, which is then projected back on itself to create its own logocentric self-imagination. Calligraphy, in contrast, free of the need for fidelity to phonetics, alludes to eternity. Certain Buddhist texts are themselves holy objects that can transmit virtue and offer protection. The radical difference between writing and calligraphy calls into question the supposed universality of a large body of logocentric assumptions, which have long structured and stabilized modern Western consciousness: language and speech; intelligence and nonsense; cosmos and chaos; divinity and secularism; spiritual embodiment and materialism; passivity and agency; and history and eternity. *Traces of Words: Art and Calligraphy from Asia* introduces works and techniques from different periods and places that offer a different lens through which to imagine the world.

จักรวาฬ และโลกันตนรกนั้นอยู่นอกกำแพงจักรวาฬไส้ อยู่ห
เขาจักรวาฬภายนอกเรานี้จึงบ่มิได้เห็นหนไส้เพื่อดังนั้นแล
เพราะว่าเดือนและตะวันมิได้ส่องไปได้เพราะว่าปลายเขายุคน
นั้นเห็นหนทางเดือนตะวันส่องไปนั้นแหละถ้าและว่าต่อเมื่
โพธิสัตว์ผู้จะลงมาอุบัติตรัสสัพพัญญุตญาณนั้นและ
ท่านเสด็จลงเอาปฏิสนธิในครรภ์พระมารดานั้นก็ดี และเมื่อท่าน
ภพจาตุโกรรธนั้นก็ดี แลเมื่อพระพุทธเจ้าตรัสแก่สัพพัญญุตญาณ
นั้นก็ดีแลเมื่อพระพุทธเจ้าตรัสเทศนาพระธรรมจักรนั้นก็ดีนั้นแลเมื่
พระพุทธเจ้าเสด็จเข้าสู่นิพพานนั้นก็ดีในกาล ๕ ทีนี้ในโลกันตนร
จึงได้เห็นหนแท้นักหนา คนซึ่งอยู่ในนรกนั้นจึงได้เห็นกันแล
ลกันตนรกก็คิดว่านั้นนี้ก็เดียวว่าแต่กูมาอยู่ที่นี่คนเดีย
นาธรรมจัก
เล่ายจึงวายเรื่องคนผู้ ก่อนกระทำ แม่และลู
นพราหมณาจารย์ผู้มีศีลและยังพระสงฆ์ให้ผิดกันครั้น
ตายไปเกิดในนรกอันชื่อว่าโลกันตนรกนั้นและตนเขาให
นักหนาโดยสูงได้ ๖๐๐๐ วา เล็บมือเล็บตีนเขานั้นดังคั่งคาว
ใหญ่ยาวนักหนาสมควรด้วยตัวอันใหญ่นั้น เล็บนั้นเสมือนนัก
ผิและเกาะแห่งใดก็ติดอยู่แห่งนั้นเขาเอาเล็บเขานั้นเกาะ
แพงจักรวาฬนั้นหน่วงอยู่และเขาห้อยตนอยู่เขาอยู่ดังค้าง
นั้นแล เมื่อเขาอยากอาหารไส้เขามิไปเพื่อจะหากินครั้นได้
มือกันเข้าไส้จเขานึกว่าเขากินก็จับกุมกันกินคนผู้หนึ่งก็
ว่าเขากินจึงคนทั้งสองนั้นก็จับกุมกันกินต่างคนต่างตระครุบ
นก็รัดเอาตัวกันทั้งสองคนในน้ำอันเย็นแผ่นดินแตกบห
ละไปต้องน้ำนั้นได้สักคาบหนึ่งเลยและน้ำนั้นเย็นนักหนาค
ตกลงมาในน้ำนั้นบัดเดียวใจไส้เห็นปานนั้นตนเขาก็เปื่อยเ
ออกไปสิ้นดังก่อนอาจมซึ่งตกลงในน้ำนั้นก็ตายบัดใจแล้วจึง
เป็นตนเขาขึ้นอีกเล่าโสดเขาจึงปีนขึ้นไปเกาะกำแพงจักรวา
ายนอกนั้นอยู่ดังก่อนเล่าแลแต่เขาทนทุกขเวทนาอยู่ที่
ช้าหิงนานนักชั่วพุทธันดรกัลปหนึ่งแท้ ภูมิ
สิ่งอันดีนั้นคือราชสีห์อันว่าราชสีห์นั้นมี ๔ สิ่ง ๆ สิ่งหนึ่ง
ติณะสิงหะ สิ่งหนึ่งชื่อกาลสิงหะ สิ่งหนึ่งชื่อ

Introduction
Traces of Words

FUYUBI NAKAMURA

THE VISUAL AND PHYSICAL PRESENCE of words has a special significance across Asia, which has the greatest diversity of languages in the world. Writing, especially calligraphy, has been revered as an aesthetic form and has played an important social and political role in Asian traditions ranging from religious texts in Sanskrit to Islamic and Chinese calligraphy. "Calligraphy is woven into the fabric of everyday life" in many parts of Asia (Alain George, see page 39). The significance of words, both as text and as image, has continued to inspire contemporary artists.

Produced in various materials and styles—from calligraphy and painting to digital and mixed media—the words presented in the exhibition *Traces of Words: Art and Calligraphy from Asia* are physical traces of time and space, embodying what is ephemeral and also what is eternal in our life. We leave traces of ourselves throughout life, be they visible or invisible. Words, whether spoken, written, imagined, or visualized, are traces unique to humans. Some words disappear while others remain only in memory or leave physical traces as writing or text. These traces are the theme of the exhibition.

The exhibition showcases varied forms of expression associated with writing and words throughout Asia from different periods: from Sumerian cuneiform inscriptions, Qur'anic manuscripts, Southeast Asian palm leaf manuscripts, and Chinese calligraphy to graffiti art from Afghanistan and contemporary artworks using Japanese calligraphy and Tibetan and Thai scripts. Different media for writing—paper, silk, clay, woodblock, or projected screen—evoke different responses to the words. By treating words themselves as material culture, not merely as text, the exhibition invites us to consider the cultural significance and artistic representations of Asian words and writing.

Between Oral and Written Traditions

Despite the ubiquity of script, it is important to remember that many calligraphy and manuscript cultures evolved from *orality.* They also have a close relationship to religion. As Alain George discusses in chapter 3, Islam, closely linked to Islamic calligraphy, initially arose from oral traditions. For the mostly nomadic pre-Islamic Arabs, oral poetry was the ultimate form of art. As George explains, the Qur'an was perceived by the first Muslims as "surpassing every previous linguistic achievement" (George, see page 39) and was committed to memory. After the demise of the Prophet, a canonical text of the Qur'an was issued, which marked the beginning of the calligraphic tradition in the Islamic world. The earliest extant manuscripts of the Qur'an are thus the oldest-known books in Arabic.

◂ **PHAPTAWAN SUWANNAKUDT**
Three Worlds 9 (detail)
2009
Acrylic on canvas
135 × 65 cm
PRIVATE COLLECTION; COURTESY OF THE ARTIST

وقضينا الى بني اسرائيل في الكتاب لتفسدن في الارض مرتين
و حکم کردیم بسوی بنی اسرائیل در کتاب هر آینه تباهی خواهید نمود در زمین دو بار
ولتعلن علوا كبيرا ۞ فاذا جاء وعد اولىهما بعثنا عليكم عبادا
و هر آینه گردنکشی کنید گردن کشی بزرگ پس چون آید وعده نخستین آنها فرستادیم بر شما بندگان
لنا اولي باس شديد ۞ فجاسوا خلال الديار وكان وعدا مفعولا
ما که بودند خداوند قوتی سخت در کارزار پس گشتند بطلب غارت در میان سراهای شما و هست وعده کرده شده
ثم رددنا لكم الكرة عليهم وامددناكم باموال وبنين وجعلناكم
پس باز گردانیدیم بر شما دولت که غالب شدید بریشان و مدد کردیم شما را بمالها و فرزندان و گردانیدیم شما را
اكثر نفيرا ۞ ان احسنتم احسنتم لانفسكم وان اساتم فلها فاذا
بیشتر از ایشان در جمعیت اگر نیکی کنید نیکی کنید برای خود و اگر بدی کردید پس مر اوراست پس چون
جاء وعد الاخرة ليسوءوا وجوهكم وليدخلوا المسجد كما دخلوه
آید وعده دیگر هر آینه تیره کردند رویهای شما و تا در آیند مسجد را چنانکه در آمدند آنرا
اول مرة وليتبروا ما علوا تتبيرا ۞ عسى ربكم ان يرحمكم وان
اول بار و تا هلاک کردند آنچه گردنکشی کردند هلاک کردنی شاید پروردگار شما که رحم کند شما را و اگر
عدتم عدنا وجعلنا جهنم للكافرين حصيرا ۞ ان هذا القرآن
دیگر کردید وعده کردیم و گردانیدیم دوزخ را برای کافران بندی بدرستی که این قرآن
يهدي للتي هي اقوم ويبشر المؤمنين ۞ الذين يعملون الصالحات
راه نماید مر آنکه آن راست ترست و مژده میدهد گروندگان را آنانکه میکنند کار نیک
ان لهم اجرا كبيرا ۞ وان الذين لا يؤمنون بالاخرة اعتدنا لهم عذابا
که ایشانراست مزدی بزرگ و آنکه آنانکه نمیگروند بآخرت آماده کردیم برای ایشان عذابی
اليما ۞ ويدع الانسان بالشر دعاءه بالخير وكان الانسان عجولا ۞
دردناک و میخواند آدمی ببدی خواندن او به نیکی و هست آدمی شتابان
وجعلنا الليل والنهار آيتين فمحونا آية الليل وجعلنا آية النهار
و گردانیدیم شب و روز را دو نشانه پس محو کردیم نشانه شب را و گردانیدیم نشانه روز را
مبصرة لتبتغوا فضلا من ربكم ولتعلموا عدد السنين والحساب
روشن تا بجویید فضل از پروردگار خود و تا بدانید شمار سالها و حساب
وكل شيء فصلناه تفصيلا ۞ وكل انسان الزمناه طائره
و هر چیزی را بیان کردیم اورا بیان کردنی و هر آدمی را لازم او گردانیدیم قلاده
في عنقه ونخرج له يوم القيامة كتابا يلقاه منشورا ۞ اقرا
در گردن او و بیرون آوریم برای او روز قیامت نامه ببیند اورا گشوده شده بخوان

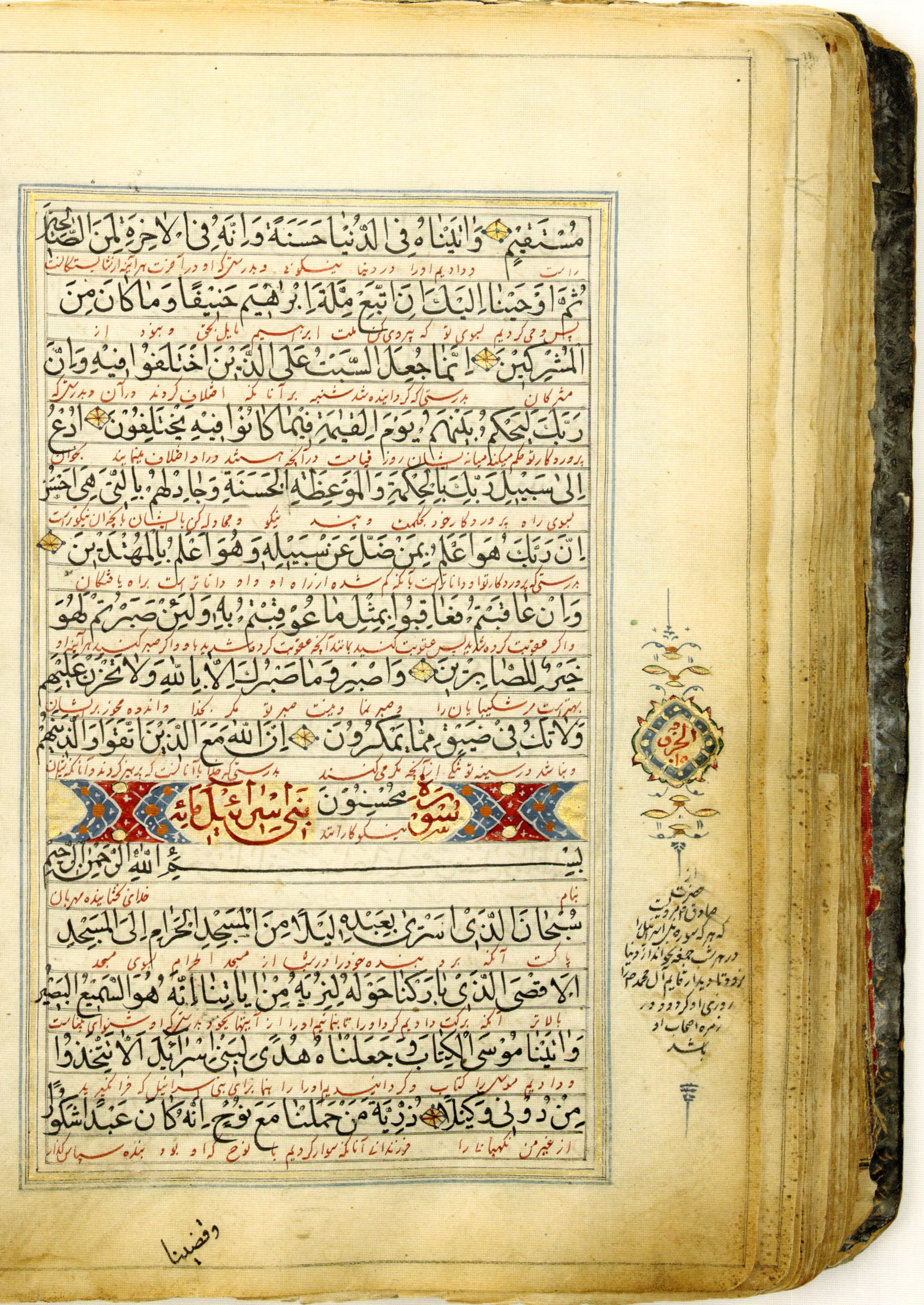

مستقيم ۞ وآتيناه في الدنيا حسنة وإنه في الآخرة لمن الصالحين
ثم أوحينا إليك أن اتبع ملة إبراهيم حنيفا وما كان من
المشركين ۞ إنما جعل السبت على الذين اختلفوا فيه وإن
ربك ليحكم بينهم يوم القيامة فيما كانوا فيه يختلفون ۞ ادع
إلى سبيل ربك بالحكمة والموعظة الحسنة وجادلهم بالتي هي أحسن
إن ربك هو أعلم بمن ضل عن سبيله وهو أعلم بالمهتدين ۞
وإن عاقبتم فعاقبوا بمثل ما عوقبتم به ولئن صبرتم لهو
خير للصابرين ۞ واصبر وما صبرك إلا بالله ولا تحزن عليهم
ولا تك في ضيق مما يمكرون ۞ إن الله مع الذين اتقوا والذين هم
محسنون

سورة بني إسرائيل

بسم الله الرحمن الرحيم

سبحان الذي أسرى بعبده ليلا من المسجد الحرام إلى المسجد
الأقصى الذي باركنا حوله لنريه من آياتنا إنه هو السميع البصير
وآتينا موسى الكتاب وجعلناه هدى لبني إسرائيل ألا تتخذوا
من دوني وكيلا ۞ ذرية من حملنا مع نوح إنه كان عبدا شكورا

وقضينا

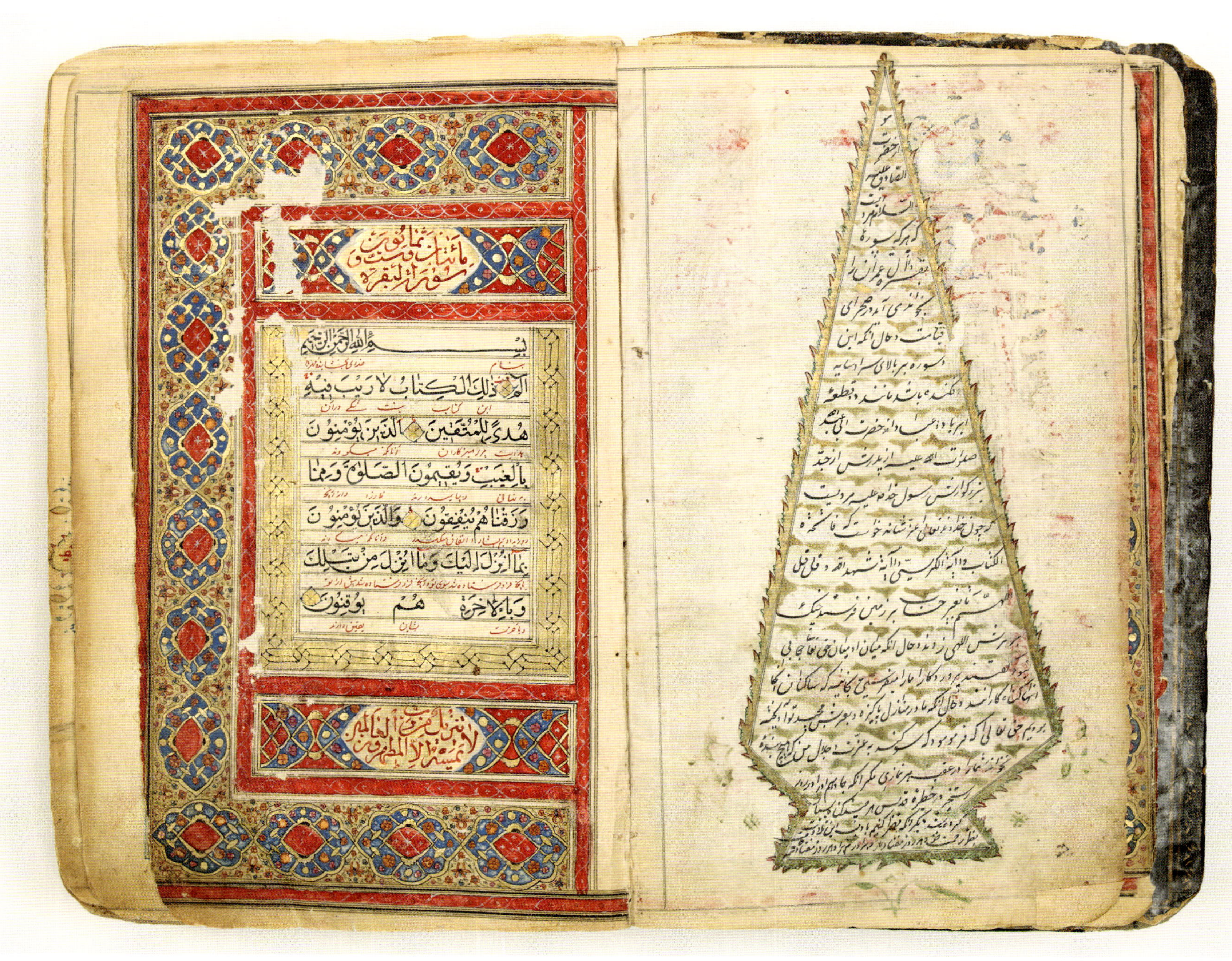

Qur'an
Iran • May–June 1839 (Rabi' I 1255)
Ink, pigments, and gold on paper; leather and silk fibre
20.4 × 13.7 × 3.8 cm (closed)
MOA COLLECTION, 3039/1

This manuscript is typical of Qur'an production in nineteenth-century Iran, with its relatively bold calligraphy in naskh *script and its illumination dominated by red, gold, and blue. It was written by one Muhammad Hasan al-Khawanari (or Khawansari), son of Muhammad Tahir. Between the black lines of the Qur'anic text is a word-by-word Persian translation in red ink. The book has an original lacquer binding with flower motifs.*

Sanskrit, the most widely used language in pre-modern India, has no native script of its own but has instead been written in many different scripts. In chapter 4, Adheesh Sathaye aptly illustrates the "oral literacy" of Vedic culture in India where an intricate system of poetry and ritual culture flourished. The sacred Sanskrit texts of the Vedas were, like the Qur'an, memorized and transmitted orally. However, as Sathaye explains, in order "for a text to truly exist, to be given public life, it has to be transformed from oral to written form." But even after the tradition of writing had emerged by the onset of the Common Era, Sanskrit manuscripts as physical objects remained closely linked to the world of orality and performance.

Despite the cultural significance of writing in many Asian societies, anthropology historically did not give much attention to the study of written cultures or literate societies. The collection of calligraphy in anthropological museums around the world is thus limited, but the Museum of Anthropology at UBC is fortunate to have some significant items in its collection.

Words as Objects

The act of incising on clay or turtle shells and animal bones marked the beginning of "writing" in ancient Mesopotamia—a region around the Tigris and Euphrates Rivers, located mostly in today's Iraq—and in China. These incised traces survived on material objects and are considered a record of writing (pages 9 and 122). As Yuehping Yen describes in chapter 1, the earliest inscriptions from China are called oracle bone script and were used as a ritual device of divination.

A piece of writing is a material object. In our increasingly digital media–dominated society, the practice of physical writing, using more traditional writing tools such as pencil, pen, or brush, is being sidelined. Our relationship with writing is no longer the same. Yet writing always entails material attributes and substances—whether it involves a keyboard and computer screen or paper and pen. The main purpose of writing is to transmit information and knowledge, which it does through material traces. These material traces and substances are usually considered secondary to the main message, or not considered at all.

In recent years in the study of written communication, however, materiality and visual effects have attracted increased attention. Perhaps this is partly in reaction to modes of analysis such as New Criticism, which treats the production of literary meaning solely in terms of language. Roger Chartier proposed that in order to understand a text, it is necessary to "identify the effect, in terms of meaning, that its material forms produced. . . . When the same text is apprehended through very different mechanisms of representation, it is no longer the same."[1] Conversely, the importance of the materiality of words has frequently been discussed in the historiography of East Asian calligraphy.[2] In emphasizing the importance of the visual effects of Chinese calligraphy, Yu-kung Kao notes that "the physical presence of words, not their content, is the object of appreciation."[3]

If it is not purely imaginary, envisaged only in one's mind, anything *visual* is also a *material* object. Visual systems or visible forms—such as the alphabet—are realized via material objects. The material object then becomes the stage upon which the visual can act as a main character. This is the creation of specific cultural forms. Discussing how semiotic analysis can apply to

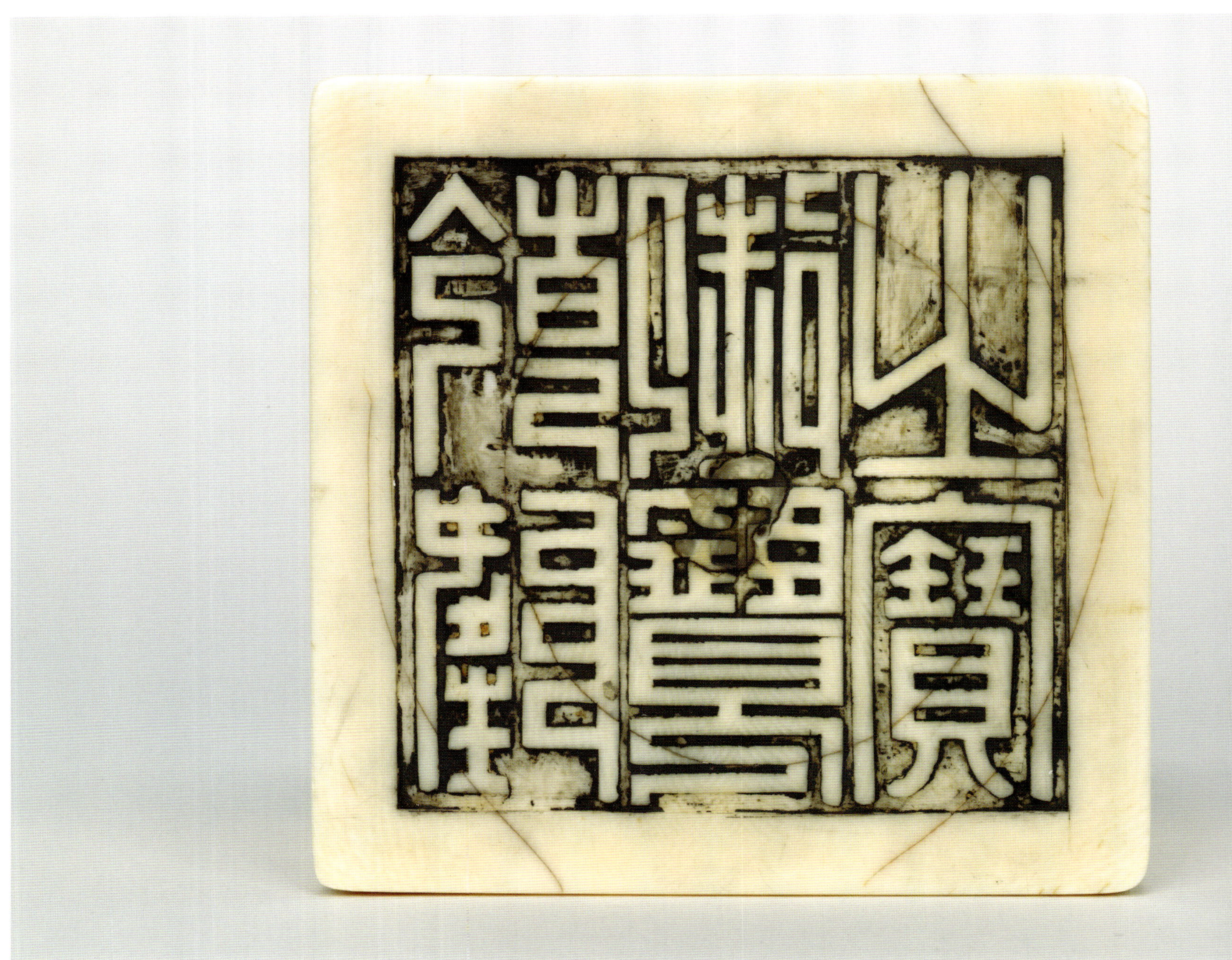

▲ ▶ **Seal**
China • Qianlong era
(1735–96)
Carved ivory
16.0 × 7.2 × 7.2 cm
MOA COLLECTION, N1.266

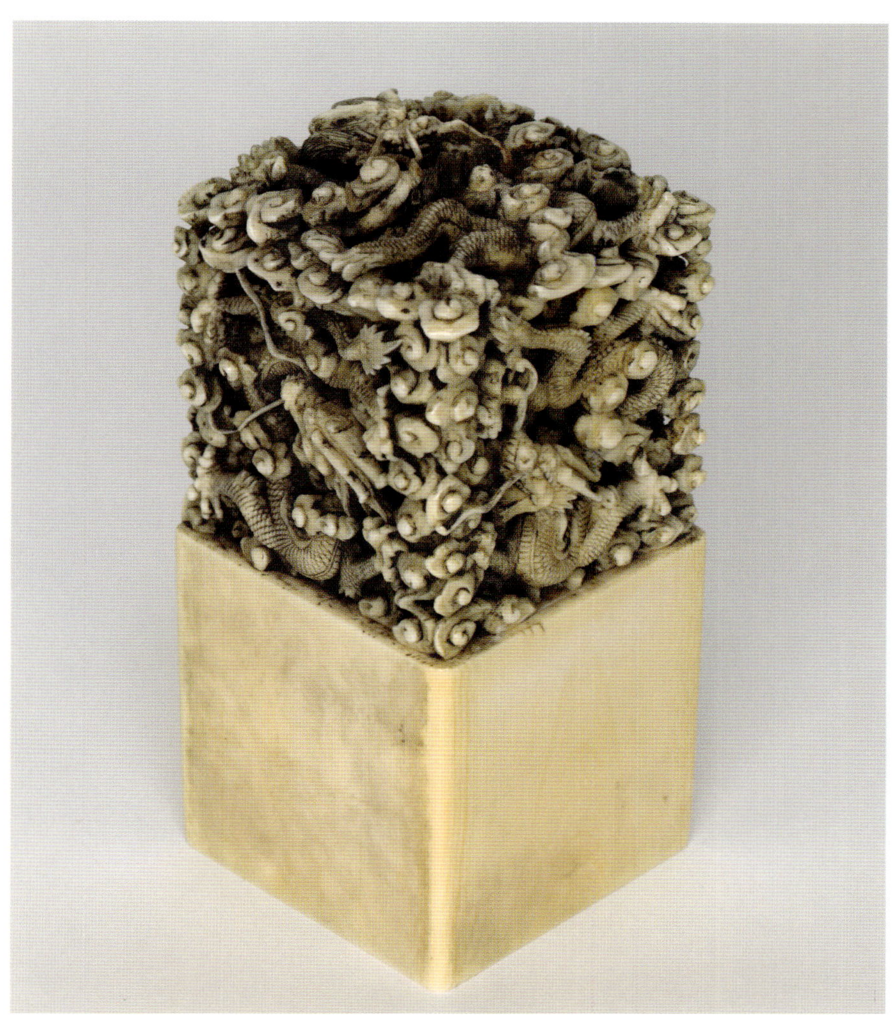

Carved with five-clawed dragons—symbols of the emperor—this seal may be one of approximately eighteen hundred seals commissioned by the Qianlong emperor (1711–99) of the Qing dynasty. The Qianlong emperor was an artist, a poet, and an avid collector of artworks who embraced the arts of other cultures. Seals were an important marker of authority and identity in imperial China. Every emperor and official used both official seals bearing his title and individual seals bearing his name. Imperial seals from this period were produced from various materials, including jade, bronze, crystal, amber, ivory, and bamboo. The art of seal engraving dates back to 1600 BCE, and it was added to the UNESCO Intangible Cultural Heritage list in 2009. Seal imprints were affixed to documents as a personal signature or sign of authority as well as to mark the authorship or ownership of artworks such as calligraphies or paintings; this particular seal was designed to mark works from Qianlong's collection. Seals are often considered artworks in their own right and are sought after by collectors.

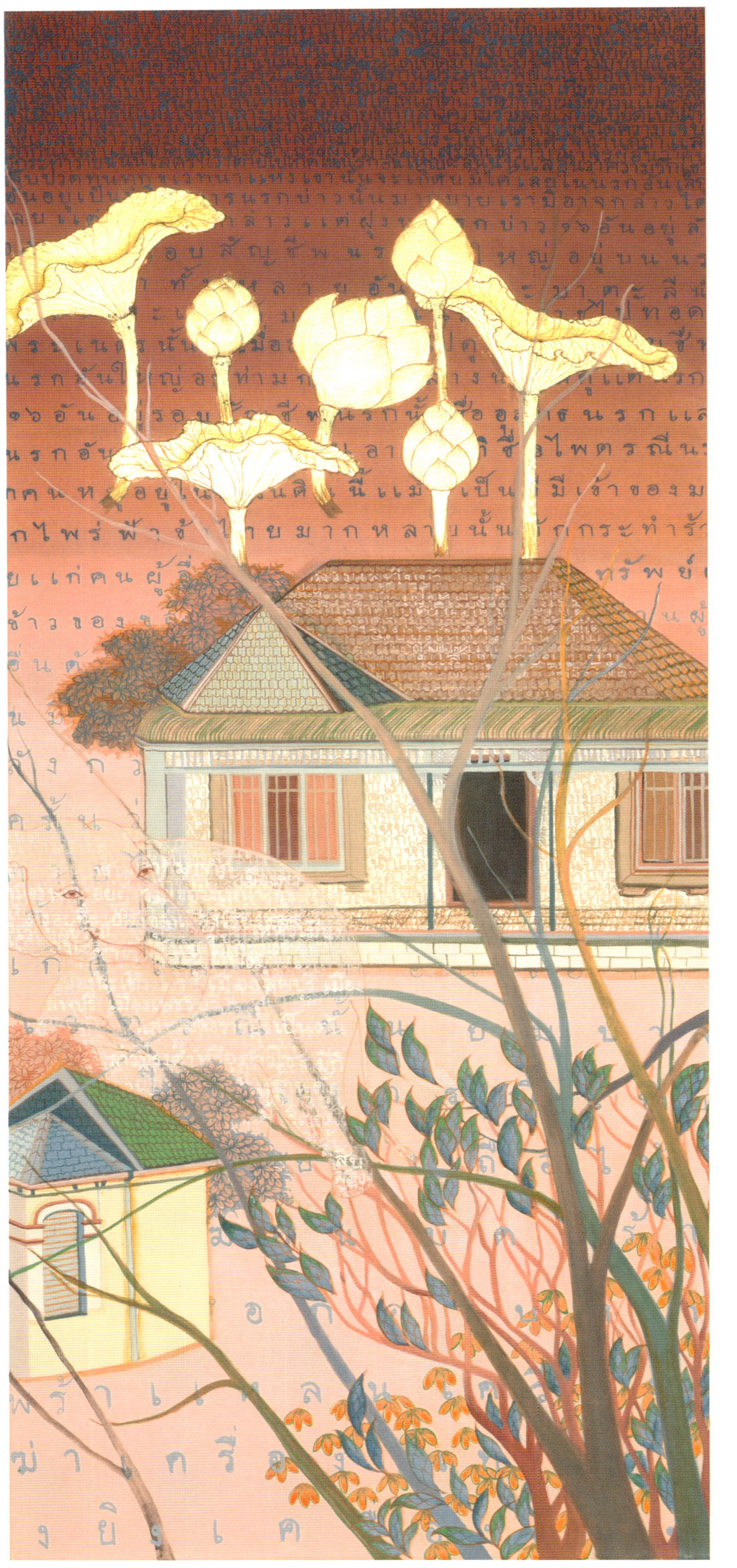

◀ **PHAPTAWAN SUWANNAKUDT**
Three Worlds 1 2008
Acrylic on canvas
135 × 65 cm
COLLECTION OF THAI PARLIAMENT; COURTESY OF THE ARTIST

▶ **Stamped Brick**
Eridu, Iraq • 2112–2004 BCE
Clay brick
6.9 × 26.6 × 26.1 cm
MOA COLLECTION, M4.29

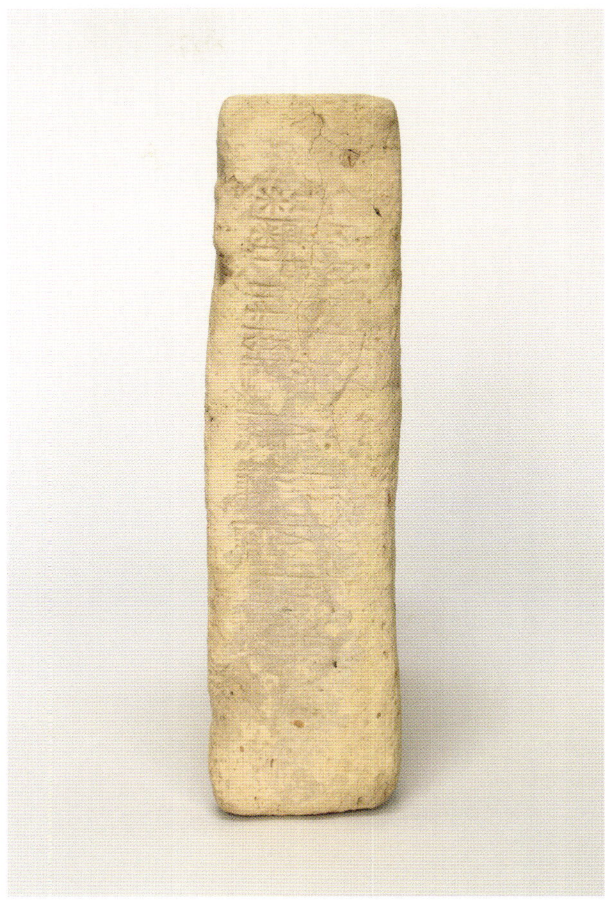

visual language, Johanna Drucker points out that "what visual arts had to offer to semiotics was a clear-cut case of the role of materiality."[4] Webb Keane argues that the Saussurean model dematerializes or abstracts signs (removes them from their context) as if "they were merely the garb of meaning,"[5] separating the sign from the material world, but there should be "a better understanding of the historicity *inherent* to signs in *their very materiality*."[6] For instance, you can have a statue carved in marble, and then the same image cast in soap or carved in wood, and the meaning would clearly be different. But it is more difficult to conceive of such a distinction in linguistic forms. In written language, the material attributes—that is, the material on which the written language leaves a trace—are subject to the historical condition of how the material produces meanings.

Encountering and Touching Words: Contemporary Art in the Exhibition

A number of contemporary Asian artists incorporate writing and calligraphy in their work. As if to reflect the history of writing, the texts many of these artists use are often religious. Calligraphy remains one of the popular sources of inspiration for a number of contemporary artists (as discussed in chapters 2 and 5). Words are not treated merely as symbols—that is, visual and/or written representations of the meanings of things. Rather, they are often regarded almost as physical entities. Once created, calligraphic words gain an existence of their own in the eyes and hands of the artists. Words resonate with the act of handweaving in the works of Phaptawan Suwannakudt (pages x, 8, and 82–85). By weaving fabric for her work in the *Cast-Off* series, Suwannakudt also wove the layers of meanings and memories to be found. In these works, the process of writing was for her like observing a wakeful moment in Buddhist meditation.[7] She grew up in temples and trained in mural painting under her famed artist father, Paiboon Suwannakudt, and so Buddhist imageries and narratives have been an important part of her work. The writing in her *Three Worlds* series is from *Traiphum Phra Ruang* (*Three Worlds of King Ruang*), a Thai Buddhist cosmological text (pages x, 8 and 85). Layers of writing overlay each other and often include secular motifs (such as urban houses) in a way that resonates with her experiences, as she makes connections through her artistic practice with her two home countries of Thailand and Australia (pages x, 8 and 85).

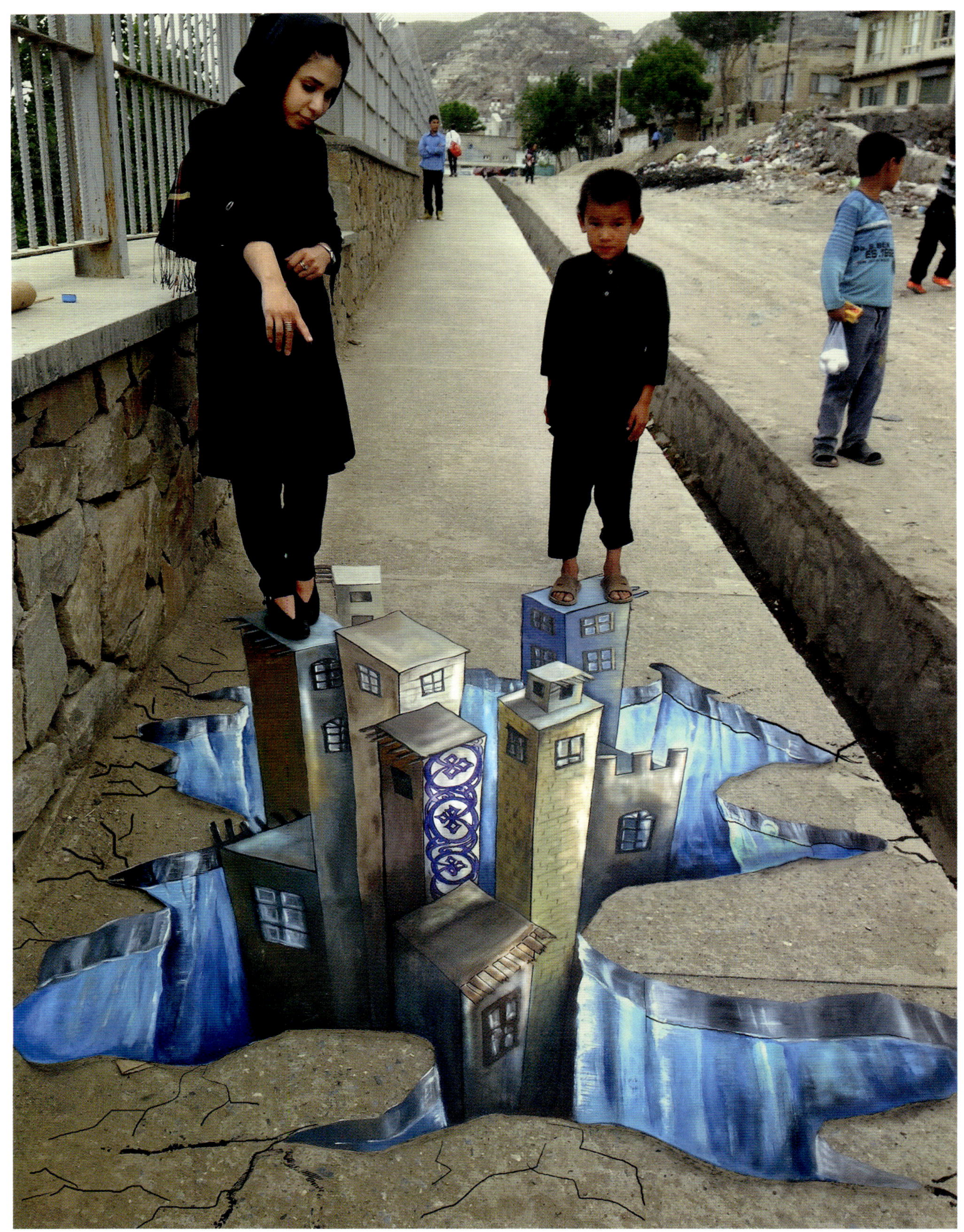

◂ **SHAMSIA HASSANI**
Magic 2014
Paint on ground in Kabul, Afghanistan
COURTESY OF THE ARTIST

Regarded as the first female graffiti artist of Afghanistan, Shamsia Hassani has gained international attention in recent years (pages 10, 77, and 86–93). I met her at a symposium on the relationship between word and image that was held in New Delhi, India, in 2012. Her evocative talk about calligraphy, and its accompanying images—as well as her personality—left a strong impression on me. Hassani considers her calligraphy to be a special kind of image. Her work involves writing on both real and imagined landscapes in Dari (Afghan Persian/Farsi) script, and her graffiti on the ruins, walls, and streets of Kabul are meant to colour over memories of the wars that have ravaged her country (page 10).

The use of script in works by Tibetan artists has attracted my attention since my first encounter with a contemporary Tibetan artist in the late 1990s in England. On my visit to Lhasa in 2010, I was fortunate to meet several Tibetan artists active in the city, including Nortse (pages 74 and 94–97). Nortse's recent works engage with the fate of the Tibetan language and appear to be asking "if language is the most fundamental marker of culture."[8]

The delicate but provocative works by Japanese calligraphers Kimura Tsubasa and Yugami Hisao combine traditional art forms with modern aesthetic sensibilities in innovative ways (pages 34–35 and 98–101; and VI, 13, 26, 33, 37, and 108–11, respectively). The strokes and words created by their brushes are a trace of time and history as well as a search for the future. Kimura and Yugami constantly seek new revelations while employing their skills from years of training in traditional calligraphy (see chapter 2).

Digital artworks by teamLab give a different twist to Japanese calligraphy. teamLab, a large collective of over four hundred "ultra technologists" or collaborators including programmers, engineers, computer-graphics animators, mathematicians, architects, graphic designers, and visual artists, was formed in 2001 by a group of five young engineers led by Toshiyuki Inoko. (teamLab is also a company, and Inoko is its CEO.) teamLab's work is characterized by creative collaboration, interactivity, and the aesthetics of digital worlds, notably with reference to traditional Japanese art, including calligraphy. They have been creating a series of digital works entitled *Spatial Calligraphy* 空書 for about a decade now. It reconstructs Japanese calligraphy in a three-dimensional space, which they call Ultra Subjective Space, allowing for a novel experience. Their work is inspired by a spatial perspective adopted in traditional Japanese pictures that does not privilege any particular viewing position.[9] In their interactive digital work *What a Loving, and Beautiful World* (2011), calligraphic words transform into images associated with the meaning of these characters when activated by viewers' shadows (pages 102–7). Works by Kimura, Yugami, and teamLab point to a new direction for contemporary Japanese calligraphy.

Artwork transforms writing—a form of communication that is often looked through rather than looked *at*—into visualized and materialized words. Viewers may experience and sense, rather than read and translate, script in new ways and gain an appreciation for the cultural significance of Asian writing beyond mere legibility.

Words in Art

Why might words evoke different responses when presented differently? The same words can be presented in various ways, such as in print or on the computer screen. We need to identify the effect of the material form to fully understand writing. The presence of writing in these works is intended to capture the spectator's attention, to raise the question of what the writing means in its particular visual context. Be it the semantic meaning of the words or something that is perceived more visually, the presence of writing opens the linguistic meaning in these works to speculation.

What do words do in these works? The artists are not necessarily trying to convey specific meanings as if it is simply text to be read. Instead, they are expressing words visually and materially. Meanings of words—their own or someone else's—guide the artists to produce works. The materialized words in this exhibition might not be intelligible to us, but the presence of meaning remains vital for the making of these works. Words and self seem inseparable as the two entities work together to become creative energy. Through the eyes and hands of these artists, new types of words are created through their words' visually transformed appearance.

This exhibition displays these different works experimentally to show the way in which words and writing may resonate in different fields and media and how they inspire creation in certain ways. It also aims to reconsider the place of words and writing in an era when the physical trace of words is often obscured by continuous waves of digital media. Despite the constant movement of people and objects in a globalized world, location remains an important reference point when viewing the images.[10] These works refer to certain cultural locations from whence these languages come. At the same time, the works embrace Asian writing, words, material, and visuality to present something different, perhaps a new language we can all share, highlighting the interaction between the meaning and material substance. Do we need to understand the semantic meaning of the writing to appreciate the artwork? The exhibition explores what is underneath or is embraced by the writing with which the artists have chosen to work. Viewing and feeling these works is like listening to songs in a foreign language we may not understand: we can still appreciate them precisely because there is more to them than the meaning of the lyrics.

YUGAMI HISAO
***Chō* 蝶 (Butterfly)** 2008
Sumi ink on Kent paper
21 × 29.5 cm
MOA COLLECTION, 3186/2

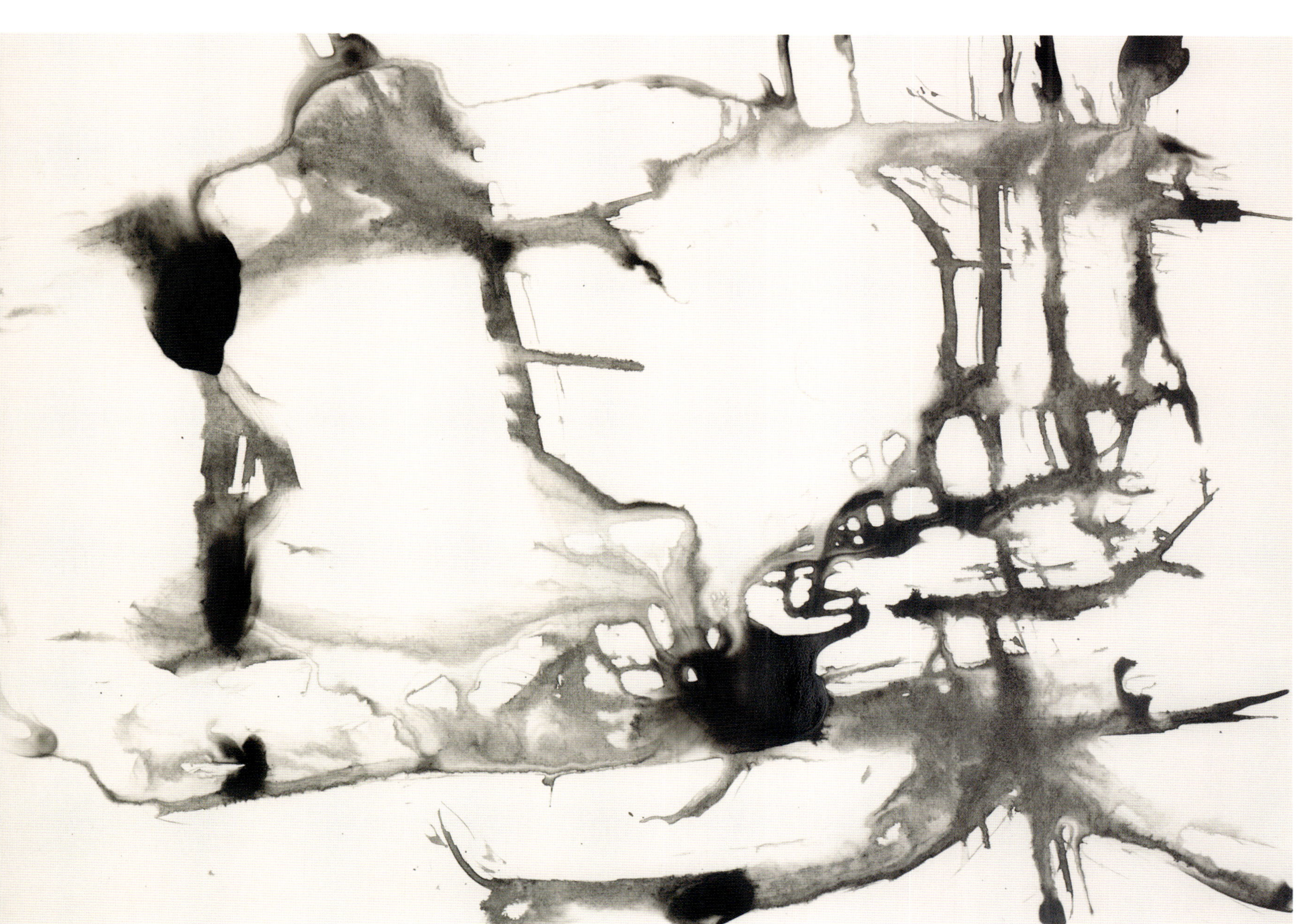

疆之性黍稌播種之宜節候早晚
之殊蝗蝻捕治之法素爰咨詢知
此甚悉雖聽政時恒與諸臣工言之於
豐澤園之側治田數畦環以溪水阡
陌井然在目桔槔之聲盈耳岸收
嘉禾數十種隴畔樹桑傍列蠶
舍浴蘭繅絲恍然如茅簷蔀屋

1
Writing the Unwritten
Chinese Calligraphy beyond Text, Image, and Art

YUEHPING YEN

THE CREATION OF CHINESE WRITTEN WORDS was considered a historical moment of cosmological significance. According to myth, when the four-eyed demigod Cang Jie created Chinese written characters, the sky started to rain grains, and ghosts wailed in the night because the knowledge of Heaven was being leaked through the characters. This mystical association has a historical origin. When the earliest corpus of extant written characters appeared in Bronze Age China, it was as animal bones being incised as a ritual device of divination. This earliest script is called oracle bone script. The birth of Chinese written characters has a direct mystical link. In fact, the association of Chinese written characters with something extraordinary, be it divine or human, has never been completely cast off since their creation. The mysticism lies at both the origin and the final destination of Chinese characters. In this essay, I show the different dimensions of Chinese characters—as text, as image, and as art, and ultimately as a transformative practice that takes one well beyond text, image, and art into the spiritual realm where the distinction between subject and object is eventually obliterated.

In our postmodern world, we are accustomed to breaking down conceptual boundaries. In the world of art, sometimes one sees the boundary between text and image blurring. It should therefore be no surprise that in the context of the visual culture of China, China's distinctive writing system could be subject to this scrutiny. After all, it is commonly said that Chinese written characters are little pictures in themselves. What illustrates the distinction and tension between text and image better than the writing of stylized pictures? Is Chinese writing an inherently visual system? Given that it started as a set of pictographs and ideographs, the answer seems immediately and intuitively apparent: yes. But let us take just one step back. Are not all writing systems in the world inherently visual, in the sense that they are all meant to be seen and read and that they convey meanings? So perhaps a more pertinent question would be, what do we mean when we say that Chinese writing is inherently visual?

A Quick Sketch of the Chinese Writing System

Chinese characters are traditionally regarded as ideographs or ideograms—written characters that symbolize a thing without indicating the sounds of their spoken form. These include pictographs—pictorial symbols for words or phrases. This popular idea of Chinese writing is shared by Chinese and non-Chinese. However, only a tiny fraction of Chinese characters derive from pictographs. And about 90 percent of Chinese characters contain a phonetic code. The majority of characters still in use today are constructed according to two

◂ **Illustrated manuscript (detail)**
China • undated reproduction of the 1696 edition
Hand-painted woodblock prints in ink on paper; accordion album
29 × 26.5 × 5 cm
MOA COLLECTION, N1.553

principles that have pronunciation as their basis. Many Chinese characters actually do not indicate ideas, or reveal knowledge linked to these ideas, through their visual forms. As with English script, a big chunk of Chinese script relates to how words originally sounded. (Except that, as a result of the huge diversity of dialects and the natural transformation of language through time, the supposedly phonetic components have become more and more detached from their modern pronunciation.)

This shows that Chinese characters do not constitute an entirely visual system as is popularly believed. But as a legacy of this misconception, some believe that Chinese characters "speak directly to the mind," implying that one can grasp their meaning just by looking at them. This overconfidence, it seems to me, derives from the same misunderstanding of how images convey meaning. If any untrained eye can grasp the meaning of any image as intended, why would paintings ever need a title, and why would anything ever be written about them? Between image and text, there is sometimes rough water to cross. Similarly, it is quite obvious that people who have not learned Chinese writing would not understand what a written character means, even characters that have evolved directly from pictographs. Meaning and idea do not simply reveal themselves to the perceiving eye. This misconception about image metamorphoses into a misconception about Chinese writing.

So, does all this demystification show that Chinese writing is not a visual system? Not quite. I would argue that Chinese writing is a visual system—but for different reasons. The compulsive search for meaning is not restricted to the realm of language and text; it is a human tendency that applies to all aspects of life. The semiotic theory of art is a strong testament to this. Images are often treated as little parcels of meanings, such as symbols. But unlike text, the meanings of images are more fluid, and their articulation does not follow the linear mode that is dominant in text. Here, I would argue that Chinese characters present a fecund visual field in the way they produce a form of culturally specific knowledge.

Consuming Written Characters as Images

In Chinese societies, written characters are often consumed as images. This is manifested in two major ways: in the artistic practice of calligraphy and other forms of handwriting (pages 17 and 18) and in a culturally specific type of knowledge formation through Chinese script. The first has been discussed extensively in writings on Chinese calligraphy. Here, I am concerned with the second—a particular type of folk etymology that serves as a source of knowledge in general.

Written characters are treated as graphic images. Characters are often, but not always, made up of more than one graphic unit. These units can be individual characters in themselves, or they can be units that serve as either phonetic or semantic codes. These standard parts can be found in many different characters. In other words, each character is unique in the sense that it combines units from a limited stock in a way that is never repeated in other characters. The parts of a character can be cut and detached, and then moved around or grafted onto or juxtaposed with parts from other written characters. The new images (not necessarily genuine written characters) resulting from these graphic operations can often signify valid information about absolutely anything.

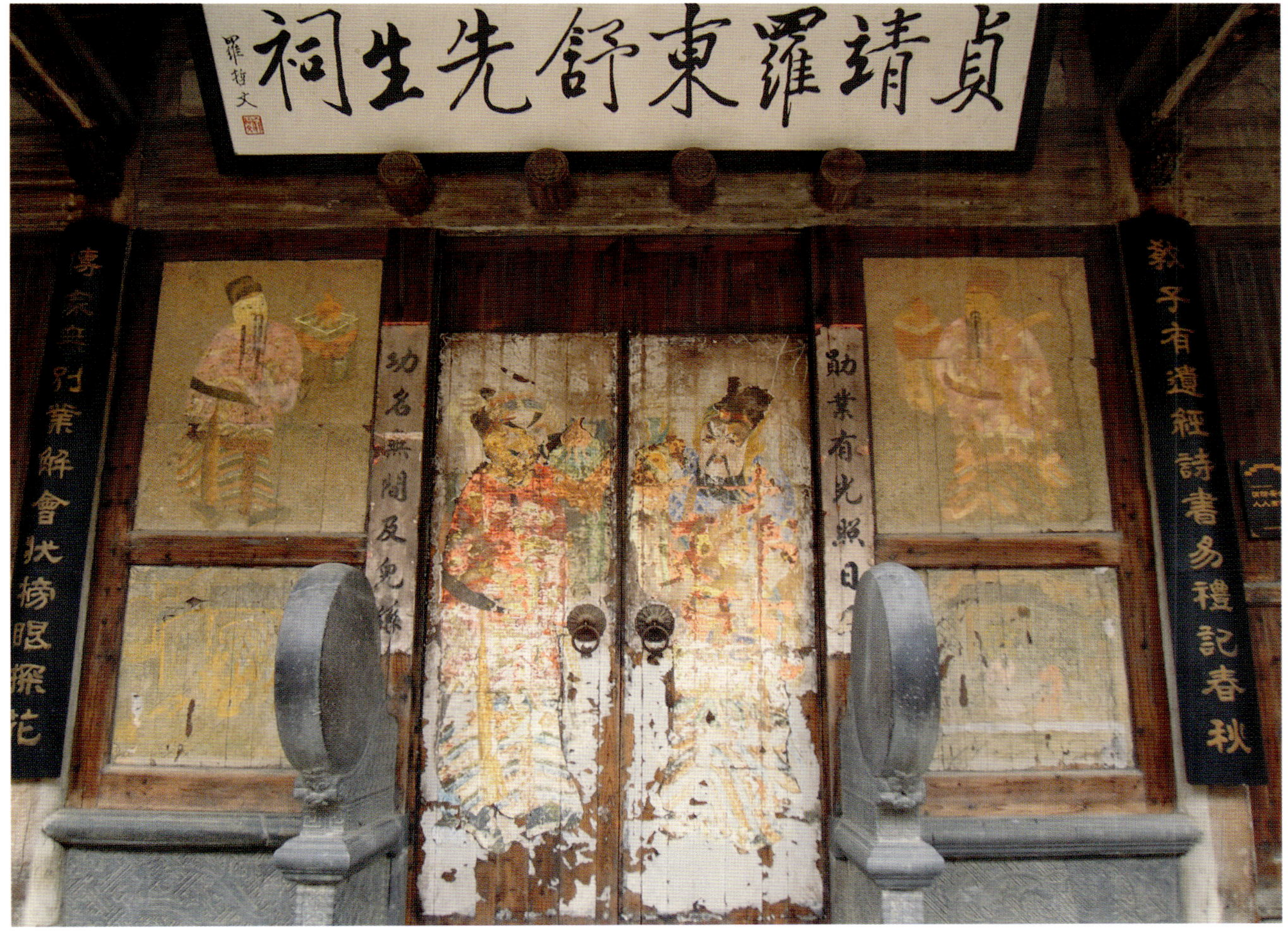

Calligraphy is an aesthetic experience that is part of everyday life in China. Pictured is the Zhenjing Luo Dongshu Ancestral House located in the old village of Chengkan (呈坎) *in Huizhou, Anhui province, as it stood in 2003. The house, built in 1539, was the largest of its kind in the Jiangnan region.*

A good example of an entire system of notation created this way—different graphic operations on the individual parts of written characters—can be found in traditional Chinese musical notation. The musical notation of the ancient seven-string Chinese instrument *guqin* is created entirely from different combinations of the graphic elements of several characters from written Chinese. (It is a tablature known as shorthand *qin* tablature, or *jianzi pu* 減字譜.) One composite character, which is not a genuine written character, usually defines one note but sometimes defines multiple notes. A single composite character can contain complicated information about finger positions and stroke techniques, including the string numbers, plucking techniques for the right hand, and which finger of the left hand to lightly touch or press down firmly at a specific position of a string. The composite characters, which may look like regular written characters, often appear completely unintelligible to those unfamiliar with the musical tradition (page 21).

Written characters are also a living record of many forms of knowledge and information from Chinese history. For instance, the pictorial origin of many characters is an excellent record of the social structure and cultural practices of antiquity. Moreover, root components, or *radicals*,

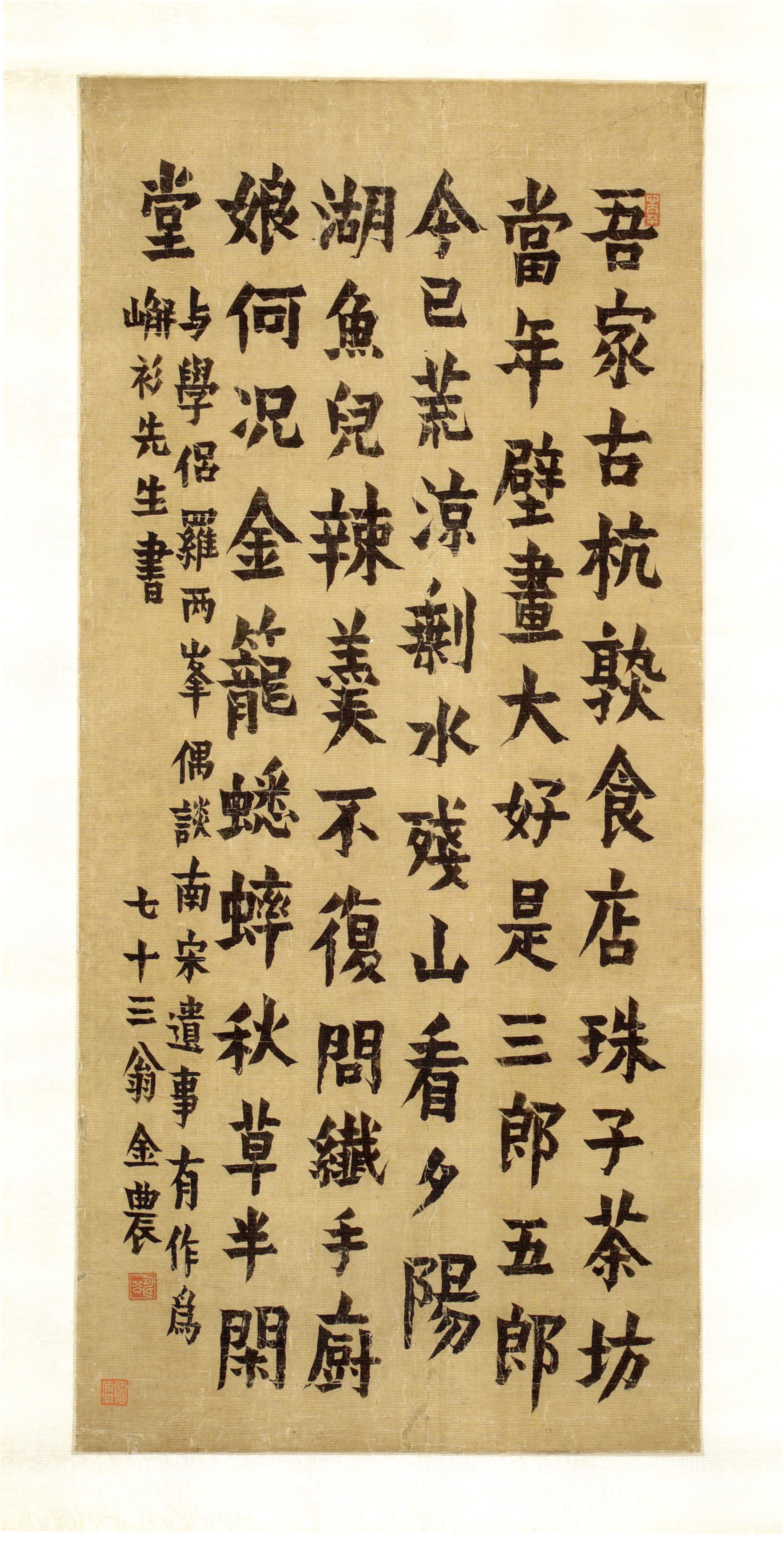

Calligraphy scroll by Jin Nong
China • 1760
Ink on silk mounted on a silk hanging scroll
231.5 × 44.5 cm
MOA COLLECTION, N1.572

Jin Nong 金農 (1687–1763) was born in Hangzhou, China, and was a calligrapher, painter, poet, and scholar. His literary and courtesy names include Jin Dongxin 金冬心 and Shoumen 寿門. He was one of the Eight Eccentrics of Yangzhou—a group of artists active in Yangzhou during the Qianlong era (1735–96) of the Qing dynasty, whose calligraphy and painting were innovative in style. Early in his life, he specialized in clerical script, but later he created a new type of script, known as "lacquer script," derived from early medieval Chinese stele inscriptions, a script that is shown in this work. This radical and individualistic style, notable for its angular brush strokes, marks an important development in the history of Chinese calligraphy. This piece was written after a conversation between Jin Nong and his student Luo Ping 羅聘, another of the Eight Eccentrics of Yangzhou. They lament the decline of Yangzhou as represented by the fate of a tea house there and a fading painting on its walls. —Fuyubi Nakamura of a character also serve as a transparent system of taxonomy. The radical in a character can place the thing or concept represented by the character firmly under a taxonomic category. For example, characters that represent names of trees have the "wood" radical (*mu* 木) in their graphic makeup, and the "metal" radical (*jin* 金) appears in characters that represent iron, copper, and money. But written characters carry more than a static stock of knowledge to be revealed and understood. When treated as images, they become a source of knowledge that is constantly evolving and expanding. As images, written characters provide an inexhaustible fuel source for knowledge production. All in all, Chinese characters occupy an interesting position between text and image. On the one hand, as with all components of language and text, these characters inspire a linear mode of thinking. On the other hand, being inherently visual, they open themselves to all kinds of graphic manipulations enjoyed by images. By exploiting the graphic potential for the enrichment of interpretation and meaning, Chinese characters behave like true images.

The Deep Knowledge within Written Characters

Words, spoken and written, are a human creation that dominates and shapes human consciousness. Language and written characters were created as the medium between our immediate experience and the abstract version of experience (in our minds). It is practically impossible to experience the world without the frameworks that language and writing have built into our cognitive mechanism. Once words were separated from immediate experience and became independent entities, they were gradually endowed with more and more meaning. On the linguistic level, written characters represent or signify "something." But they are not the "something" that is represented or signified. They are the bridge that links the world of immediacy with the world of mental constructs and manipulations. From there, written characters become covered in layers and layers of meaning accumulated through time while they become further and further removed from their origin—that is, the immediate experience.

Beyond the dense layers of meaning, written characters are regarded as containing some sort of "deep knowledge," which is essential to the true understanding of Chinese writing. Different people might have different opinions about how to unravel the deeper meaning of written characters. What matters is that there is assumed to be an almost "theological" version of the deep meaning behind written characters. I discuss this in a previous book:

> Linguistic or semantic meanings of written characters are of secondary order. They are appearance within which the essence of a character is buried. . . . Written characters are seen to be unbelievably deep, much deeper than human intelligence or comprehension ever will be.[1]

There are three standard approaches to extracting the deep knowledge of written characters: through philosophical interpretation, through the unearthing of antiquated semantic meanings (i.e., the etymology of Chinese characters), and finally, through "doing" calligraphy. The first two are interpretive approaches, and the last one experiential and phenomenological. I have discussed the first two approaches in my previous work.[2] Here, I want to focus on the third.

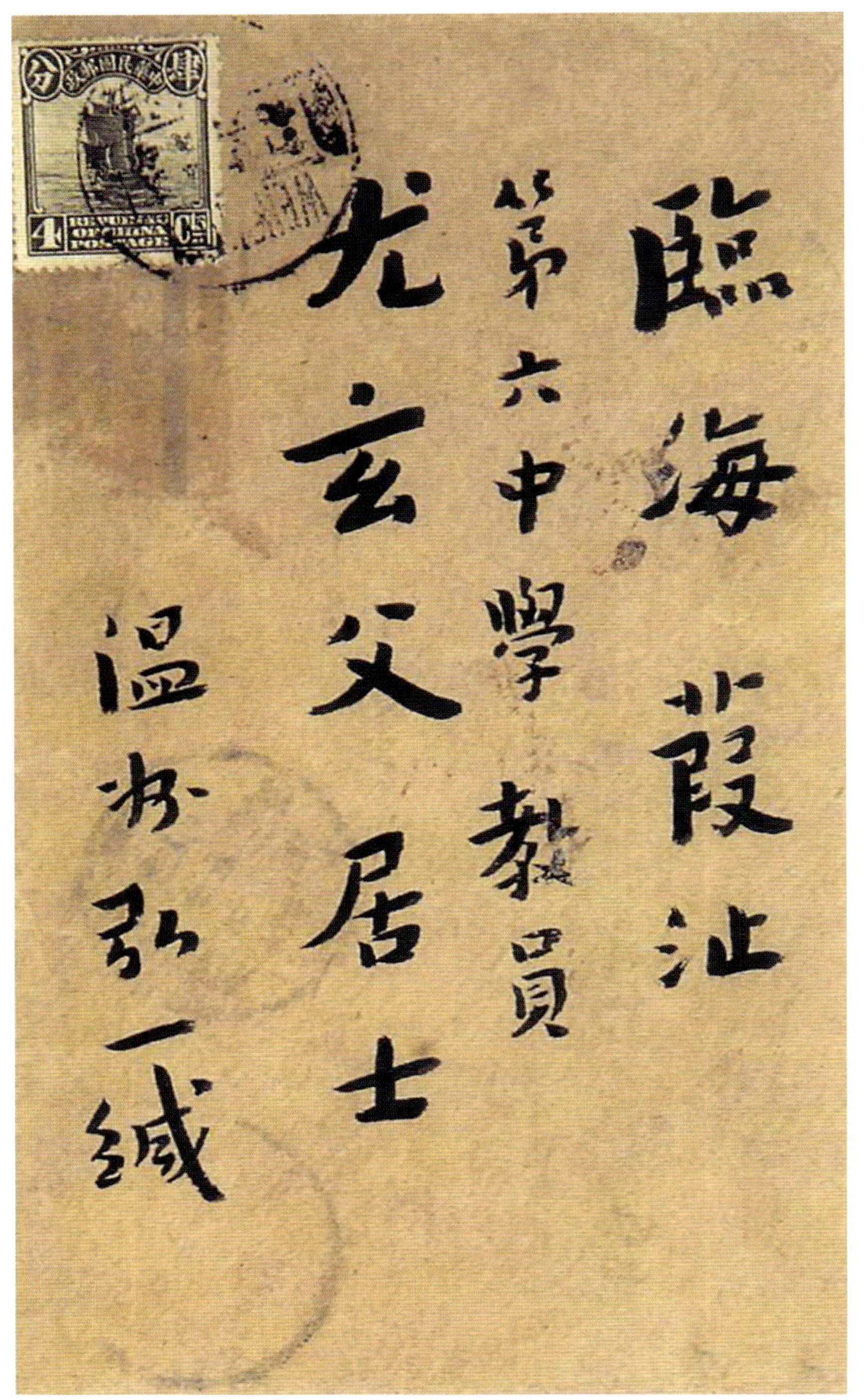

無上慧堅固
功德華莊嚴
大方廣佛華嚴經句
歲次鶉火書仲 晚晴老人

▲ **Calligraphy by Hongyi Fashi on a postcard**
China • n.d.
COURTESY OF YIXIN FASHI

The postcard is addressed to You Xuanfu (also known as You Mojun), a teacher and writer.

▲ **Inscription by Hongyi Fashi**
China • n.d.
Ink on paper
62 × 16.5 cm (each)
COURTESY OF YIXIN FASHI

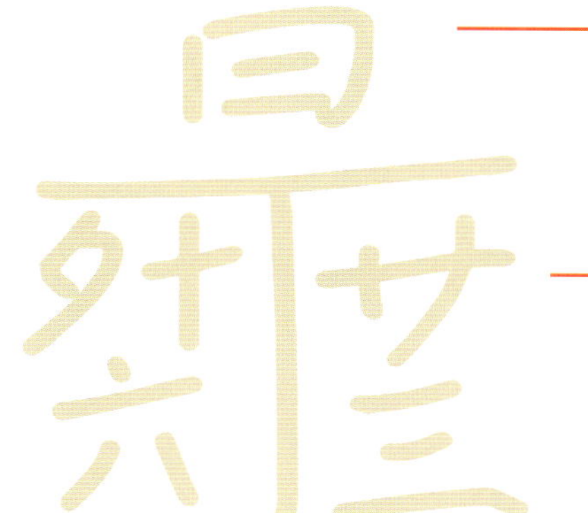

The 夕 symbol is derived from the Chinese character 名—press down the fourth finger of the left hand. The character 十 (ten) to the right specifies the tenth hui *position marker; the character 六 (six) below means the sixth string is pressed down.*

The 早 symbol is derived from the Chinese character cuo *撮—pluck two strings with two fingers of the right hand at the same time.*

The 艹 symbol is derived from the Chinese character 散—pluck an open string. The string number is indicated by the Chinese character 三 (three) below. Together they mean pluck the third string without pressing it down (an open string).

Beyond Text and Art: A Calligraphic Path towards the Summit

There are many ways in which Chinese written characters can be produced or reproduced. Characters when printed, typed, or handwritten (not with brush and ink) do not share the same aesthetic elevation and social agency as calligraphy. They are "mundane." But when Chinese characters are written with brush and ink, they become a highly empowered cultural form—a tool of social power (see the calligraphy by Sun Yat-sen on page 119), an extension of the person, and a way in which to interpret one's relationship with the world and extract deep knowledge.[3]

The calligraphic writing process begins with the calming of the body and mind. Fresh ink is prepared by grinding the ink stick in water on an ink stone in a slow, circular, repetitive, and monotonous movement. The grinding process releases pine soot very slowly from the ink stick and mixes it with water. At the same time, the other ingredients in the ink stick, including camphor or musk, are gradually released, and their fragrances fill the air and the calligrapher's nose. Meanwhile, in the background, the calligrapher can hear what sounds like two pieces of very smooth stones rubbing very gently against each other, lubricated by a small dollop of water. The calligrapher's gaze focuses on their hand movement, the ink stick, and the ink stone. The circular motion of their hand continues until the ink has reached the right consistency and quantity. The process has a meditative effect on the calligrapher. Focusing their body and mind on a single movement, a single sound, a single smell, and a single sight helps them to purify their senses and gather their thoughts. The preparation of ink also prepares the calligrapher's body and mind in a way that is required for calligraphic writing—that is, a state of relaxed concentration and clarity. But this is only the initial preparation. The transformation of the calligrapher's body and mind carries on.

When the mind fidgets and lacks concentration, it moves from one subject to another in extremely short intervals. It is scattered and wandering. Meanwhile, the body tends to make many unnecessary and small movements: small jerks of the hand, fiddling with the hair by the cheek, gentle twisting of the back and the waist, little flicks of the eyelids in response to a faint noise nearby, and so on. Normally we are not even aware of any of these small yet incessant movements. The body is often in sync with the mind, even though we often cannot perceive their moving at the same pace and rhythm. When one writes with a soft brush and ink on highly absorbent paper, the paper registers faithfully all traces of the writing process: how the brush twists and turns, how it presses and lifts, the speed it travels over the paper, the thickness of the ink, the evenness of ink on each hair of the brush, and the smoothness of movement and execution of force, down to every moment of slight hesitation and pause. Once a stroke or a character is written, it must not be retouched or altered afterwards. Chinese calligraphy is therefore truly an art of the fleeting moment. It is not difficult to imagine that if the calligrapher's body is erratic and flutters in the same way as in everyday situations, their inked strokes would also be full of unexpected marks and flaws, obvious to perceptive eyes.

Now the calligrapher settles down to write. After the initial stilling of both the mind and the body during the grinding of the ink, the calligrapher has probably already trimmed and smoothed off quite a lot of unnecessary small movements. The initially scattered mind is also a little bit more gathered and focused. As the mind stabilizes and a higher degree of concentration is reached, the sensory faculties become sharper and the perception clearer; an unperturbed surface of water reflects the world more clearly. The calligrapher can now see what goes through their own mind. They can see how their calligraphic strokes respond to the thoughts that pass and flip through them at the moment of writing. They become calmer and more perceptive to the nuances of the calligraphic strokes, and their mental stability and concentration consolidate even further, resulting in even more awareness and perceptual clarity. The concentration and clarity feed into each other and enhance each other. This is the gradual deepening process that will eventually bring the mind and the body into a harmonious and integral whole. As the experience deepens further, it could lead to a state of open awareness coupled with total relaxation and perfect stillness.

When a good calligrapher practises writing, they are not just trying to produce visually pleasing ink strokes. On top of the mastery of brush techniques, calligraphic writing is above all a process of gradual self-discovery and rectification. The heightened state of mind allows the calligrapher to inspect their intention more clearly. For example, a very slight pause and hesitation could come after a faint and fleeting desire to create a certain graphic effect more pleasing to the eye—or to create a calligraphic effect that could be interpreted as reflecting a certain personal trait that they crave. When a calculating thought such as this occurs, the mind is not pure. Being aware of their own hidden desires means that they can know themselves better and rectify their flaws. The heightened awareness of their own bodily movements, the inked traces, and their fleeting thoughts allow the calligrapher to examine themselves in greater detail. Every discovery such as this can lead to a corrective measure to purify their intention and to distill their mind. They can cut loose wandering thoughts and illusions, shake off the fixations that their mind and body cling to. In the inked traces, there lies a terrain of mind with all its crooks and creases: the lurking desires that normally escape one's attention, the subtle disgust and exaggeration that occur when one is offended by something minor, and the arrogance that comes in many forms. They do not allow themselves to be pulled along blindly by the automatic motion of the hand and the flow of inked traces, nor by any hidden deliberation of the heart. They are on a journey of continuous self-examination, self-discovery, and self-rectification.

With tireless practice and determination, the calligrapher may eventually be able to still their mind to such unfaltering stability that they are not distracted or perturbed by what passes by, and to distill their mind to such clarity that they can experience the world in a way that is not warped by prejudice, illusion, or expectation. With the endless chattering of internal debates subsided, a world of immediacy begins to emerge. The calligrapher's mind, body, and calligraphic characters are all at ease, not seeking or grasping at any

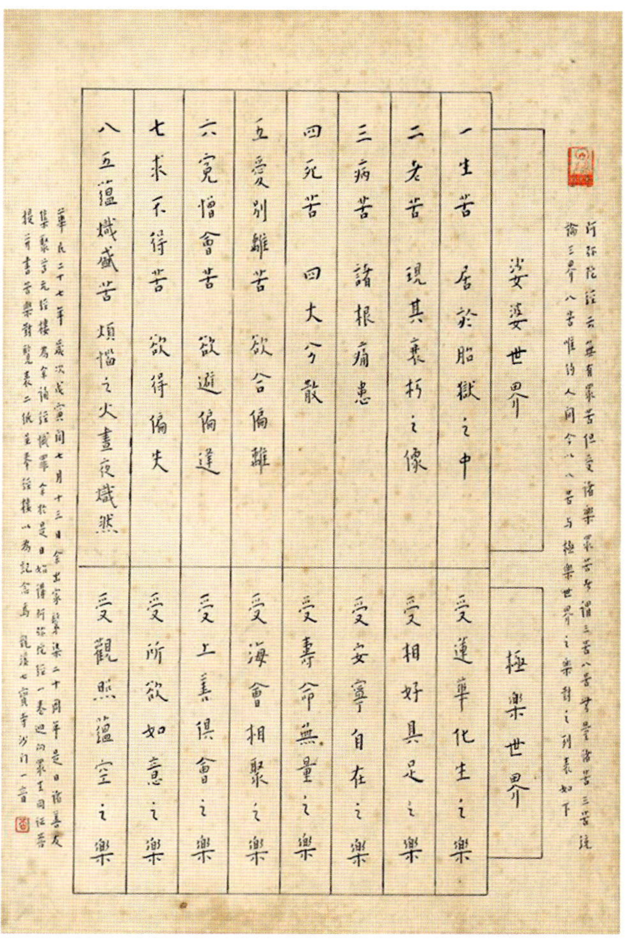

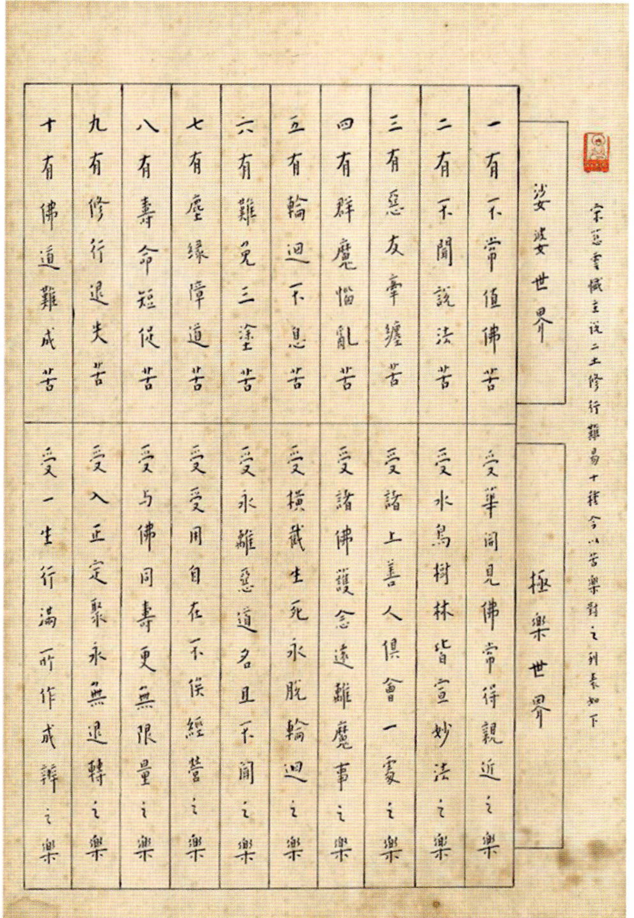

Calligraphy by Hongyi Fashi
China • 1938
Ink on paper
COURTESY OF YIXIN FASHI

The difficulties of Buddhist practice in the two realms (Samsara and Western Pure Land) are being compared.

preference, nor rejecting any undesirable outcome. They simply flow in the act of writing. Leaving conceptual reasoning and discriminating thoughts behind, the calligrapher returns to experiencing unmediated bodily sensations as a whole person—all sensations at the same time. Their mind is in the present moment. The brush and the hand that holds it become an inseparable part of the calligrapher's body, which is inseparable from their mind. Their mind is no longer turbid and churning with deluded thinking. It is free from the invisible forces that pull it automatically into various directions that the calligrapher otherwise has no control over. Their mind is in unison with their body and their environment. It merges with the great vastness, the great flux, that is the backdrop of all happenings—a continuous and never-ending coming and going, arising and disappearing, congregating and dissipating. In this flux, their mind, their body, and their brush are an integrated whole, and so are the inked traces on the paper. The calligraphic writing is no longer an object left behind by a separate experiencing subject. As the deepening process continues, the distinction between the subject (*wo* 我) and the object (*wu* 物), a distinction that we believe to be the foundation of all knowing and cognition, may eventually, or at least temporarily, become obliterated. It is a world of no opposites, including the knowing and the known, the writing and the written. Things are just there as such, and the calligrapher's presence is part of that.

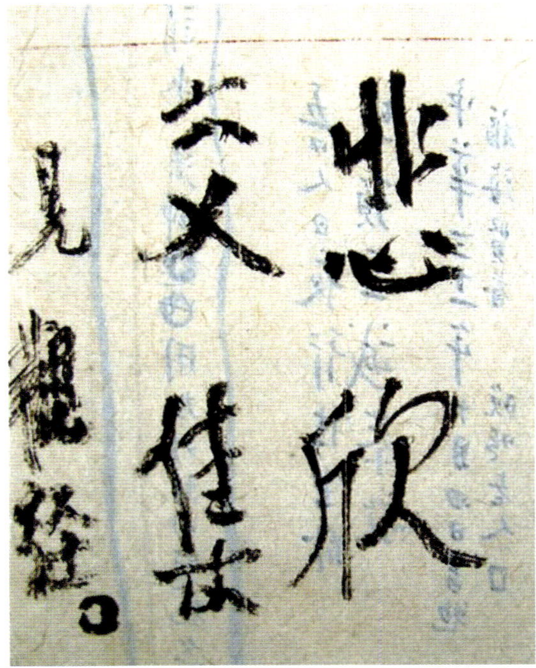

Calligraphy by Hongyi Fashi
China • 1942
Ink on paper
COURTESY OF YIXIN FASHI

This is Hongyi Fashi's last piece of calligraphy. The text reads, "Worldly joys and sorrows are intertwined," written three days before he passed away.

At this point, calligraphy has gone well beyond text and image, and even art. Descriptions of the pinnacle of calligraphic achievement teem with images of absolute smoothness, and of effortless, harmonious, and unimpeded flow. It is depicted as highly focused and moving without signs of hesitation or stagnancy. This state of absolute spontaneity is often described by Chinese calligraphy theorists as the exhibition of nature's mystery (*tianji* 天機) and cannot be forced in any way or planned with any effort. Tapping into nature's mystery is indeed one of the deepest forms of knowledge that can be acquired. And this kind of deep knowledge in written characters changes the way one perceives the world, and one's relationship with the world. It can only be achieved through "doing" calligraphy, rather than thinking about it.

A Journey Well Taken

This may all start to sound rather inconceivable. There are, however, examples of calligraphic masters who have gone very far along the path, such as the Buddhist monk Hongyi Fashi (1880–1942).[4] As one of the most talented and celebrated "full spectrum" artists in modern China, he enjoyed great achievements in many fields in both traditional and Western art forms. After leading some pioneering projects in theatre, music, and painting, he drastically altered his course to become a Buddhist monk. But he was no ordinary monk. He was a towering figure in modern Chinese Buddhist history, respected for his profound scholarship in monastic rules (Vinaya) and the depth of his religious practice. A pre-eminent Buddhist teacher of his era, he was later regarded as the eleventh-generation heir of the Nanshan Vinaya tradition in China and one of the four greatest Buddhist masters of modern China.

Like most members of the wealthy and educated class at that time, he began his training in classic literature, calligraphy, and other literary art forms very early in childhood. Before adulthood, he was already highly accomplished in all these art forms. After his ordination to become a monk, he gave up all forms of artistic practice except calligraphy. His calligraphy is often likened to lotus flowers growing above a muddy water surface, gently gesturing in the wind that brushes through them. They are the image of serenity, purity, and elegance without pretension (page 20).[5] The somewhat naive strokes demonstrate a subtle playfulness without spillage. His calligraphic writing is poised and relaxed, never stagnant or flabby. Despite being highly adept in techniques and well versed in all styles of calligraphic history, he developed a unique style that is unadorned, genuine, and extremely sophisticated at the same time. You cannot detect in it any intention to please, or to flaunt certain desirable qualities. Professionally trained in Western sketching and painting, he had a natural appreciation of form, composition, and graphic balance (affected by the speed and force of writing). Despite his innate ability in aesthetic forms, he did not devote his attention to the standard formal qualities of calligraphy valued by most calligraphers.[6] If his calligraphy shows form and composition, it does so without premeditated intent through his utmost devotion to every single calligraphic stroke. No stroke is too insignificant to be treated flippantly. Every movement is a movement of significance. Every movement comes from the heart, free from any deluding thought, attachment, and discrimination. If you concentrate and follow the traces of the brush in his work, you can see that the soft brush moves very slowly and gently on the paper, and you can sense his steady and barely perceptible breathing in the background. Looking at his calligraphy, you can almost feel a consistent and delicate breeze of fresh air gently wafting through the characters and strokes (page 20).

When he wrote, he kept others at a distance to avoid being disturbed. One of his students, Liu Zhiping, who later became an influential figure in the modernization movement of music in China, described what he saw when Hongyi Fashi wrote the text from *Amitābha Sūtra* for him as a gift: "My teacher was completely focused. The execution of the piece was done very slowly. Each dot and stroke was given his full energy. The piece of five-*chi* high (about 153 cm) took him about two hours to complete."[7] A rough calculation shows that his average speed for this work was about one minute for each of these one hundred and twenty characters. Each character is on average 6.5 × 6.5 centimetres in size. This is a very slow speed of writing, especially for a highly accomplished calligrapher. To write an entire piece at this pace for a full two hours would take an extremely calm and concentrated mind. His calligraphy does not show any trace of either being scattered or unexpected swerves. All of this confirms the state of his mind—steadfast concentration and acute awareness (page 23). We do not know for sure whether he achieved such a peak of experience, in part because this particular state is both inconceivable and indescribable to those of us who have never experienced it. To our naive and inexperienced eyes, however, there is no doubt that he has gone very far on the journey towards the peak (page 24).

Some of us may be inclined to dismiss this immediately as calligraphic mysticism, especially those of us who have not spent a long time with the calligraphic brush. However, for devoted calligraphers intending on pursuing a supreme goal, the peak may lie beyond sight, but the path towards it is there. Bit by bit, the raw, crude, frittering, and temperamental body is gradually transformed into a subdued yet alert, withholding yet relaxed, unaffected yet uninhibited body by the practice of calligraphic writing. Meanwhile, the scattered and wandering mind that is full of preconceived notions, expectations, calculations, hidden agendas, and conflicts is also undergoing a slow and gradual transformation. As if gathering in all the frayed ends of a piece of fabric, it is smoothed into a relaxed but focused, serene but acutely aware and spontaneous mind—a mind that is neither seeking nor devising. At the beginning of the journey, the body, the mind, and the world are all fragmented and separate. And the distinction between subject and object cannot be clearer to us rational beings. At the end of the calligraphic journey, however, all of these things become united. Is this calligraphic path pure mysticism or a genuine possibility of self-transformation? One would not know for sure until one set oneself on the spoken path. After all, the immediate reaction to dismiss it may turn out to be nothing more than one of one's numerous mind games at play.

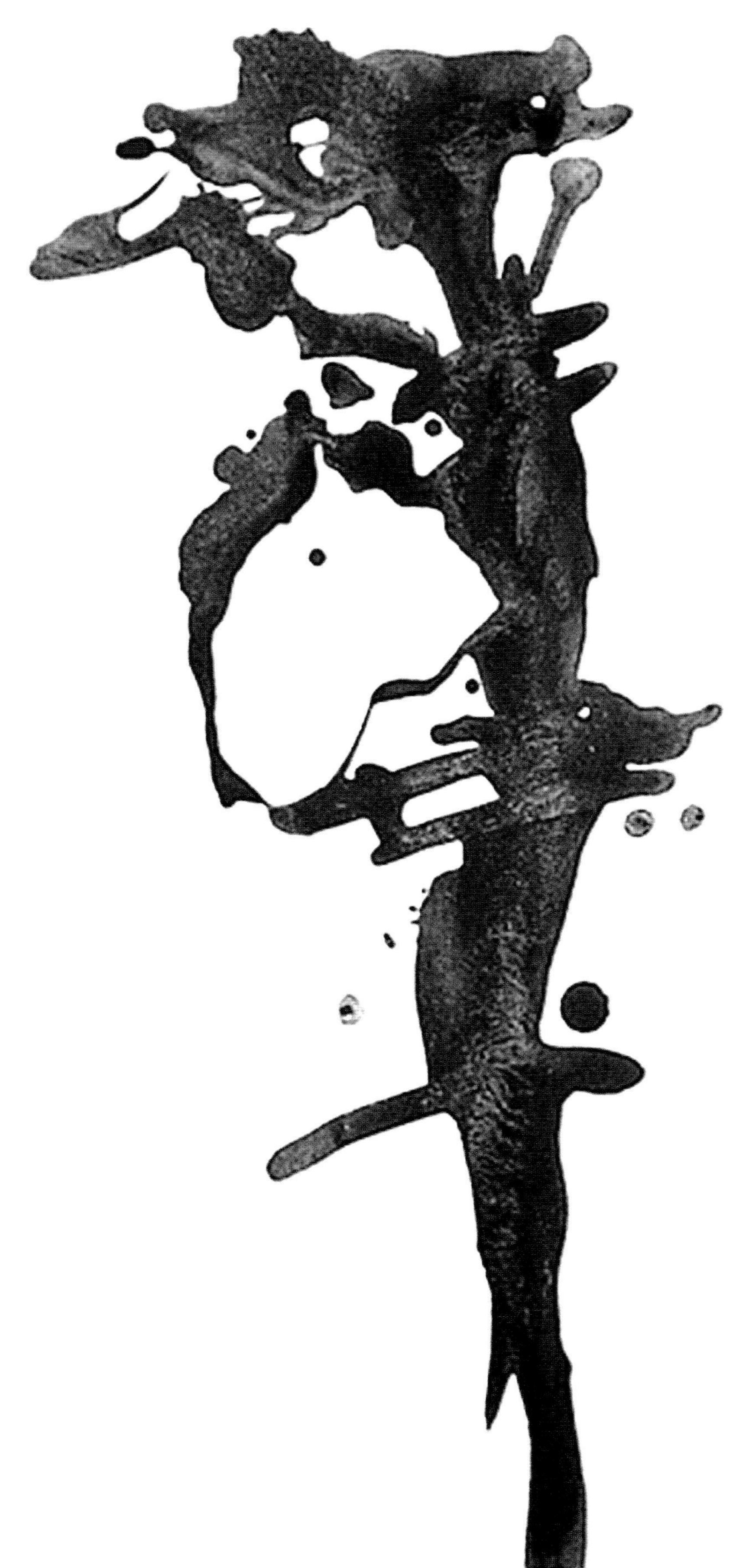

2
The Infinite Possibility of Words in Japanese Calligraphy

FUYUBI NAKAMURA

SUPPOSE YOU TAKE A MOMENT and *look at* the facing image. Perhaps you will focus on its visual aspects—colour, shape, and texture. You may wonder if it is an abstract picture or some sort of writing, since the title of this chapter includes the words "Japanese calligraphy." And if you conclude that it is indeed a piece of writing—or, more specifically, a work of Japanese calligraphy—you might wonder, what does it say? While it is a valid question, let us forget whether the image is a word, a Japanese character, or a type of writing for the time being.

The Visualized Word as a Problem

W.J.T. Mitchell talks of the "struggle for dominance between pictorial and linguistic signs" in the context of modern Western theories of art and literature.[1] With Japanese calligraphy, however, we are faced with an additional problem, because a *written* word itself may construct an image. What we see is an internal struggle within the visualized word. There is no split in Japanese calligraphy between word and image, in the sense used by Mitchell: one does not claim authority over the other, but rather word and image negotiate and coexist as one visible entity.

Japanese calligraphy is frequently regarded as *written* text that is artistically and visually expressed. This perception is historically undeniable. There was traditionally no separation between writing, literature, and calligraphy, and historically important calligraphers were predominantly fine poets. Calligraphy had a close relationship not only with poetry but also with painting. First developed in China, "the three perfections"—painting, poetry, and calligraphy practised together in works of art—emerged in the culture of the literati[2] and had a profound influence on the development of Japanese art.

However, although most contemporary calligraphy in Japan features the written word (no matter how illegible), its aim is not necessarily to act as written text—that is, convey a specific message and attach lexical meanings to words. Instead, it is to give words material and visual expression. For the calligrapher, words are what often trigger creation; they are the sources of inspiration. This remains the case even when a calligrapher is not writing actual words. One can easily forget that written language cannot exist without a material presence. When writing is illegible, as in the facing image, this material presence is accentuated.

Legibility is no longer critical in contemporary calligraphy: when words are present in calligraphy, they can entail new meanings and roles. "Writing is sensible: it has material form that can be perceived and appreciated independently of semantic content."[3] If visualizing words is a large part of contemporary calligraphic expression, it is possible for a calligrapher to even *destroy* the referential function of words.

◀ **YUGAMI HISAO**
The Stains/07, *Mumi mushu* 無味無臭 (No taste, no smell), from The Stains of Words series 2002
Sumi ink on paper
29.7 × 21 cm
PRIVATE COLLECTION; COURTESY OF THE ARTIST

The linguistic meaning of a word can become redundant, but the calligraphic words can acquire new meanings. Contemporary calligraphers are not necessarily aiming to faithfully convey the meanings of the words that they write.

What, then, do "words" *do* in calligraphy if they do not carry linguistic signification? How does the *presence* of words affect the production of calligraphy? How do we understand those works of contemporary Japanese calligraphy that consciously avoid writing words? Do we consider it graphic art, but with words whose meanings are redundant? (See chapter 1, on Chinese calligraphy.) Is the presence of words necessary for calligraphy to be *calligraphy*? We need to ask what *makes* calligraphy.

What Is Japanese Calligraphy?

In our time, Japanese calligraphy has an ambiguous and complicated status as art.[4] Once calligraphy lost its place as a medium of written communication (in the modern period), it went through a series of dramatic transformations. Japanese calligraphy is not just an artistic activity; it carries a social significance and has various functions in society. Japanese calligraphy is an artistic practice and social practice, and these two aspects are not mutually exclusive. Contemporary Japanese calligraphers practise and produce styles ranging from the traditional to the avant-garde, usually depending on which school they belong to. Historically, there are six styles of scripts, which developed in China in different periods: oracle bone script, seal script, clerical script, semi-cursive/running script, cursive script, and standard script. These styles challenge contemporary calligraphers to explore different aesthetic and artistic possibilities.

The definition and understanding of calligraphy vary, depending on the calligrapher or the calligraphic school. Japanese calligraphy is commonly known in Japan as *sho* (書), *shodō* (書道), *shohō* (書法), *shosha* (書写), or *shūji* (習字), depending on the context.[5] These terms are not rigid, and each connotes different meanings. *Sho* frequently refers to calligraphy that is consciously executed as art or fine art; it also means "writing" or "book." *Shodō* literally means "the way of *sho*"; additionally, it refers to calligraphy as art or as traditional cultural form but also reflects the religious and spiritual aspect of calligraphy. It is perhaps the most common term for Japanese calligraphy in general. *Shohō* is the method of calligraphy. *Shosha*, which literally means "copying of *sho*," and *shūji*, "learning words," are usually used in an educational context, reflecting the way in which calligraphy is taught or learned.

Importantly, in both China and Japan, calligraphy has been thought of as a "picture of the heart" (*shinga*), which is said to reflect or embody the personality of the calligrapher. This is known as *sho wa hito nari*, literally "calligraphy is the person." This perception that calligraphy and the person who writes it have a special relationship is an important aspect of understanding calligraphy.

Calligraphy is an intrinsic part of life in Japan. It is still part of the compulsory educational curriculum in Japan. It is also taught in the secondary and tertiary education sectors, and many people attend private calligraphic schools. It is, however, unusual to take up calligraphy as a purely artistic pursuit. Those who consciously define calligraphy as art remain at the margin.

The experience of learning and doing calligraphy has attracted the public, and so numerous private calligraphic schools have sprung up throughout the country. Many people start taking private calligraphy lessons because they want to have good handwriting; sometimes children are sent by their parents. Some may find calligraphy therapeutic; others may regard it as a form of mental or spiritual training. What many practitioners enjoy is the actual act of calligraphy—it is believed to induce certain effects not only on the body but also on the mind. It involves more than the act of writing (see chapter 1). There is much to experience or gain from the act of practising calligraphy, and for the typical Japanese person, awareness of the potential rewards are an incentive to start learning.

The Shifting Status of Calligraphy: A Brief History

The history of Japanese calligraphy is, in a way, the history of writing in Japan, although historians dispute exactly when and how writing was introduced in Japan.[6] Modern Japanese is written with three sets of script: *hiragana* and *katakana*, the two syllabic scripts; and *kanji*, a logographic script imported from China. Written Chinese, which consists of approximately fifty thousand characters, is at least thirty-five hundred years old and has been in use for about fifteen hundred years in Japan. This writing system is a rare example of a written form of communication in continuous use since its creation.

The inscription *Kan no Wa no Na no kokuō* (漢委奴国王) engraved on a gold seal is generally agreed to be the earliest record of writing that arrived in Japan from China, supposedly in 57 CE.[7] However, it took a few hundred years until a system of writing was adopted in Japan after the arrival of inscribed objects. The Chinese writing system was imported to Japan via Korea sometime in the fifth and sixth centuries, in the wake of Buddhism. Originally, the main purpose of calligraphy was to allow the copying of Buddhist texts.[8] Chinese characters were initially used without modification but subsequently altered to better suit the Japanese language, as the linguistic structures of the two languages differ. The indigenous syllabic scripts *hiragana* and *katakana*—developed from *manyōgana*, the first system to represent the Japanese language phonetically—were in use in the seventh century. As a result, Japanese calligraphy developed a distinctive style during the Heian period (794–1185 CE). With the addition of these two indigenous scripts, Japanese calligraphy generated new forms previously not seen in China: the strokes of *kana* link one script to another, creating a continuous and rhythmic flow of the brush (page 30; see also pages 140–41).

The Heian period was characterized by the court aristocracy; it was followed by a period of shoguns ruling the country. Calligraphy during the feudal period was strongly influenced by Zen Buddhism, which had a profound impact on Japanese society from the thirteenth century onwards. Zen-inspired calligraphy, known as *bokuseki* (ink trace), is marked by its bold and expressive style, distinct from the elegance and refined technical mastery of Heian calligraphy. The tea masters of the Muromachi period (1392–1573) favoured long scrolls with *bokuseki* calligraphy, which they displayed in the alcoves of tea houses, a practice that continues to the present day in tea ceremonies. Calligraphy gained public popularity during the Edo period (1603–1868) because it was practised by members of high society and by Buddhist monks in earlier periods.

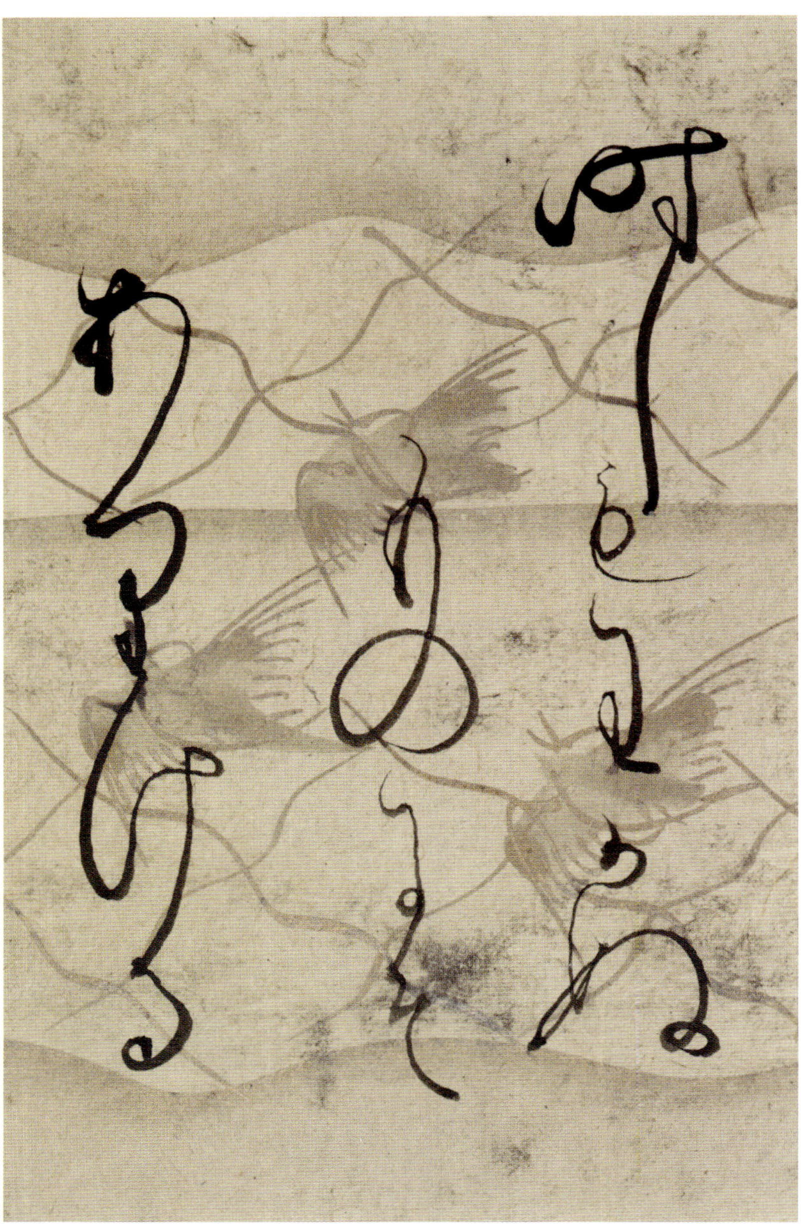

▲ **A card from *Ise monogatari uta karuta***
伊勢物語うたかるた
(*The Tales of Ise* poem cards)
Japan • mid-17th century
8 × 5 cm
UBC LIBRARY COLLECTION, PL787.I52 1700Z (RBSC)

However, calligraphy's status became contentious during the Meiji period (1868–1912), with the introduction of European concepts of art and the emphasis on calligraphy's practical skill in the newly structured education system. Calligraphy was included in the art section at the Domestic Industrial Exposition of 1881, which prompted the influential critic and educator Okakura Kakuzō (also known as Tenshin, 1863–1913) and the artist and educator Koyama Shōtarō (1857–1916) to debate whether calligraphy fit within European notions of the "fine arts." New expressions in calligraphy emerged, not only because of European influences but also because of the discovery of Chinese calligraphy classics from the Six Dynasties period (the third to the sixth century). The calligraphy of the calligrapher Nakabayashi Gochiku (1827–1913) and the politician Soejima Taneomi (1828–1905), with their innovative style and creative forms of written characters, were inspired by these particular Chinese classics and can be seen as a precursor to post–Second World War avant-garde calligraphy.[9]

Following the Second World War, Japan was occupied by the Allied Forces, led by the United States, until 1952. Traditional arts, including calligraphy, were seen as conservative or nationalistic and became linked to negative images of right-wing imperialism. Artists working in traditional media (such as calligraphy) had to break away from the old traditions in order to continue their art. Some calligraphers explored innovative modes of expression, which resulted in an active avant-garde calligraphic movement. However, avant-garde calligraphy, or *zen'eisho*, was not entirely novel in the postwar period, as the Shodō Geijutsu-sha (The calligraphic art group), led by the disciples of Hidai Tenrai (1872–1939)—known as the father of

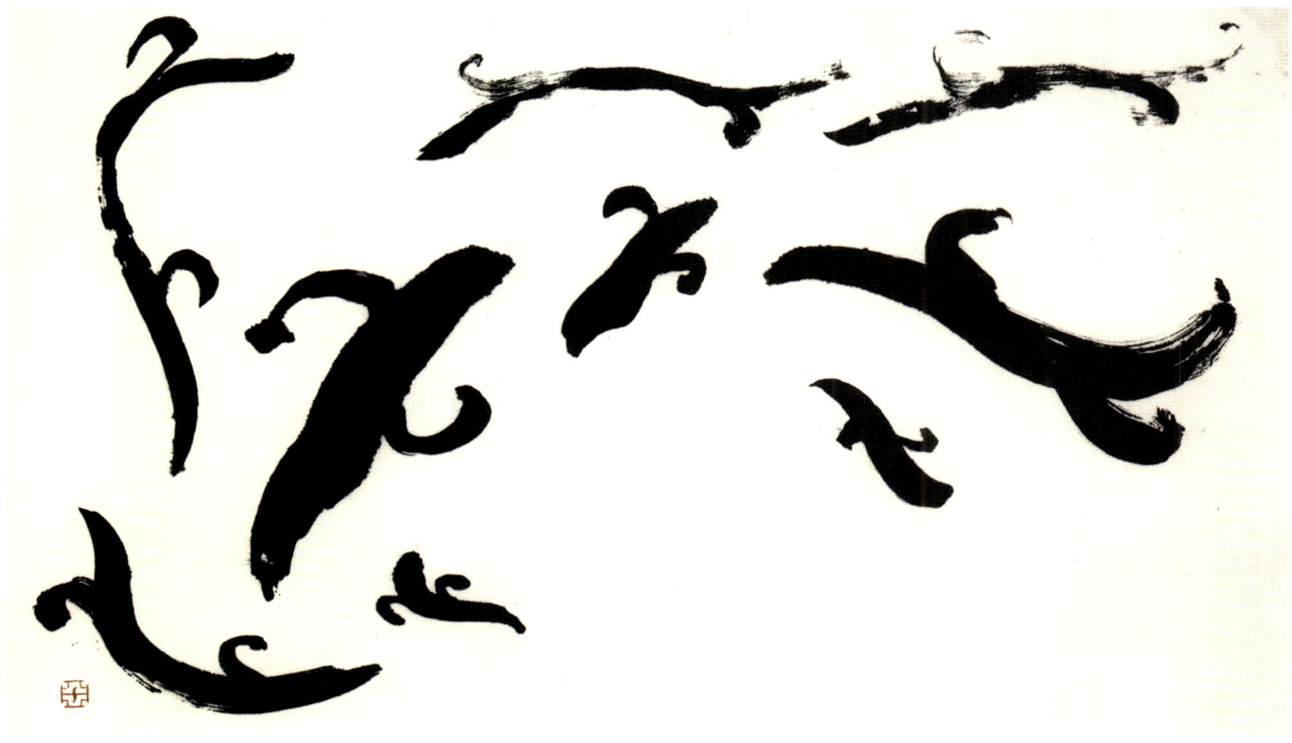

Hidai Nankoku, Work I:
Den no variēshon
電のヴァリエーション
(Variation on Lightning)
1945
Sumi ink on *gasen* paper
42 × 63 cm
CHIBA CITY MUSEUM OF ART, JAPAN; COURTESY OF TENRAI SHOIN

modern Japanese calligraphy—had already begun to produce experimental works in the 1930s.

Shodō Geijutsu-sha included calligraphers such as Ueda Sōkyū (1899–1968), Uno Sesson (1912–95), and Hidai Nankoku (1912–99). Another prominent group was Bokujinkai (Ink people group), established by Morita Shiryū (1912–98) and Inoue Yūichi (1916–85) in 1951 in Kyoto. These calligraphers were keenly aware of the artistic movements and developments in the West. For over twenty years following the end of the Second World War, Japanese calligraphers and Western artists—particularly those involved in American Abstract Expressionism and its European equivalent, Art Informel or Tachisme—looked to each other for inspiration. This period produced many works of innovative artistic expression.[10]

Hidai Nankoku was the first calligrapher to not write "words" as we know them. Hidai created *Work I: Variation on Lightning* (1945) by deconstructing the character for "lightning" (電) in various styles of script in order to construct new forms. This work is part of his *Spirit Line Works* (*Shinsen sakuhin*) series, whose title recalls the belief that calligraphy is a "picture of the heart." His father, Hidai Tenrai, proposed that one should return to the classics whenever stuck for inspiration; similarly, to create this work, Hidai Nankoku studied and used the varied styles of the character 電 listed in the Chinese dictionary, *Gu zhou hui bian* (古籀彙編; in Japanese, *Kochūihen*). Although the brush strokes appearing on the paper have their origin in a particular word, they can no longer be discerned as being related to a word. This conscious departure from the writing of words was considered revolutionary in the world of calligraphy. At the same time, this experimental development paradoxically prompted calligraphers to reconsider the role of words in calligraphy. Even after calligraphy and writing went in separate ways, "words" remained at the core of calligraphic works.

Materializing Words

Beginning in the 1940s, the innovative use of materials marked a new wave of calligraphic expression. Of course, materials and tools have always played a crucial role in the creation of calligraphic works. The calligrapher's equipment is referred to as *bunbō shihō*—the four treasures of the studio, or the calligrapher's four treasures—and consists of *fude* (brush), *kami* (paper), *sumi* (ink), and *suzuri* (ink stone). Calligraphers past and present have expressed personal and sometimes intimate relationships with these treasures, which have been at the heart of calligraphic production.

The four treasures are not merely equipment but rather an integral part of the process and outcome. It is difficult for the calligrapher not to regard the *bunbō shihō* items as a "body-part, a prosthesis, something invested with his (or her) own social agency *vis-à-vis* other social agents."[11] *Bunbō shihō* do not just reflect the calligrapher's "personhood"; the items themselves have their own personhood, as tools or materials. Among the *bunbō shihō*, the *fude* (brush) directly expresses the calligrapher's ideas and intentions. It is frequently referred to as "an extension of the calligrapher's body" and has "its own particular life force."[12] The *fude* is likened to a human being—its component parts are called *nodo* (neck), *hara* (stomach), *koshi* (hip), and so on. A few hairs placed at the tip of the *fude* are called *inochige*, or "life hair."

Calligraphy, often regarded as belonging to the domain of traditional art or culture, was given a new twist with calligraphers exploring materials and their potentials in unprecedented ways—different *sumi* (ink) effects, for example. Of particular note are Hidai Nankoku's attempts to use unconventional materials such as oil paints and nitrocellulose lacquers, or to use conventional media in novel ways. Though he continued to experiment with materials, factors such as the graphic forms of scripts and their meaning, and the application of technical skills, remained important to him. Like a pendulum, Hidai "swung back and forth between the temptations of modern art and the powerful pull of classical calligraphy."[13] He would choose a new medium to demonstrate that it was *not* the material that was of utmost importance to calligraphy. "A disciplined stroke," as Hidai calls it, is what makes calligraphy *calligraphic*. He continued to experiment with new materials and techniques. However, despite his fascination with the texture of various substances, he remained uneasy about the adoption of these "foreign" materials and methods of calligraphy.

The interplay between traditional and modern in contemporary calligraphy becomes acutely evident when we examine the materials used: either traditional material in an innovative manner, or modern material in a conventional way. The manipulation of a medium is thus often at the core of the contemporary calligrapher's experiments. It is nevertheless important to remember, though, that calligraphers are reluctant to surrender completely to the power of medium alone.

Contemporary Japanese Calligraphy

Following in the footsteps of these innovators, contemporary calligraphers continue to experiment with media. Yugami Hisao experiments with various *sumi* effects by preparing his own *sumi* mixture.[14] In his series entitled *The Stains of Words*, Yugami shows how words leave their "stains" on the writing surface. Indeed, the surface is often considered to be "where solid substance meets the space of action."[15] However, the process of creating a calligraphic work is not as straightforward as it seems. There is an element of the unknown, or "accidentality," because the outcome is determined not only by the calligrapher but also the properties of the *sumi* used.

In the case of Japanese calligraphy, inked words display a kind of agency of their own by leaving ink traces on paper after the calligrapher has executed their work with the brush. Colloid particles in the *sumi* move around when suspended in water, and the natural movement of the *sumi* shapes the outcome (this page). How the *sumi* behaves and how it leaves stains or traces behind cannot be fully controlled by the calligrapher. The *sumi* seeps into the paper, creating *nijimi* (blotchy) ink effects. Meanwhile, the friction between the brush, *sumi*, and paper leaves *kasure* (scratchy) ink effects, beyond the calligrapher's control. It is similar to baking pottery in a kiln. The potter creates a pot in a specific shape, but the final outcome is determined by the interaction of materials, temperature, and the potter's technique. Calligraphic works are created by the interaction between human agency (the calligraphers and their techniques) and the agency of things (nature and materials). In other words, calligraphy is the result of how human creativity resists, controls, embraces, or prompts the "natural" creativity of materials.[16]

▼ **YUGAMI HISAO**
***Ketsuniku* 血肉 (Blood and flesh)** 2007
Sumi ink on *gasen* paper
22 × 42 cm
COURTESY OF THE ARTIST

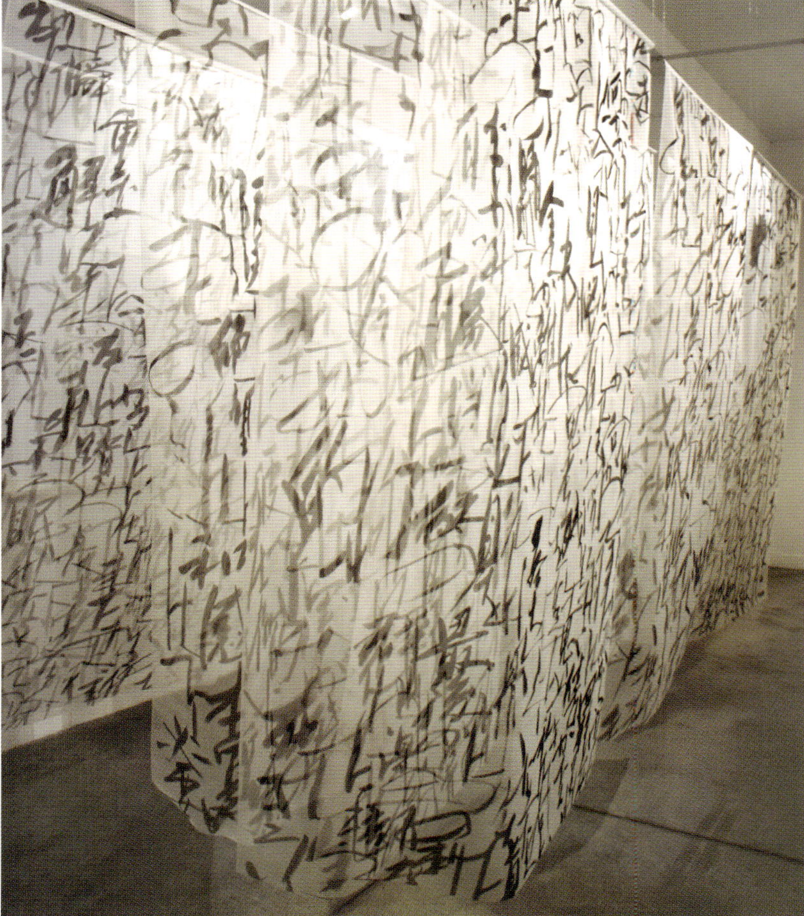

◀ **KIMURA TSUBASA**
Crowded 2006
Sumi ink on organdy
15 sheets, each 107 × 196.5 cm
COURTESY OF THE ARTIST

Despite his efforts in creating various *sumi* effects, Yugami remains uncertain to what extent he should rely on them in creating new expressions. It is a question of how much his agency as a calligrapher matters.

Kimura Tsubasa has practised Japanese calligraphy for thirty years, since the age of seven. Once equipped with traditional skills—acquired through more than a decade of training—she began seeking her own style in 1998.[17] Through her oeuvre, Kimura explores what calligraphy communicates and the interaction between meaning and non-meaning, the legible and illegible, the parts and the whole of characters and texts. She explored these themes in a series of exhibitions entitled *Crowd*.[18] The "crowd of words," as Kimura calls it, is a visual spectacle that fills the exhibition space in a way that threatens to overwhelm the viewer. This crowded style has been,and continues to be, a characteristic of her work (this page). Space or "writing surface" in contemporary Japanese calligraphy is not limited to the space within the paper, fabric, or water onto which the inked words reside. The space is much broader and freer because of the ephemeral nature of materials.

While each character has its own form and meaning, its role within the larger context changes its original meaning or allows it to be read in new ways. In *Outline* (2007), Kimura's work in this exhibition, columns of words mingle and overlap, giving a jittery edge that in turn creates a tense atmosphere (pages 98–101). Here Kimura inverts traditional understandings of space in Japanese calligraphy—she emphasizes the role of the art object as an agent, one that looks at and embraces the viewer rather than the other way around. In this space, it feels as if one is facing something huge and enigmatic. And the spacing within the calligraphic characters draws attention to the movement between one stroke and the next. Kimura believes that only calligraphic strokes make it possible to express her ideas about Japanese calligraphy. Recently, however, Kimura's work has begun to change, evincing a preoccupation with calmness and balance rather than busyness.

The Big Bang and Black Hole (2009) exemplifies Kimura's new interest in composure (page 35). This work has two components, one with legible script and another with abstract expressions in ink. Kimura writes the *Iroha uta*—a poem that is said to have been written sometime during the late Heian period (794–1185 CE) and is about the transitory nature of things in this fleeting world and expresses the Buddhist notion of impermanence[19]—to create

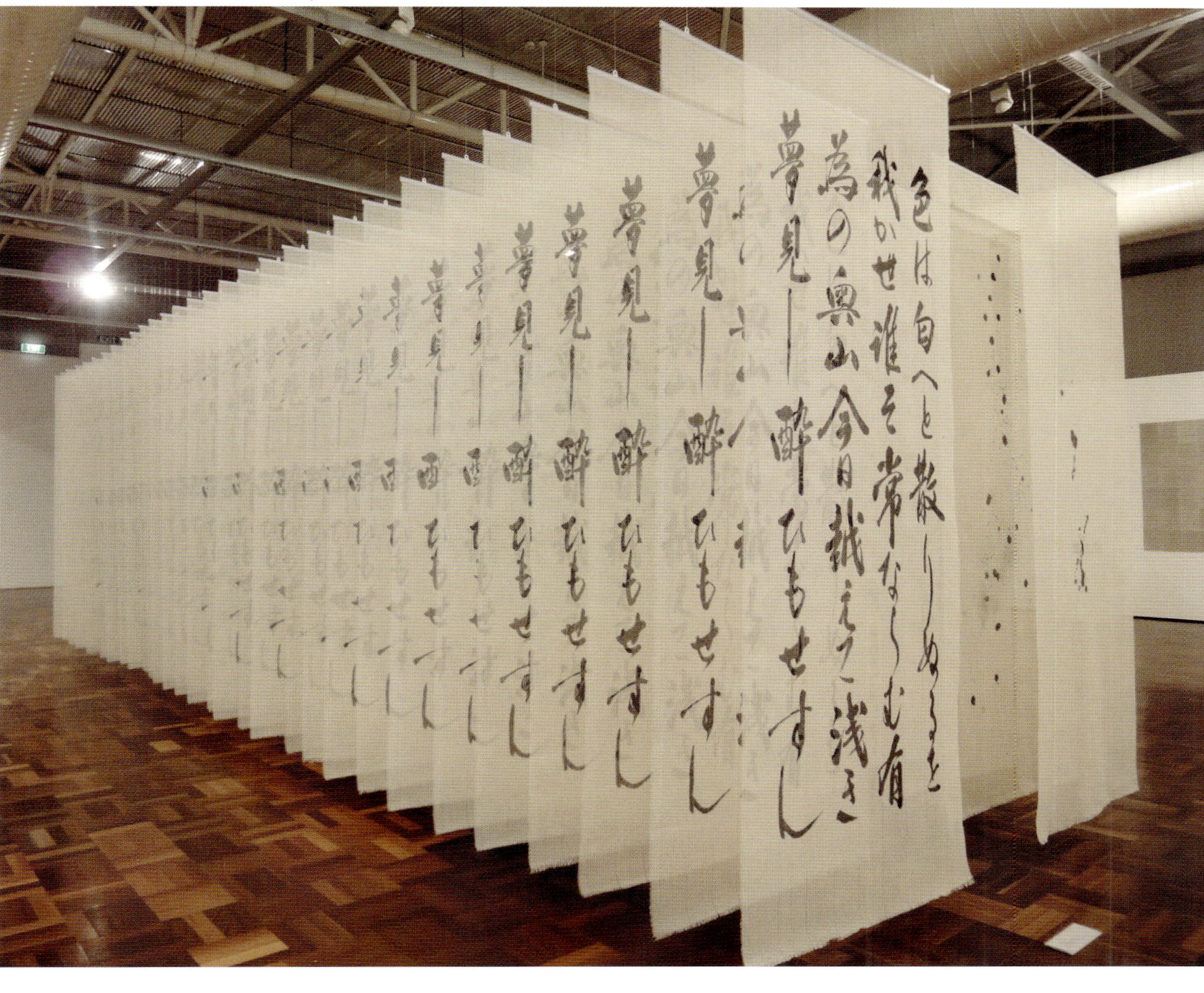

KIMURA TSUBASA
The Big Bang and Black Hole
2009
Sumi ink on *shifu* (fabric woven from paper threads)
60 sheets, each 100 × 264 cm
COURTESY OF THE ARTIST

the legible component. It is also a mnemonic verse, originally consisting of the *hiragana* syllabary, with forty-seven syllables (forty-six syllables are used in contemporary Japanese), each used only once in the poem. By exploring the concept of impermanence, Kimura expresses a kind of eternal sequence or reincarnation in her work.[20] With its combination of *kanji* and *hiragana,* Kimura's work performs a reincarnation of calligraphy that contains traces of a unique Japanese calligraphic history. That is, by combining different scripts and referencing Chinese characters and Japanese syllabary, it speaks to a Japanese tradition that originated in China and later developed its own particular style.

The title *The Big Bang and Black Hole* refers to the universe within Kimura herself. The beginning and the end, light and darkness, and internal and external spaces are expressed through the calligrapher's use of *sumi.* Just as the Big Bang refers to the origin of the universe, the various characters, each with their ancient origin story, are connected through splashes of *sumi.* It is as if Kimura were representing preliterate expressions in abstract forms. On the other hand, the idea of an ever-expanding black hole articulates the infinite possibilities of calligraphic expression. Instead of focusing only on black hues, and to represent the infinite world of light that emerges out of darkness,

▸ **YUGAMI HISAO**
***Tsuki* 月 (Moon)** 2015
Sumi ink on Kent paper mounted on wood panel
22.8 × 15.8 cm
MOA COLLECTION: 3186/3

Kimura draws attention to *sumi*'s myriad hues, which encompass even *white* hues. Here, we can see how Kimura's interest has shifted from creating work that fills the space to creating space within her work.

To maintain the integrity of calligraphic works as calligraphy or *sho*, calligraphers need to abide by certain rules or traditions. The tradition in calligraphy demands an adherence to the content (i.e., words), which "*dictate[s]* the movements of the brush,"[21] unlike a purely abstract picture detached from its precedents. Therefore, even avant-garde calligraphy tends to stay within the accepted canons, as contemporary calligraphers continue, in many ways, to follow traditional methods. Kimura says, "In order for *sho* to be *sho*, the calligraphic methods need to be consciously employed."[22] In this way, she feels she connects to the ancestors who created these characters when the calligraphy that had taken place before her is reanimated through writing.

Unlike lines in paintings or drawings, calligraphic brush strokes or lines have a certain rhythm. To compose a character, a calligrapher follows a notation or ordering of strokes, thus incorporating some sort of *predetermined action* in the process rather than merely producing strokes visually. Just as "the musical phrase is an expressive gesture shaped in sound" and the physical trace is "an almost incidental by-product," calligraphic lines are expressive gestures that are shaped as traces on paper. It is "the movement of forming these words that counts."[23] In Kimura's view, working within calligraphic conventions paradoxically offers infinite possibilities for new expression. Kimura remains determined to be a custodian of this age-old tradition as well as a creator of novel practice. In this way, her work carries *sho* into the twenty-first century.

IT IS IMPORTANT TO REMEMBER that while there is a certain degree of material agency or a sense of "accidentality" in the outcome of the examples I have shown, the practice of calligraphy involves extensive knowledge of materials and techniques to achieve the intended results. By understanding the materiality and performativity of words, we can consider Japanese calligraphy not only in terms of what we see but of what we know actually takes place during the time the inked words negotiate and resist the space and leave their traces in the final work.

The question remains whether the works discussed in this chapter can still be regarded as *calligraphic*. The avant-garde calligraphy movement has left a legacy of how "words" can be visualized and materialized in calligraphy. At the same time, it has presented various possibilities as to how the substance might create the form as well as the meaning through the interaction between human and non-human agents. Not only do organisms contained in materials such as paper and ink grow, but also cultural artifacts and artworks *grow* in culture as long as we go beyond merely looking at them. Contemporary calligraphers such as Kimura and Yugami are inventing new forms of visualized words and keep expanding the possibilities of the role and place of Japanese calligraphy.

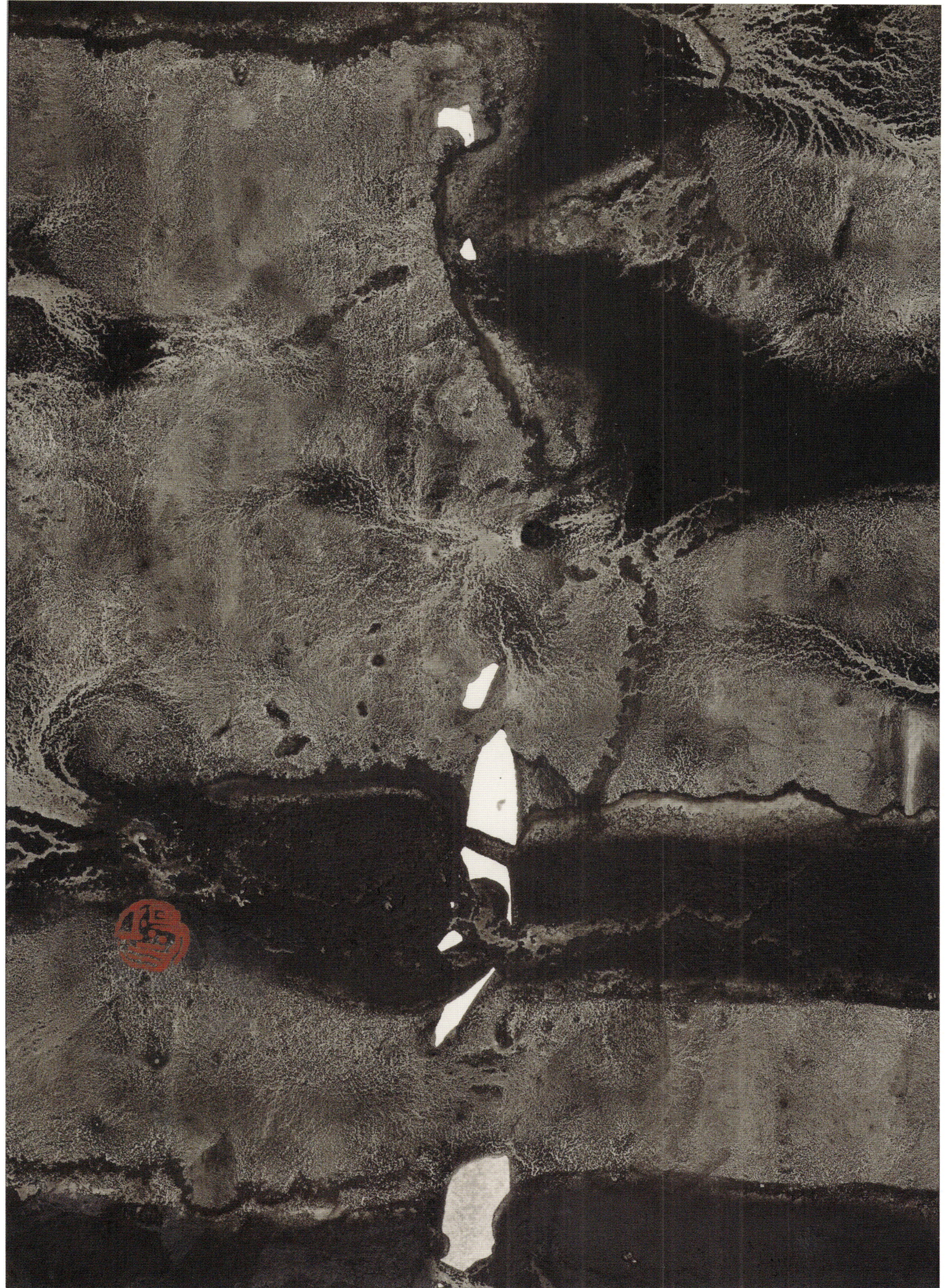

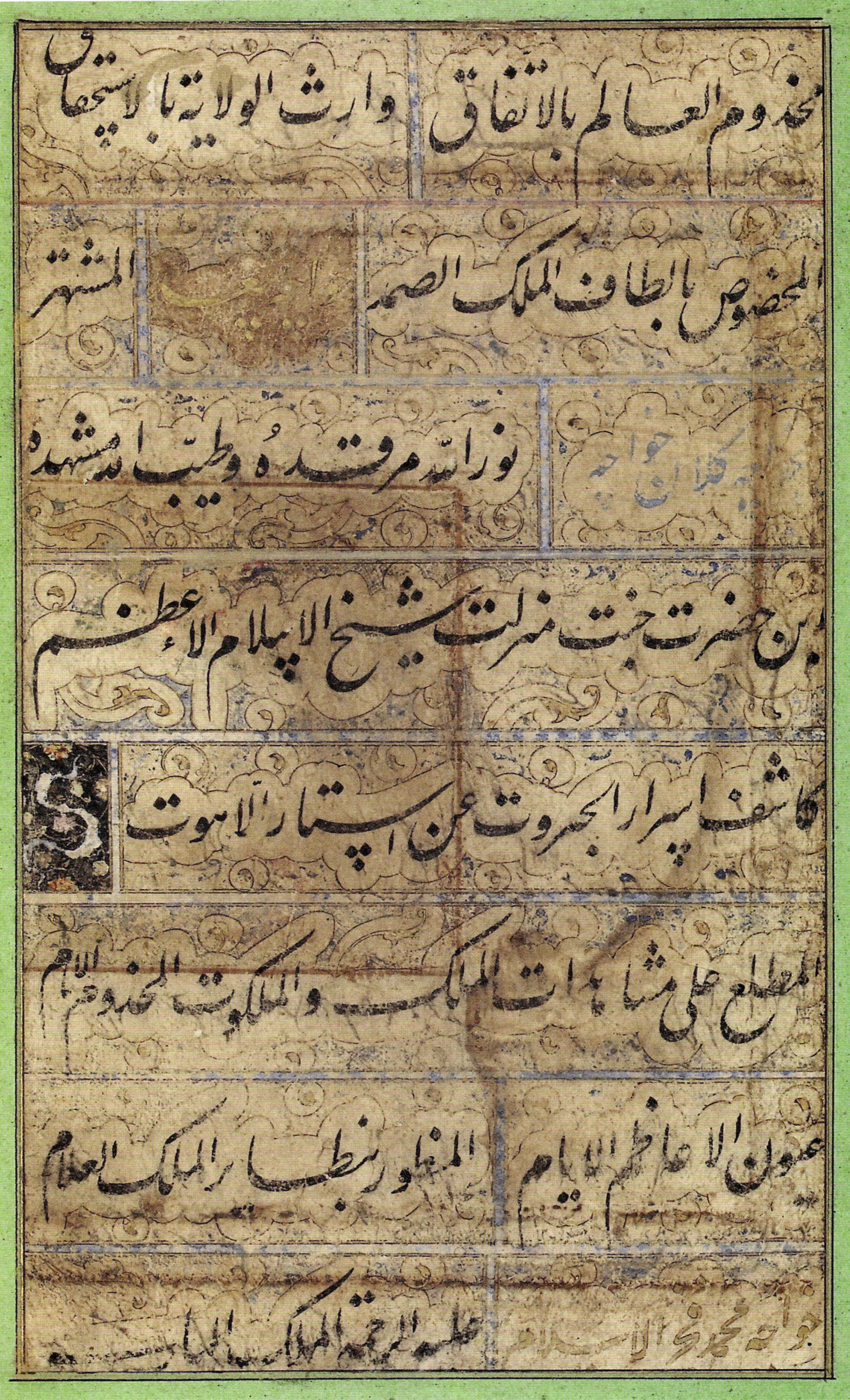

مخدوم العالم بالاتفاق وارث الولایة بالاستحقاق
المخصوص بالطاف الملک الصمد المشتهر
نور الله مرقده وطیب الله مشهده
ابن حضرت جنت منزلت شیخ الاسلام الاعظم
کاشف اسرار الجبروت عن استتار اللاهوت
المطلع علی مشاهدات الملک والملکوت المخدوم الامام
عیون الاعاظم الایام المنظور بنظر الملک العلام
خواجه محمد فخر الاسلام علیه الرحمة

3

Islamic Calligraphy and Its Spread across Asia

ALAIN GEORGE

IN CITIES IN THE ISLAMIC WORLD, calligraphy is woven into the fabric of everyday life. From Beirut to Karachi, it can be seen at every corner, on mosques, in shops, and on street walls, but also in newspapers, on websites, and in countless other media. If the Muslim call to prayer, uttered five times a day from mosques, is a unifying feature of soundscape across these regions, then the same can be said about the visual impact of calligraphy, in its various shades and textures, on their streetscape. This essay will sketch out the emergence of this art form, its key principles, and some major stylistic developments in Asia.

The Emergence and Codification of Islamic Calligraphy

To seek the origins of Islamic calligraphy is to seek the roots of Islam. The monotheist religion proclaimed by the Prophet Muhammad (d. 632 CE) in Arabia, at the very western end of Asia, initially arose from a culture of orality. Poetry was the primary art form of the pre-Islamic Arabs. It expressed the genius of language, of words composed according to strict rules of meter to evoke a multiplicity of images, with a power to move the listener. In a population that was mostly nomadic, verses were carried "in the breasts of men," as the Arabic language has it, without the burden of objects.

The Qur'an was perceived by the first Muslims as surpassing every previous linguistic achievement; and like poetry, it was initially committed to memory. But with the passing of the Prophet, and then of his Companions, came the risk of losing parts of the sacred text and of seeing conflicting variants enter into circulation. It is at this point that a canonical text of the Qur'an, the so-called Uthmanic recension, is said to have been issued—and that the history of Arabic calligraphy begins. The earliest extant manuscripts of the Qur'an, which are also the oldest-known Arabic books, are datable to around the second half of the seventh century. They were written on large parchment leaves, but their script remained akin to individual handwriting, with its natural flaws and irregularities. While they were suitable for recording the text, they could not fully match the majesty of the age-old scribal traditions of Christians and other religious groups of western Asia (what we call the Middle East today).

By the 690s, the empire of Islam had expanded to the regions between North Africa and Iran, and successful military campaigns were soon launched into the northwest of the Indian subcontinent, Central Asia, and Spain. During these crucial decades of the late seventh to the early eighth century, less than a century after the death of the Prophet, the caliphs of the Umayyad dynasty (661–750) built the first great monuments of

◂ **Persian calligraphy in *nasta'liq* style (detail)**
Iran • 16th to 17th century
Ink and pigments on paper
MOA COLLECTION, 2645/3

Islam, widely recognized as masterpieces of world architecture: the Dome of the Rock, built in 692 on the Temple Mount in Jerusalem; and the Great Mosque of Damascus, completed in 715, set within the colossal walls of a Roman temple of Jupiter. Through these realizations, Muslims were asserting their symbolic appropriation of lands steeped in centuries of civilization. As part of the same process, Arabic calligraphy was deployed in the public sphere, from the large scale of monumental inscriptions to the minute one of coins, thereby proclaiming in visual terms the identity of the new faith to a world hitherto permeated by Christian crosses and icons.

Before calligraphy could assume this iconic character, it had to undergo a seminal reform that made geometry (for letter forms) and proportion (for the relationships between these forms) its cornerstones. These principles, first applied to Arabic script at the turn of the eighth century, found a natural resonance not only in the Qur'an and its praise of the harmony of God's Creation, but also in classical antiquity. One work by Plato is particularly significant in this respect: *Timaeus*, his allegorical account of how the world came to be. In this work, which would later be translated into Arabic, Plato asserts that the Demiurge, the Creator, used geometry and proportion as the founding principles of the physical world, from the microcosmic level of atoms to the macrocosmic level of the planets. In Plato's perspective, proportion was not a mere synonym for harmony, but rather a scientific concept based on quantifiable musical intervals. The notion was ultimately derived from the striking observation, made in earlier generations and confirmed by modern physics, that simple numerical ratios underlie musical consonance.

These concepts had a profound influence on Mediterranean civilization. Proportion was notably a key principle of Greco-Roman, Byzantine, and Islamic architectural design. But early Muslims were the first to systematically transpose them to script and page layout. To this day, geometry and proportion remain the theoretical cornerstones of Arabic calligraphy, although the practicalities of their application have changed. The title *Music for the Eyes*, chosen by the contemporary American calligrapher Mohamed Zakariya for an exhibition pamphlet,[1] could well have met the approval of Qur'anic scribes at Baghdad a millennium ago.

Once its founding principles had been established under the Umayyad dynasty, Arabic calligraphy went on to flourish for some three centuries, evolving into a wide range of angular styles known collectively as Kufic (see the Qur'an manuscript on page 41). Then, between the tenth and thirteenth centuries, it underwent a radical transformation: the highly formalized Kufic styles, which had been reserved for copying of the Qur'an, were merged with cursive tendencies derived from ordinary handwriting. Geometric codifications were still applied, but with more flexibility. During this period, as a result of a gradual process of conversion, Muslims were also beginning to make up the majority of the population in societies from Iran to Spain. The new cursive scripts had the added advantage of being more easily legible to readers who lacked specialized training.

Two names were associated, in Islamic tradition, with the onset of these trends: Ibn Muqla (d. 940), a prominent official in Baghdad at the court of the Abbasid caliphs, the foremost Islamic dynasty of its time (750–1258); and in the next generation, Ibn al-Bawwab (d. 1022 or 1031),

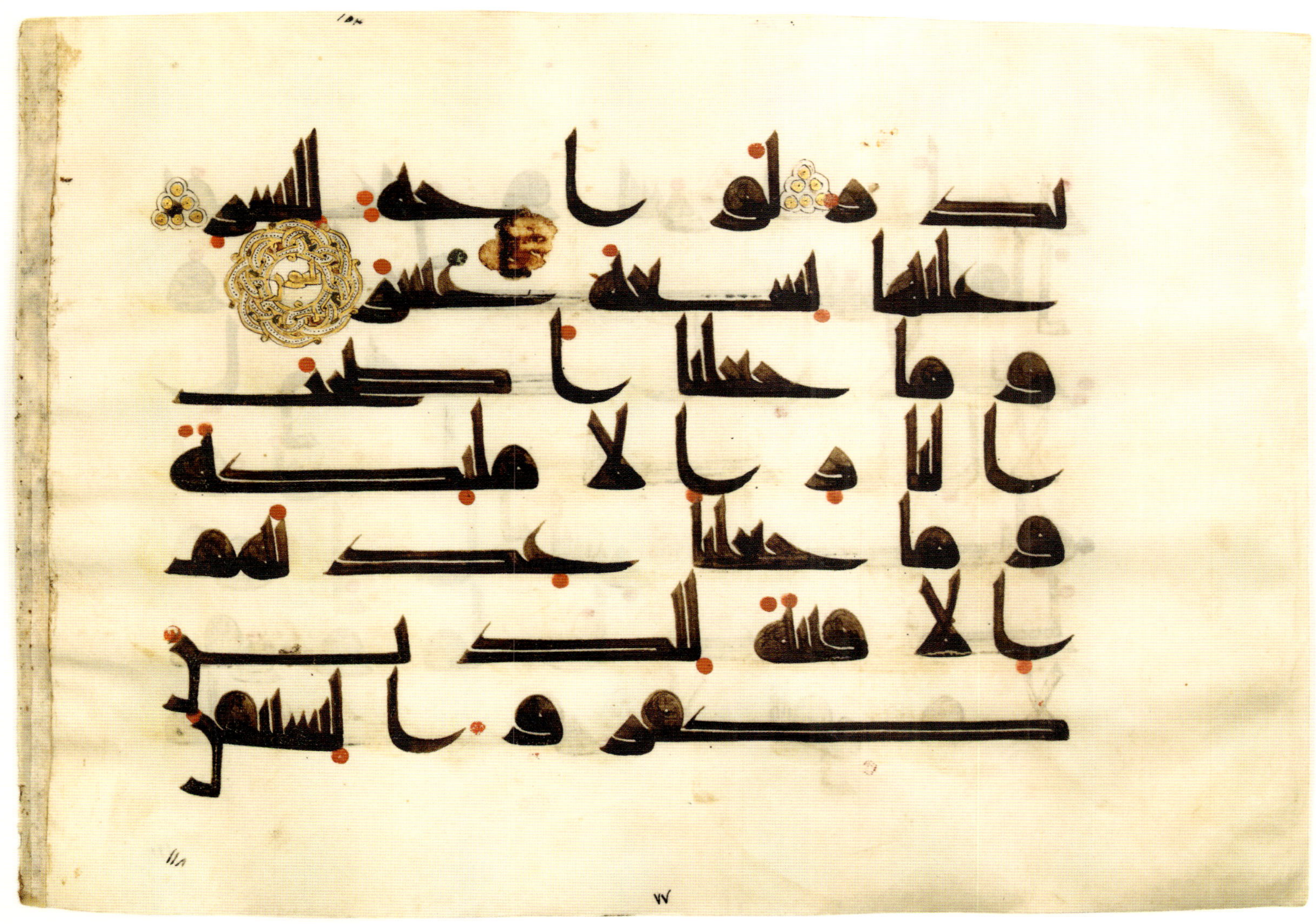

▲ **Leaf from a Qur'an manuscript in Kufic script**
Possibly Iraq, Iran, or Syria •
9th century
Vellum and ink
23.5 × 32.5 cm
MOA COLLECTION: 2988/1

This manuscript leaf with text from the Qur'an (chapter 74, verses 28–31) is in Kufic script. In the early Islamic period, Arabic calligraphy was codified according to geometrical principles. Letter forms were defined with a precision that brings to mind a modern typeface, and the whole page was also laid out proportionally. In this piece, the scribe has enhanced the appearance of the script by stretching the letters horizontally.

The absence of letter-pointing (usually consisting of thin black dashes) allows the austere, skeletal beauty of the Kufic script to be magnified. The manuscript was nevertheless intended for recitation, as shown by extensive vocalization (the notation of short vowels) through red dots. This particular page must have originally belonged to a lavish multi-volume Qur'an probably endowed to a mosque or religious institution. —Fuyubi Nakamura who worked at the court of the Buyid sultans, between Baghdad and Shiraz. The actual role of both figures is debated, with some scholars arguing that they were important calligraphers among others of their generation, rather than the wholesale creators of new trends. In either case, it is remarkable that already in this period, calligraphy was becoming the subject of art historical writing and was being collected centuries before painting or any other arts. Like their counterparts during the European Renaissance, Islamic writers on the subject emphasized the role of the individual genius as the catalyst of artistic innovation, whereas modern studies have tended to reveal more incremental processes.

The Six Pens and the Age of Yaqut

By the end of the thirteenth century, after some three hundred years of experimentation, the six classical styles that remain predominant to this day had been formed: *naskh*, *thuluth*, *rayhani*, *muhaqqaq*, *riqa‘*, and *tawqi‘*. To these, the Iranian world added in the late fourteenth century a seventh style: *nasta‘liq*. Each of these styles obeyed strict letter codifications measured by rhomboid dots reflecting the thickness of the pen nib. These rules did not ossify, however, and continued to be refined and transformed by subsequent generations. Today, the most widespread styles in the Arab world are *naskh* and *thuluth*, written according to definitions set by Ottoman calligraphers in Istanbul in the sixteenth and seventeenth centuries. Further east, *nasta‘liq* is predominantly used to write Persian and Urdu; its most revered masters were active in the fifteenth and sixteenth centuries, notably at Tabriz (Iran), Herat (Afghanistan), and Bukhara (Uzbekistan) (page 43).

The establishment of the Six Pens, as the above styles came to be known, was ascribed by Arabic and Persian writers to a single figure: Yaqut al-Musta‘simi. Yaqut is reputed to have brought the calligraphic styles to perfection by establishing a canon of forms and proportions, along with specific modulations of thick and thin strokes. Later calligraphers, many of whom traced their living artistic heritage to him through chains of master-pupil transmissions, regarded his work as a source of emulation. Dozens of manuscripts ascribed to Yaqut exist in collections worldwide today, but most are forgeries, or copies made out of reverence for the master. The nature of his actual accomplishments thus remains, at present, something of an enigma.

Yaqut began his career in the service of the last Abbasid caliph, al-Musta‘sim, to whose patronage he owed his last name, al-Musta‘simi. In 1258, al-Musta‘sim was killed at the hands of the Mongol conquerors of the eastern Islamic world, thereby bringing half a millennium of Abbasid rule to an end. Yaqut continued to practise his art under the Mongol empire, which nominally stretched from Baghdad, where he lived, to Beijing. Muslims were widely employed in the Mongol administration of China, and the oldest remaining Chinese mosques date to this period, which also saw the development of Islamic calligraphy in China.

The Diffusion of Islamic Calligraphy across Asia

This eastwards movement was not an entirely new phenomenon, as Islamic calligraphy had already been spreading for centuries beyond the core historical regions of the Islamic world, between the Nile and Oxus Rivers. The textual and archaeological record shows that organized Muslim merchant

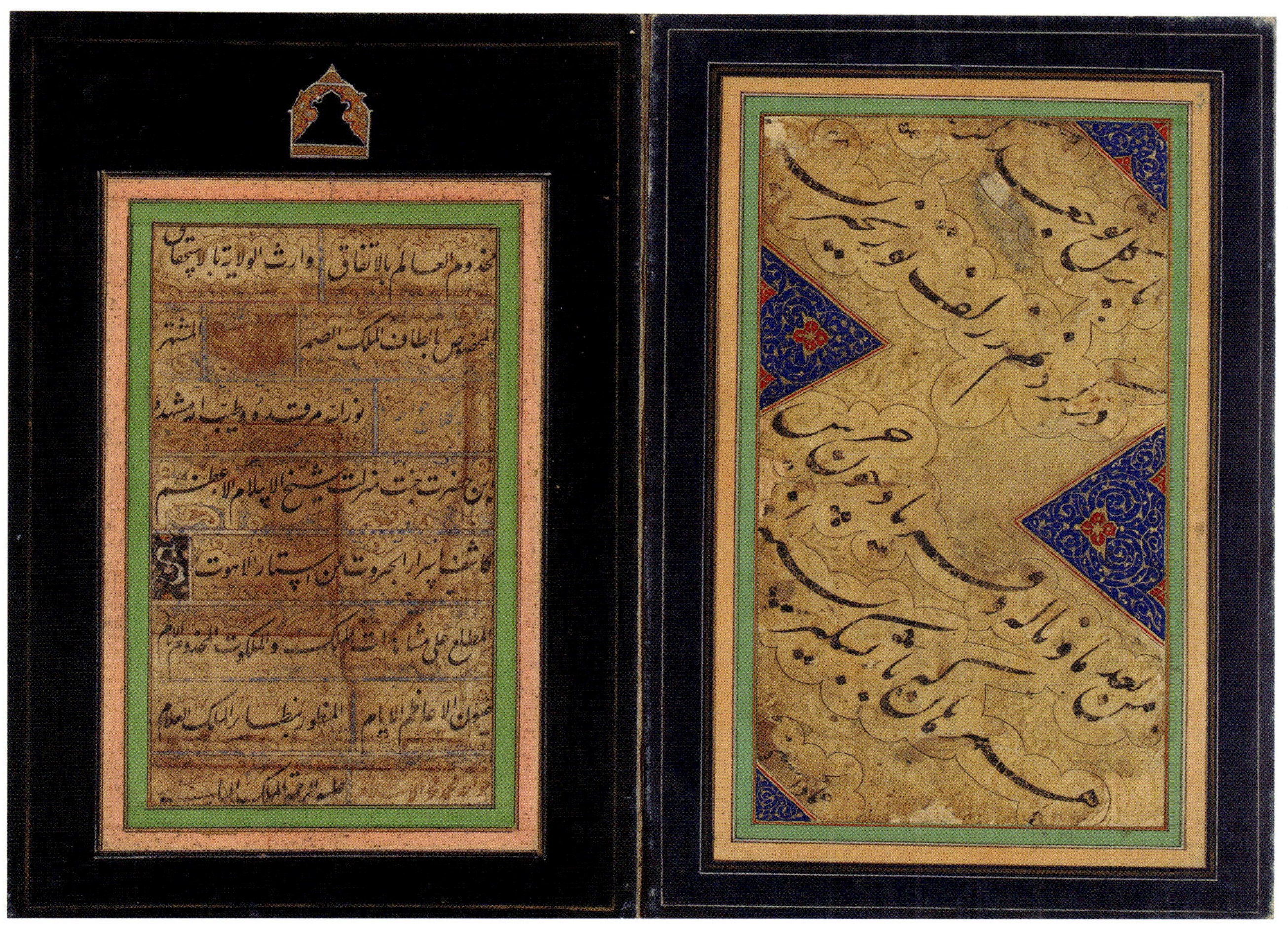

Persian calligraphy in *nasta'liq* style
Iran • 16th to 17th century
Ink and pigments on paper
31.0 × 41.8 cm (overall)
23.2 × 14.8 cm (left)
27.6 × 17.0 cm (right)
MOA COLLECTION, 2645/3

This pair of Persian album leaves contains poetry in beautiful nasta'liq *style. The one on the right is signed by 'Imad al-Hasani (d. 1615), also known as Mir 'Imad, a famous calligrapher at the court of Shah 'Abbas, in Safavid Iran, and one of the great masters of* nasta'liq. *On the left are eight lines of verse in praise of Muhammad, probably penned by a different calligrapher. Both pieces were later collected into an album, as suggested by their similar paper frames. Putting together such albums was a widespread practice in the early modern Islamic world.* —*Fuyubi Nakamura*

communities began to emerge in East Africa, western India, Southeast Asia, and southern China in the first two centuries of Islam (the seventh and eighth centuries). It is likely that calligraphy travelled along with them, although early evidence of this diffusion is rare. The trends that eventually came to predominate in these regions marked a break from the highly codified scripts of the central Islamic lands.

Chinese Qur'ans were copied, from at least the fifteenth century, in a script best described as Chinese *muhaqqaq*, as it bears features of classical *muhaqqaq*, one of the Six Pens, but is less polished in form and more expansive in articulation. While Chinese *muhaqqaq* was written with a reed pen, the normal instrument for Islamic calligraphy, Chinese Muslim calligraphers also developed a monumental style written with the brush. This style, called *sini* (the Arabic word for "Chinese") in modern times, looks winding and twisted by the standards of classical Islamic calligraphy; it is also less effusive than Chinese calligraphy, which makes it a true cultural hybrid (page 44). It was traditionally written for display pieces in mosques, on large paper sheets, on painted wooden panels, or on ceramics, and is practised to this day.

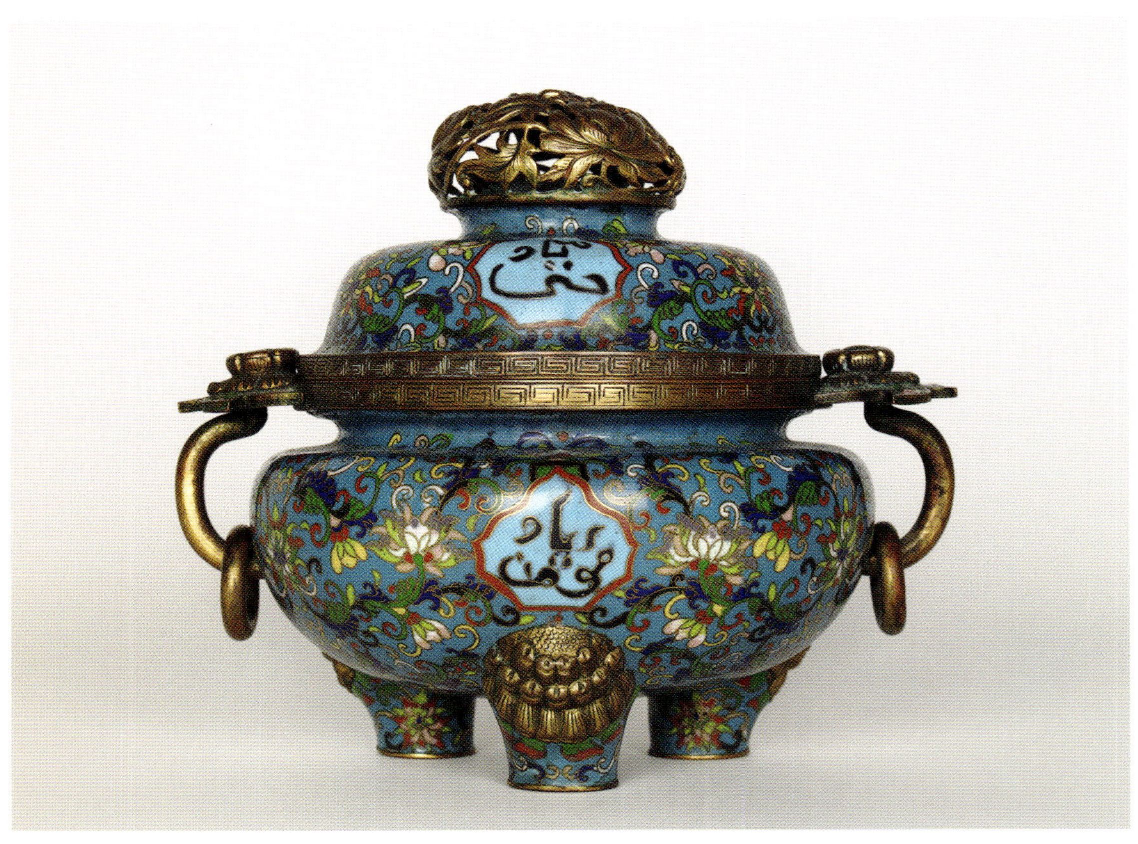

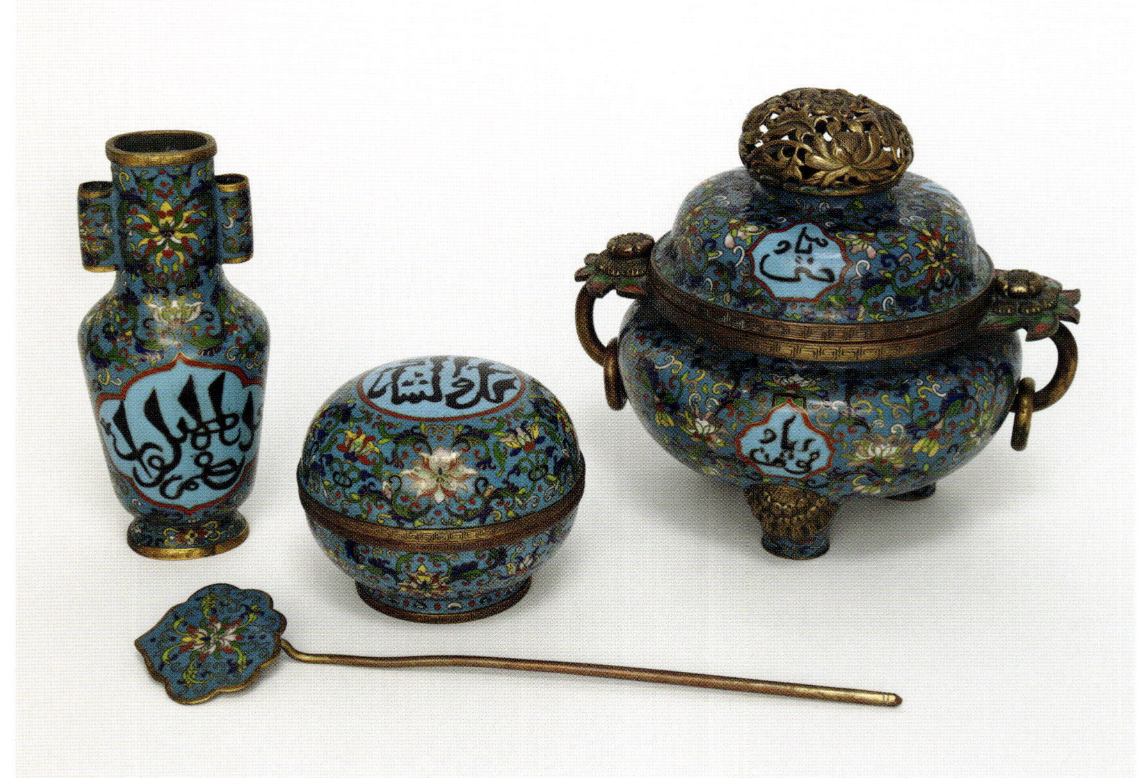

Incense set with inscriptions in *sini* script
China • 19th century
Brass metal and enamel
[Incense burner] 16 × 18 × 14.5 cm
MOA COLLECTION, 2988/3 A-B
[Incense box] 8 × 9.5 cm
MOA COLLECTION, 2988/4 A-B
[Vase] 15.2 × 7 × 6 cm
MOA COLLECTION, 2988/5
[Spatula] 1.2 × 5.5 × 24.2 cm
MOA COLLECTION, 2988/6

Incense has a significant presence in devotional life throughout the Muslim world. This incense set was probably made in Guangdong Province in southern China. The cloisonné enamel vase, incense box, and incense burner are decorated with a dense design of flowers and scrolling leaves on a turquoise ground, while cartouches containing Arabic inscriptions in the Chinese style of calligraphy known as sini *appear on a pale turquoise ground.*
—Fuyubi Nakamura

In the Indian subcontinent, a distinctive style of Islamic calligraphy had emerged by the fourteenth century: bihari. This style has a distinctive boldness, with its angularity and strong contrasts between thick and thin strokes. Its letter definitions are less precise than with the Six Pens, but this also gave its practitioners more freedom of expression, often with a palpable sense of playfulness. Bihari remained a living tradition for half a millennium, until the nineteenth century. But from the sixteenth century onwards, particularly under the Mughal and Qutb Shahi empires, calligraphers in India increasingly adopted classical styles, and the movement of craftsmen and objects between India and Iran led both traditions to converge.

Maritime Southeast Asia—Nusantara in Malay—is the coastal region between Thailand, the Malay Peninsula, Indonesia, and the southern Philippines. Here, Islamic calligraphy was typically written in forms derived from *naskh*, the most common book hand in the central Islamic lands, with more or less marked departures from established norms. The earliest preserved Islamic manuscripts from these regions date to the seventeenth century, even though the tradition they represent must have originated earlier. The Arabic alphabet was also used to write local languages, as in many other pre-modern societies across the Old World, particularly in sub-Saharan Africa.

In early modern times, as Islamic calligraphy was evolving into myriad forms in Southeast and East Asia, it reached peaks of refinement and creativity in the central Islamic lands, particularly in Istanbul, the capital of the Ottoman empire; but also in such centres as Isfahan and Shiraz in Iran, as well as Lahore, Delhi, and Golconda in India. Traditional styles, such as *naskh*, were refined, and the illumination reached fresh expressions in every period (see the Qur'an on pages 2–4). New forms also evolved, and one general trend was the development of large display pieces in monumental script. These could be composed as words set in an invisible geometrical frame; or, for instance, as mirror writing, whereby a word or phrase is replicated symmetrically across a vertical axis. There was also a shared interest, across the early modern empires of Islam, in pictorial calligraphy, in which the contours of letters and words form an image—for example, a lion (pages 48–49), a pear, or a man in prayer.

Calligraphy in Modern and Contemporary Times

Standing in any part of the Islamic world in the nineteenth century, an observer would have seen calligraphy as a vibrant, revered, and apparently immovable tradition. But its transmission and renewal were challenged by the growing cultural hegemony of European modernity. The traditional modes of learning with which Islamic calligraphy was associated were gradually being eroded by modern science, just as Arabic printed books, which had existed since the sixteenth century, were becoming so widespread as to encroach on the prerogatives of scribes, and hence on a centuries-old approach to the transmission of knowledge. Then, towards the early twentieth century, the Arabic script was replaced, in many countries, by European alphabets: Latin in sub-Saharan Africa, Southeast Asia, and the Republic of Turkey; and Cyrillic in Soviet Central Asia. This combination of factors led to a decrease in its teaching at the school level, a decline of its status, and a loss of institutional support for training at higher levels.

Even though calligraphy receded in this period, it was perpetuated in different local contexts. Its recent history in Istanbul encapsulates many of these trials. In the 1920s, the city went from being arguably the foremost centre for calligraphy in the world to one in which its most renowned practitioners had to work with little recognition, mostly in the private sphere. By the second half of the twentieth century, as a renewed interest in their art began to surface, these Ottoman masters were still alive and available to pass on their skills to the next generation. The last of them died in the 1980s, and today Istanbul is a thriving centre that perpetuates a tradition with living roots in the Ottoman era. In the present age of globalization, it attracts students from all corners of the Islamic world, from Morocco to Indonesia, but also North America, Western Europe, and Japan, to receive advanced training in classical calligraphy.

It takes several years of full-time study to master one of the Six Pens, and the process is still sanctioned today by the award of a traditional "licence," or *ijaza*, in Istanbul. The student begins by learning single letters, each with its particular articulation of forms, set of proportions, and variations of stroke width, based on exemplars set by a master (diffused today as printed booklets, whereas original works were used historically). The student then moves on to combinations of letters and eventually to whole words. At every step, his or her practice sheets are corrected by the teacher. Once fully trained, the student prepares a formal composition, usually in a set rectangular format. If approved, it is endorsed in writing by one or several masters and retained as a diploma (the *ijaza*), which confers formal permission to sign one's work in this style.

The late twentieth and early twenty-first centuries have also witnessed a burgeoning of expressions that merge calligraphy with contemporary art. This phenomenon, with origins in twentieth-century Arab Modernist painting and Iranian art movements, encompasses such diverse forms as paintings on canvas, compositions on paper, photography, installation art, and sculpture. Islamic calligraphy remains as ubiquitous as ever in everyday life. Graphic designers and typographers have brought it into their work with increasing sophistication, while more traditional commercial workshops continue to produce street banners, shop signs, film posters, and truck decorations. In the last decades, graffiti artists like eL Seed (page 47), Yazan Halwani, and Shamsia Hassani (pages 86–93) have also embraced calligraphy with exuberant vitality in such cities as Tunis, Cairo, Beirut, Kabul, and Tehran.

Thus, just as the modern art forms find an enthusiastic response in a globalized art market, the core roots represented by its traditional forms are enjoying some measure of renewal. In the same societies, from Morocco through Egypt to Pakistan, different people are producing or appreciating calligraphy in a wide variety of ways, and for different reasons: as a spiritual discipline, notably among traditional calligraphers, but also for some artists working with modern forms; as a revitalization of cultural values challenged and often sidelined in the past century, particularly in street art and graphic design; and as an identity marker that singles out work from the Middle East and Islamic world in the contemporary art market. The borders between these broad categories are naturally porous.

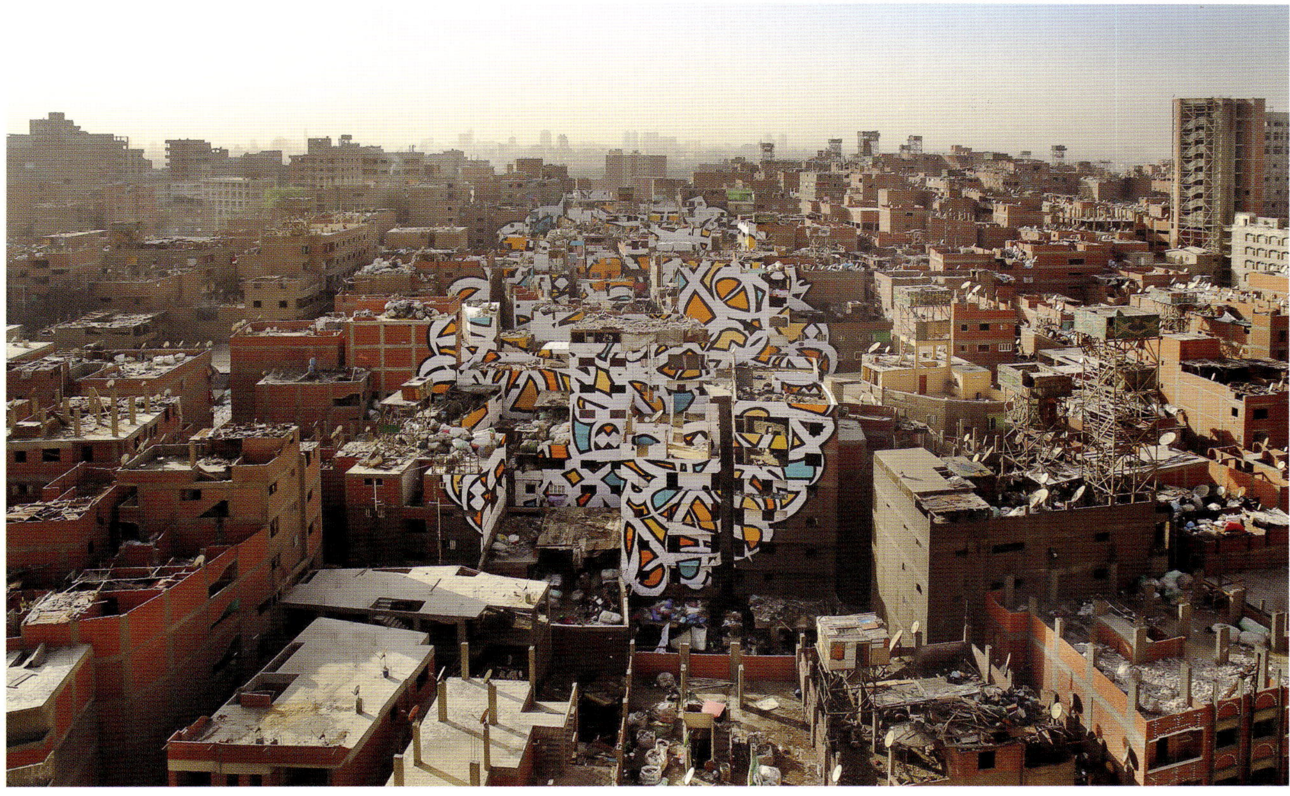

EL SEED
Perception 2016
Mural in Cairo, Egypt
COURTESY OF THE ARTIST
This monumental calligraphic mural by eL Seed, a French-Tunisian artist, was executed across nearly fifty buildings in a marginalized Christian neighbourhood of Cairo. This art piece with Arabic calligraphy is visible in its entirety only from a distant vantage point.

From Ancient Roots to the Twenty-First Century

As has become apparent, the roots of Islamic civilization plunge into late antique Arabia, the Greco-Roman world, and Iran. Islamic calligraphy reflects this heritage, being an art form ruled by rational principles and executed in slow, controlled motions. It presents a contrast, in this respect, to the flow of energy channelled through the brush in East Asian calligraphy. But the hand movements of Chinese and Japanese calligraphers can be slow and measured, and the praxis of Islamic calligraphy will often have a meditative dimension. These apparent distinctions become particularly blurred in certain styles, such as *sini* script in China, with its ample yet still relatively restrained curves, or the most free-flowing expression of Persian calligraphy, called *shikasta nasta'liq*. The connections between calligraphy and Islamic spirituality, particularly Sufism, run deep, but these connections have mostly been conveyed through oral teachings. A few treatises that express this dimension of the art exist, notably the *Adab al-Mashq* (Manners of practice) by Baba Shah, a calligrapher active in Isfahan in the late sixteenth century.

For over a millennium, calligraphy has retained a unique status in the diverse cultures of the Islamic world because of its innate association with the Qur'an and its inherent plasticity. The latter was appreciated even in medieval and Renaissance Europe, where motifs inspired by Kufic calligraphy frequently found their way into decorative arts. Today, the deceptively simple elegance of Islamic calligraphy continues to garner a near-universal appeal. Only time will tell where the current burgeoning of new and old forms will lead its evolution into the next century.

▶ **Pictorial calligraphy of a lion**
India • 17th century
Opaque watercolour, ink, and gold on paper
12 × 19.2 cm
THE AGA KHAN MUSEUM, AKM526

This splendid calligraphic lion is an example of zoomorphic writing, where calligraphers blended the arts of writing and drawing by using words to form animal and human shapes. The Arabic text is a supplication to 'Ali, the cousin and son-in-law of Prophet Muhammad. 'Ali, because of his courage and valour, was known to Muslims by the epithet "The Lion of God," which would explain the animal chosen here. The seventeenth-century calligrapher was so faithful in copying the earlier model that he also replicated the signature of the original sixteenth-century calligrapher that forms the hind leg of the lion.
—Filiz Çakir Phillip and the Aga Khan Museum staff

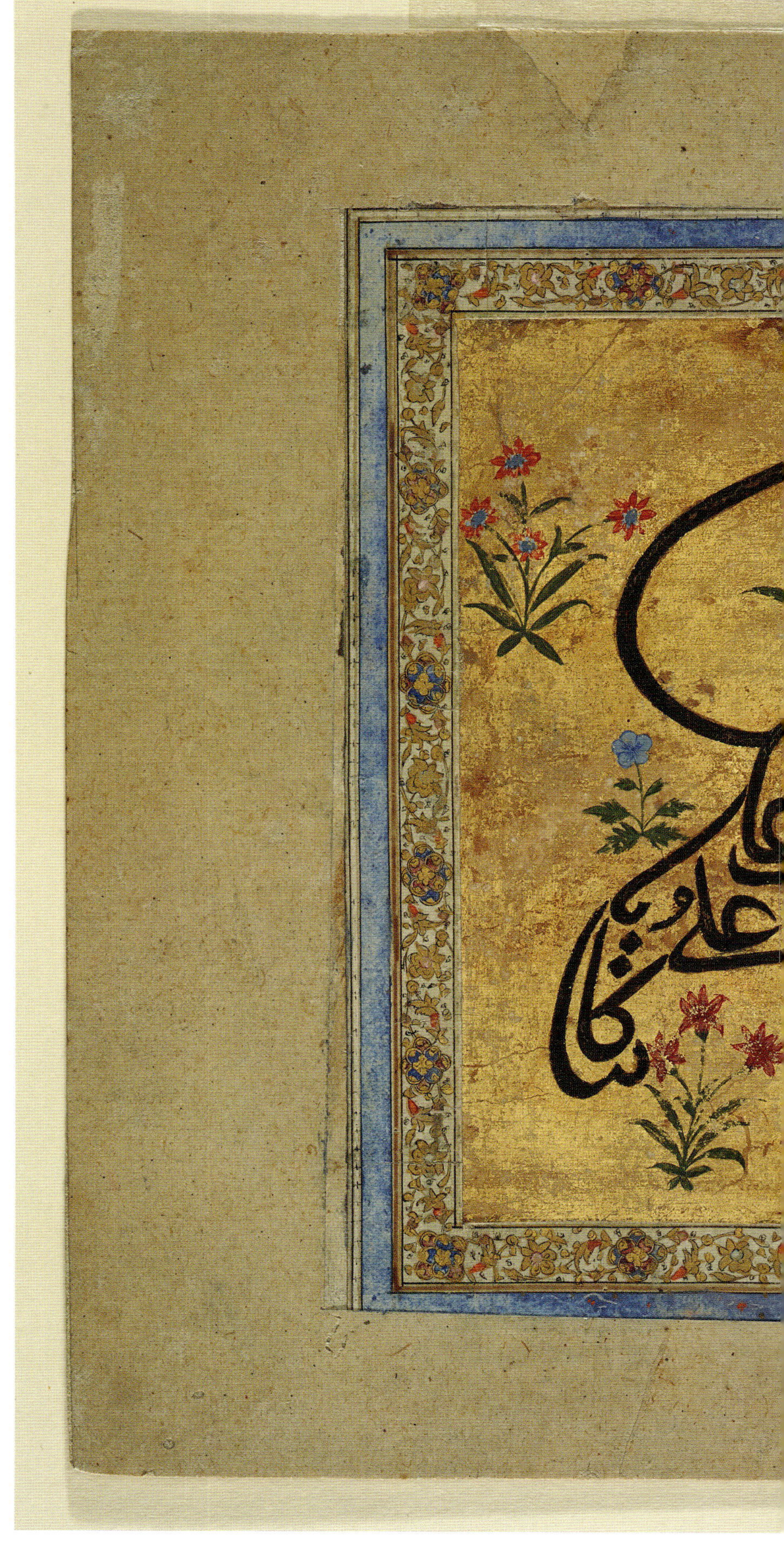

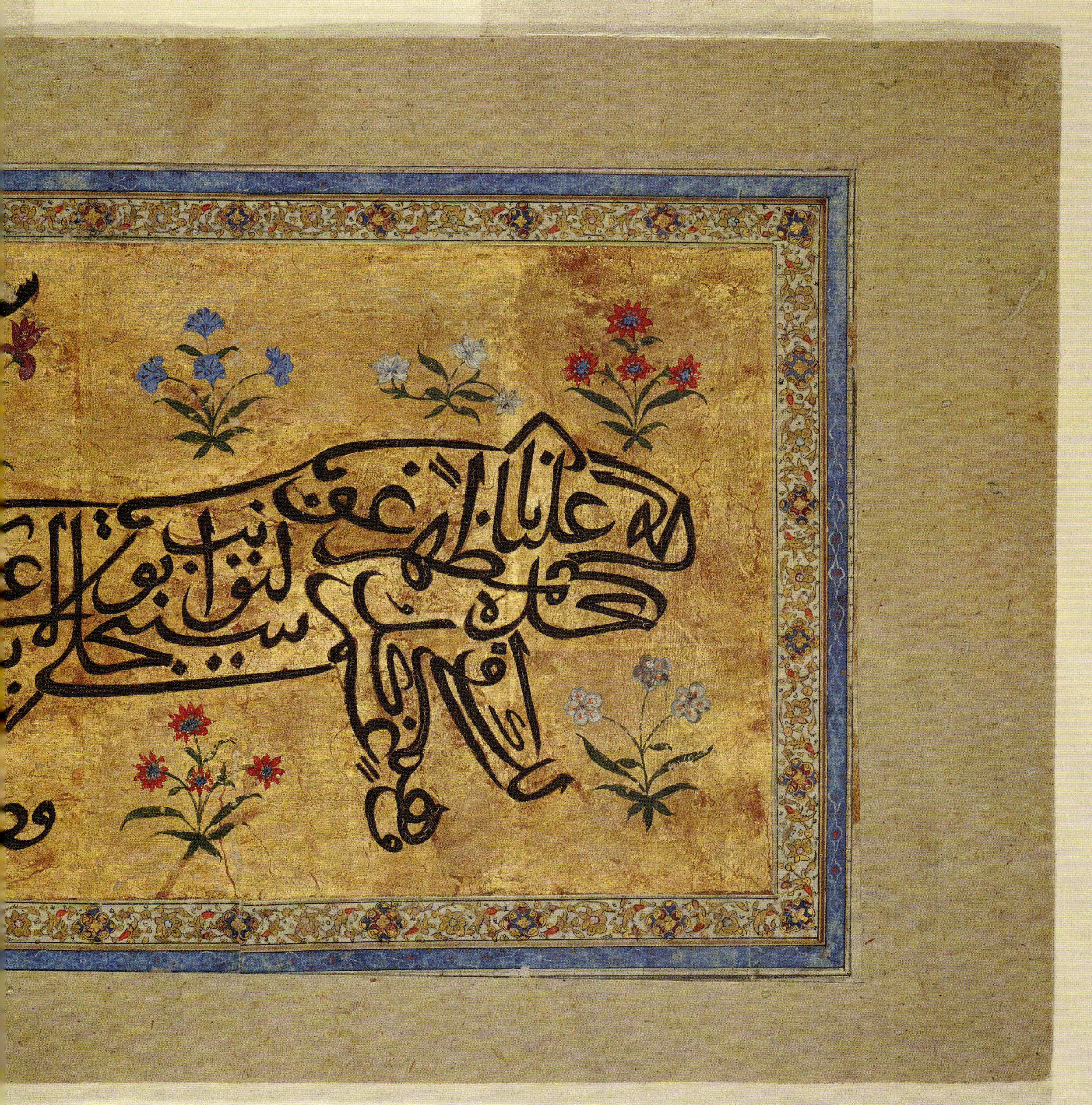

Calligraphy by Fath ʻAli Shah
Iran • ca. 1800
Opaque watercolour, ink, and gold on paper
36.3 × 26.7 cm
THE AGA KHAN MUSEUM, AKM235

This piece of Persian calligraphy in nastaʻliq *style was created by Fath ʻAli Shah (r. 1797–1834), the second ruler of the Qajar dynasty in Iran (1779–1925). He was trained in calligraphy like many other rulers, and followed the style of Mir ʻImad al-Hasani (d. 1615), the sixteenth-century master of* nastaʻliq *calligraphy. The text in this piece is a repetition of one single line: "My reed pen shames Jupiter (lord of planets) and Mercury (scribe of the heavens)." His signature appears between the first and second lines. —Filiz Çakir Phillip and the Aga Khan Museum staff*

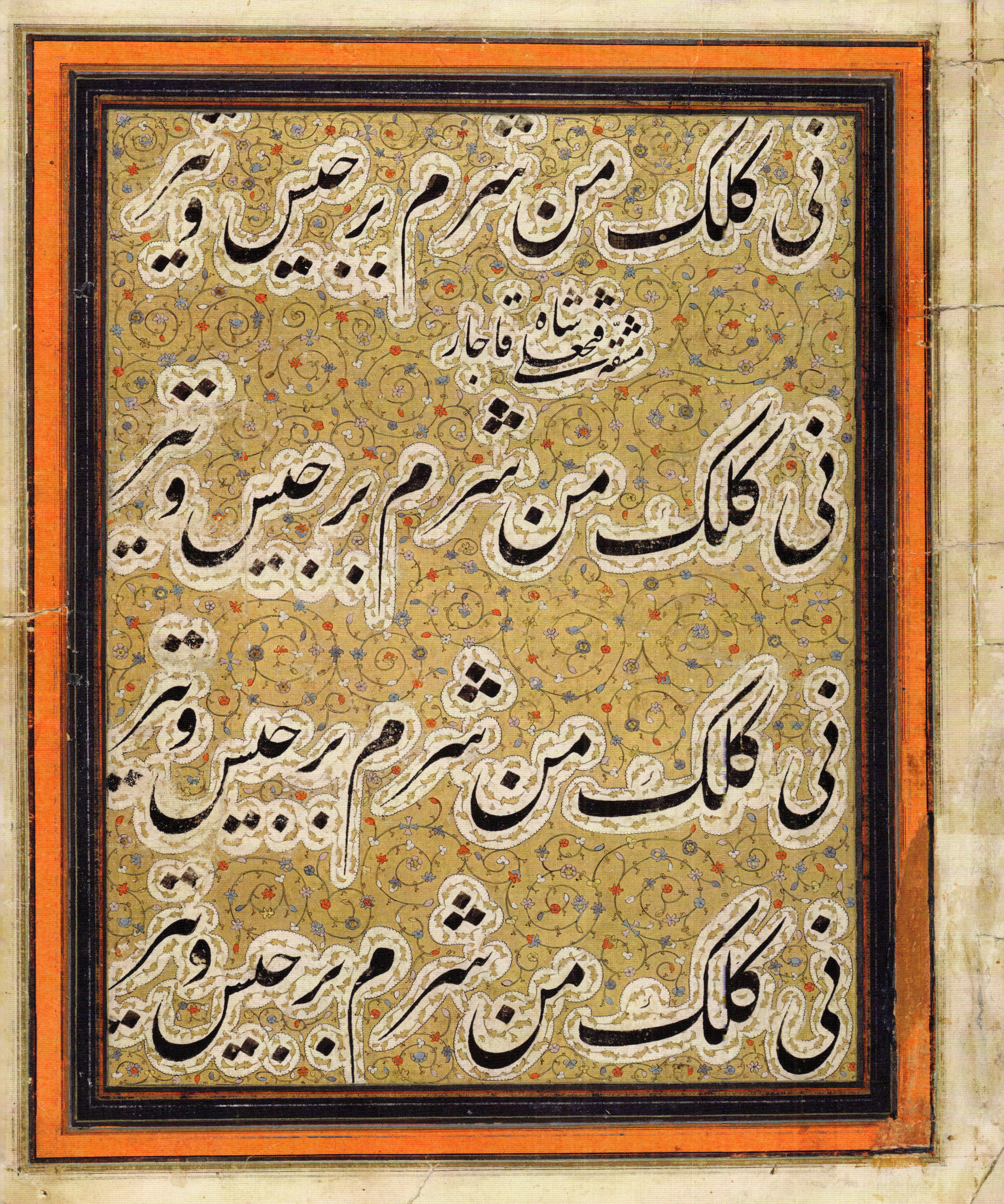
مشقه فتحعلی شاه قاجار

गणेशायनमः ॐ श्रीगुरुभ्योन्नमायनमः
निर्यस्यस्मरणमात्रतोगदाः उमादिभिषजेशे
ः ॥ रागादिरोगान्सततानुषक्तानशेषका
त्सुक्यमोहारतिदाञ्जघानयोपूर्ववैद्यायन
नआयुष्कामीयमध्यायंव्याख्यास्यामः इत
र्षयः आयुष्कामायमानेनधर्मार्थसुखसा
शेषविधेयःपरमादरः ब्रह्मास्मृत्वायुषो
ग्रहात् सोश्विनौतौसहस्राक्षंसोत्रिपुत्रादि
णादिकांस्तेतुपृथक्तन्त्राणितेनिरे तेभ्योऽति
मातनेभ्यस्थः क्रियतेष्टांगहृदयंनातिसं
बालग्रहोर्ध्वांगशल्यदंष्ट्राजरावृषान् अष्टा
स्तानेषुसंस्थिता वायुःपित्तंकफश्चेतित्रयोदो

4

The Public Life of Sanskrit Manuscripts

ADHEESH SATHAYE

THE MUSEUM OF ANTHROPOLOGY at the University of British Columbia (MOA) possesses several manuscripts composed in Sanskrit, the classical language of India, though only one of them actually hails from the subcontinent itself. For centuries, in fact, Sanskrit texts accompanied the spread of Buddhist and Hindu traditions beyond India's borders, and MOA's collection speaks evocatively to the impact that they have had in East and Southeast Asia.[1] In India itself, the classical language of Sanskrit served as the pre-eminent medium for producing and disseminating elite works of intellectual, sacred, and poetic expression for more than two thousand years. This essay will briefly explore the cultural value of Sanskrit manuscripts, their life as material objects, and how they were produced and used in pre-modern India.

First, it is worth taking a moment to appreciate the complexity of the archives that we have today and the work that Sanskritists do within them. According to conservative estimates, more than seven million manuscripts are housed in public repositories in India alone, not to mention those in Europe, North America, and the rest of Asia. And there are undoubtedly many millions more that are gathering dust (and themselves turning to dust) in private cabinets and attics throughout South Asia. Just cataloguing and preserving these manuscripts is a Herculean task, never mind saying anything meaningful about their date, provenance, or authorship. Beyond that, there is the problem of the manuscripts' textual history. Though Sanskrit had been the premier register for elite intellectual expression since at least 1000 BCE, the peak of literary activity in this language, by most accounts, came during a roughly thousand-year period between the formation of the Gupta Empire and the Delhi Sultanate, about 300–1300 CE. During this so-called Cosmopolis, documents written in Sanskrit were regularly disseminated across a vast geographical area stretching from Afghanistan to Bali, including places where the local vernaculars were totally unrelated to Sanskrit. Due in large part to the unforgiving climate of South and Southeast Asia, and the relentless work of rodents, insects, and fungi, few physical works from this era have survived. Instead, what we have today are multiple copies of the original exemplars—or rather, copies of copies of copies—that were produced by scribes of later times.[2]

Because they were handmade, these medieval copies typically contain mistakes, interpolations, and deviations from one another. And so, at its core, the modern study of Sanskrit is *philological*—the aim is to collect existing manuscript copies of any given text, to compare what they say, and to reconstruct what the original version likely would have been. Textual criticism, as this method is

◂ **Sanskrit paper manuscript in Devanāgarī script (detail)**
Eastern India • ca. 19th century
Ink on paper
WELLCOME LIBRARY, LONDON, UK, SHELFMARK GAMMA 15, FOLIO 1, VERSO

called, is rigorous and time-consuming work, and the resulting scholarly editions of Sanskrit texts are often quite expensive to publish and highly technical in their appearance. It is no surprise, then, that the field of Sanskrit studies has become marginalized in today's fast-paced, theory-driven academy; still, it is indispensable for the historically grounded study of India, for without knowing precisely what the texts were, we can say little about the contexts in which they were written down.[3]

On the other hand, for an average person today, whether in South Asia or Canada or anywhere else, the encounter with Sanskrit manuscripts is a strikingly visual one—an immediate engagement between the eyes and an obscure but fascinating set of symbols etched or drawn on pieces of handmade paper, birch bark, or palm leaf. Though few people today are able to read the texts, Sanskrit manuscripts are nonetheless treated with reverence as repositories of transcendent wisdom, as relics of an ancient, vanishing heritage, as sacred artifacts, or even as tools for fortune-telling. This was, to some extent, also true in the ancient and medieval past. Manuscripts were treasured for the information they carried, whether sacred, intellectual, or expressive, and were created and copied to preserve and transmit this knowledge in visual form. Sometimes manuscripts were lavishly illustrated and decorated, and gifted by rich patrons to temples or gurus to earn religious merit. And in some esoteric contexts, they came to have magical, occult, or mystical functions, such that the symbolic value of Sanskrit texts carried more weight than their literal meaning. We should note that in pre-modern India, the engagement with manuscripts would rarely have been a *private* one. Rather, Sanskrit manuscripts were fully couched within *public* acts of performance: writing a manuscript involved a student or scribe faithfully recording the words of the original author as he or she spoke them out loud, while reading a manuscript involved a live exposition of the text by a skilled reader and knowledgeable guru to groups of eager listeners whose grasp of Sanskrit was cursory at best. This is to say that the long history of Sanskrit manuscript culture has involved a robust and inescapable engagement with orality.

Writing In Sanskrit: A Brief History

The earliest evidence of writing in India is shrouded in mystery. The archaeological remains of the Indus Valley civilization (ca. 2400–1900 BCE) have yielded numerous seals, inscriptions, and other examples of a prehistoric writing system, but their script has not been convincingly deciphered, and in any case, did not survive the decline of this prehistoric urban civilization. The next major phase of Indian cultural history, the Vedic period (ca. 1500–500 BCE), featured a complex system of poetry and ritual culture that was decidedly oral in its nature. For centuries, the sacred Sanskrit scriptures of the Vedas were memorized and transmitted verbatim from person to person within exclusive circles of Brahmin priests using a highly sophisticated system of oral pedagogy, with no hard evidence of writing practices. The "oral literacy" of Vedic culture fostered intensive forms of linguistic, philosophical, and scientific learning, but writing does not appear to have been used for the production and distribution of these texts until well after the Vedic period.

The earliest bona fide writings from the Indian subcontinent are found in two contexts—first, a famous set of inscriptions on pillars and rock

Gāndhārī birch bark scroll
Gandhāra (northern Pakistan/eastern Afghanistan) •
1st century CE
Ink on birch bark
5 sheets, each 14 × 24 cm, laminated to form a scroll, 119 cm (length)
BRITISH LIBRARY, LONDON, DETAIL OF SCROLL OR. 14195.20; PLATES 5–6 FROM STEFAN BAUMS, "A GĀNDHĀRĪ COMMENTARY ON EARLY BUDDHIST VERSES: BRITISH LIBRARY KHAROṢṬHĪ FRAGMENTS 7, 9, 13 AND 18," PHD DISS. (UNIVERSITY OF WASHINGTON, 2009)

This is a portion of a Gāndhārī scroll containing a commentary on verses from the Dhammapāda, *the* Suttanipāta, *and other early Buddhist sources. It was composed in the Gāndhārī language using the Kharoṣṭhī script. It was discovered in the 1990s among a collection of twenty-eight Buddhist manuscripts buried in a clay pot in the Gandhāra region and is currently housed at the British Library in London,* UK.

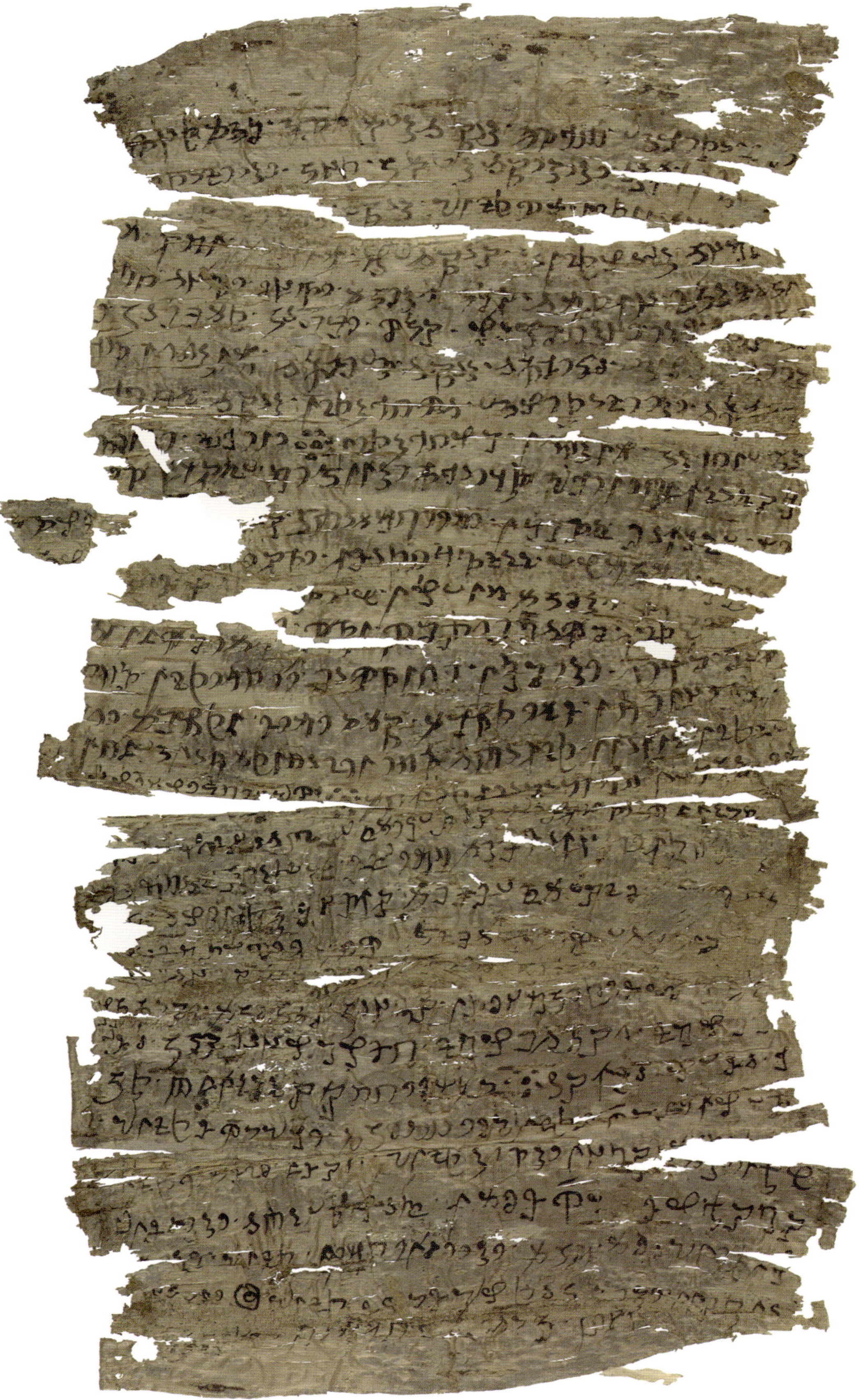

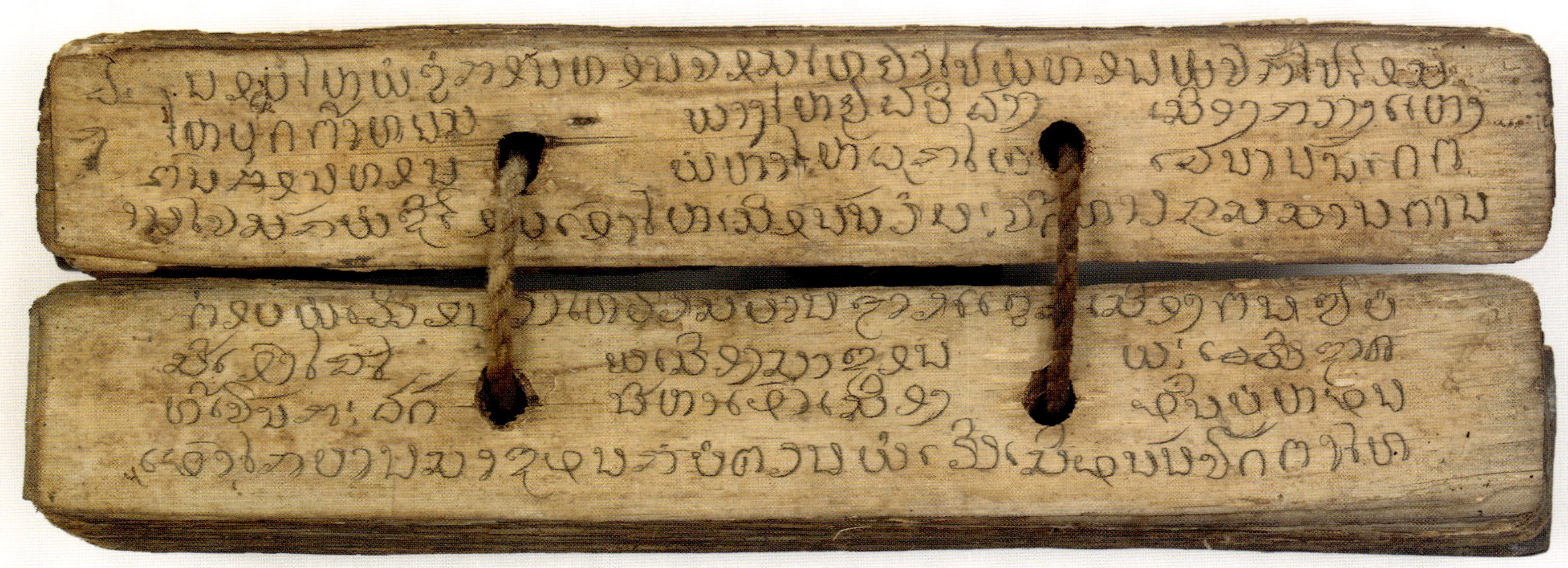

outcroppings across the subcontinent attributed to the Mauryan emperor Aśoka (r. 268–231 BCE), composed in an eastern brand of Prakrit and written mostly in the Brāhmī script; and second, a variety of birch bark manuscripts, datable to between 100 BCE and 200 CE and composed in Gāndhārī, a regional language spoken in northwest Pakistan and eastern Afghanistan and written primarily in a right-to-left script called Kharoṣṭhī.[4] Both the Aśokan and Gāndhārī materials suggest that a vibrant tradition of writing had established itself across North India by the onset of the Common Era. This technology then appears to have acted as a catalyst for a new form of elite literary culture in early India that was fundamentally anchored by fixed writings in the language of Sanskrit. This Sanskrit written culture, deeply engaged with the more nebulous oral traditions that surrounded it, was to dominate the cultural landscape of South Asia for the next thousand years.[5]

As mentioned above, the earliest South Asian manuscripts were written on materials made from the inner bark of the birch tree (*Betula utilis* D. Don), which was either prepared as separate leaves or sheets, or laminated to create long-form scrolls. Texts were inscribed using wooden or reed pens and soot-based inks. Birch bark is quite fragile, and in South Asia, the tree grows natively only in the Himalayas (page 55). And so, while birch bark manuscripts continued to be manufactured in the state of Kashmir until the seventeenth century, in the rest of India, beginning in the early centuries of the Common Era, writing materials were more commonly made from various species of palm tree, such as *Corypha umbraculifera* L. (talipot or ola palm), *Borassus flabellifer* L. (toddy or lontar palm), and *Corypha utan* Lam. (gebang palm).[6] A number of items in the MOA collection are made from the lontar palm, which grows in humid, coastal areas throughout South and Southeast Asia, and yields a thicker, broader writing surface than the other two types (this page and 128–29). To produce manuscript pages, palm leaves were dried, cut, and then seasoned by first boiling them in water or milk, burying them in wet sand, and then redrying and oiling them before polishing them with shells or stone. Depending on

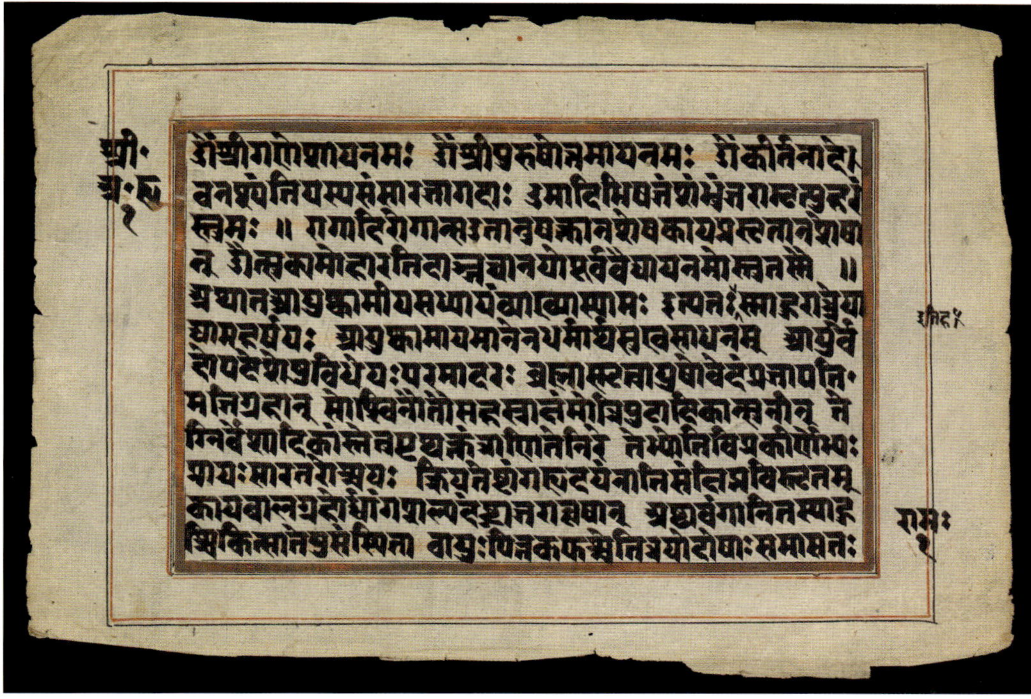

◂ ◂ **Palm leaf manuscript in Tham script**
Thailand • n.d.
Ink on palm leaf, and wood and plant fibre
10.3 × 23 × 3.8 cm
MOA COLLECTION, 2902/23

◂ **Sanskrit paper manuscript in Devanāgarī script**
Eastern India • ca. 19th century
Ink on paper
WELLCOME LIBRARY, LONDON, UK, SHELFMARK GAMMA 15, FOLIO 1, VERSO

The first folio of the Aṣṭāṅgahṛdayasaṃhitā *(Compilation on the heart of medicine) by Vāgbhaṭa, a highly influential seventh-century treatise that outlined, in more than seven thousand Sanskrit verses, the eight branches of ancient Indian medicine.*

the width of the leaves, one or two holes were bored in the middle, through which a cord would be passed to bind the book. Decorative wooden slats were affixed to both sides of the manuscript to act as a protective covering and to identify the text.

Texts were written onto palm leaf using two methods. One way was, as with birch bark manuscripts, to paint ink onto the writing material using a pen or brush. This method is found mostly in Nepal and eastern India (pages 58–59). The second way was to incise the letters into the palm leaf using a stylus made of metal or bone, and then to apply a dark pigment made from lampblack or vegetable extracts to accentuate them. This method was especially popular throughout South India and Southeast Asia and has prompted scripts from these regions to take on a more "rounded" nature than those of North India, since engraving straight lines can cause more fragile leaves to split (page 126).[7]

The earliest use of paper in the Indic context can be traced to the mid-first millennium (ca. 400–800 CE), based upon manuscripts found at Buddhist sites along the ancient Silk Road in the Xinjiang Province of China and in Gilgit in northern Pakistan. Paper manuscripts became more widespread in the subcontinent beginning in the eleventh century. In Nepal and eastern India, paper production was influenced by Chinese techniques and resembled that of Tibet and Southeast Asia, with the use of wood fibres as a raw material. In western India, especially among Jain communities in Gujarat and Rajasthan, paper began to be used for manuscripts around the twelfth century. Its manufacture was adapted from Persian methods and tended to use hemp, cotton, silk, and other repurposed textiles as raw material. Paper manuscripts were generally left unbound and were wrapped in a cloth for transport and protection.[8]

A word may be said about two distinctive visual features of certain Sanskrit manuscripts, especially those of the Jains and Buddhists: rubrication and illumination. Rubrication—the application of red or other coloured ink—was mostly used to highlight important passages, accents, colophons, verse and sentence markers, or other breaks in the text. Yellow pigment made from turmeric paste

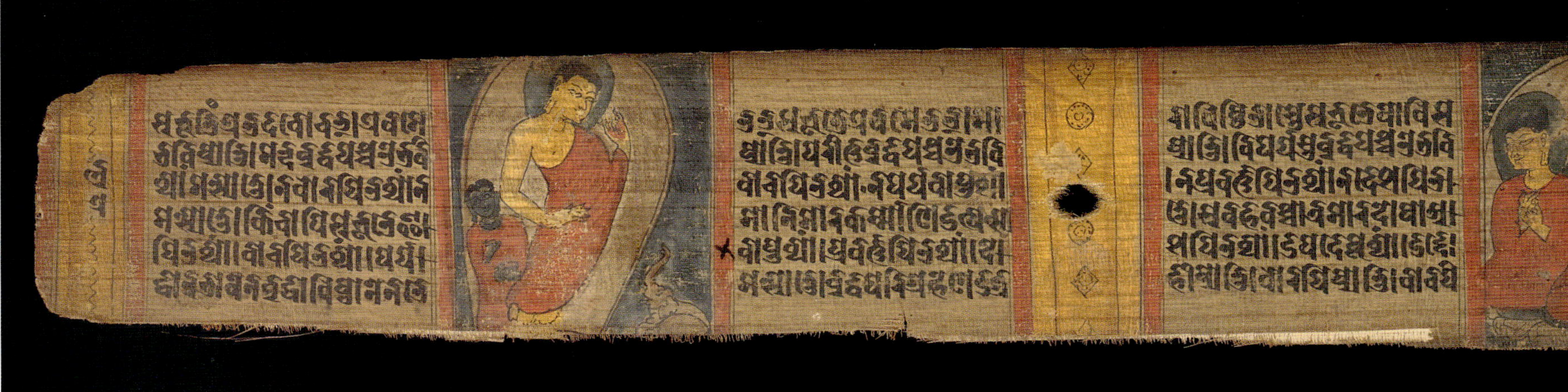

was sometimes used for highlighting or making erasures. Such embellishments are quite common even in the most rudimentary Sanskrit manuscripts. Illumination—adding illustrations to a written text—became an especially refined artistic practice among Jain and Buddhist copyists, and there is evidence that in some studios, the scribe and the artist would work independently of one another in producing illuminated manuscripts (page 60). Other types of decorative features include centre dots, fleurons, geometric patterns, and border patterns. Rubrication and illumination both appear to have gained popularity with the transition from palm leaf to paper. When creating palm leaf manuscripts, copyists had been required to leave a prominent gap in the centre of each folio where holes would later be punched for the cord that bound the book together. In paper manuscripts, no hole would be made, since the manuscript was left unbound. Copyists took advantage of this centre gap to add a large red dot to represent the hole, as well as more creative decorative shapes or geometric patterns. While we can only speculate about the motivations behind these forms of scribal ornamentation, they clearly indicate an expectation that the manuscripts would be seen by a broader public, and not just read in private.

Birch bark, palm leaf, or paper, or stone, copper, iron, or wood—no matter what the material was, and no matter the ink, script, or hand, the millions of manuscripts and inscriptions that we now possess are the material legacy of the cultural practice of writing in Sanskrit, an enduring tradition that spread across pre-modern South and Southeast Asia. In order to gain an understanding of how this Sanskrit manuscript culture worked from the perspective of the authors, readers, and copyists, we may now turn to three distinct "moments" in which Sanskrit writers themselves commented on the act of writing in Sanskrit. They also offer a glimpse into how manuscripts, as physical objects, interacted with the larger, more nebulous world of orality and performance that swirled around them, and how they would have come to constitute a pre-modern Sanskrit "public culture." First, we will turn to an origin myth told in the Sanskrit epic *Mahābhārata* (ca. 500 CE) that explained how the deity Gaṇeśa had originally written down the words of the great epic's composer, Vyāsa. Then, we will take up the writings of a celebrated Sanskrit poet named Rājaśekhara (ca. 900 CE), who argued that a good poet should always have a well-trained scribe by his side. Finally, we will look at a medieval compendium on gift giving attributed to a king named Ballālasena (1170 CE), who explained in detail why publicly donating fresh new copies of books to temples and Brahman scholars would be a good thing to do.[9]

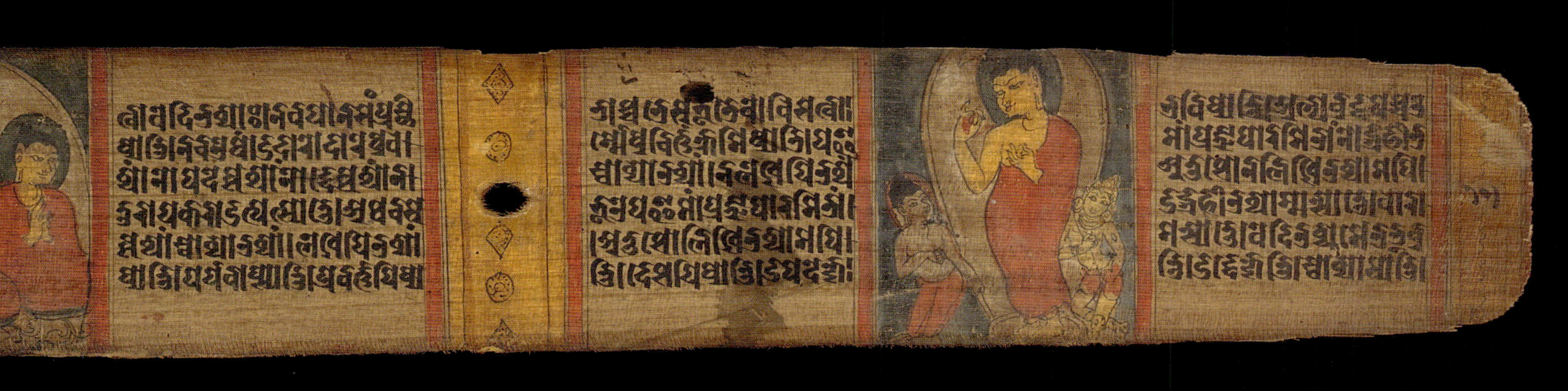

▲ **Sanskrit palm leaf manuscript in Bhujmolī script**
Nepal • 11th century
Ink on palm leaf
6 × 55 cm
WELLCOME LIBRARY, LONDON, UK, SHELFMARK EPSILON 1, FOLIO 101, VERSO

A folio from an eleventh-century illuminated prose copy of the Aṣṭasāhasrikā-prajñāpāramita-sūtra, *or "The Perfection of Wisdom in Eight Thousand Lines," an early Mahayana Buddhist text dating perhaps from the first century* BCE. *The manuscript contains eighteen miniature images, made with red, yellow, and green colouring. The three images shown here reflect the Buddha's taming of an elephant at Nalagiri (left), his miracle of emanating water and fire from his multiplied bodies at Śravasti (centre), and his visit to the Trayastriṃśa heaven (of the thirty-three gods) (right).*

The Primal Scribe: Gaṇeśa and the Great Epic (ca. 500 CE)

At the beginning of the *Mahābhārata*, we find a self-reflexive anecdote about how this great Sanskrit epic came to be written down by Lord Gaṇeśa, the auspicious, elephant-headed god of new undertakings. Legend has it that after the mythic sage Vyāsa had mentally created the *Mahābhārata*, he was in need of a scribe capable of transcribing his massive new poem as he recited it from memory. Brahmā, the all-knowing grandfather of the gods, felt that Gaṇeśa would be the best fit for the job and urged Vyāsa to consult the deity. Gaṇeśa agreed to take on the task, but under the condition that he would remain Vyāsa's scribe, "so long as my pen does not stop writing, even for a moment." In response, Vyāsa stipulated, "At no point should you write anything down without understanding it." This scribal challenge is used to explain why, even today, we find the occasional hard-to-understand verse in the *Mahābhārata*—it turns out that Vyāsa had intentionally placed these "textual tangles" (*granthagranthi*) in his composition to give himself some extra time to come up with the rest of it![10]

We should note here that the textual authenticity of the *Mahābhārata*'s Gaṇeśa anecdote is quite shaky, at best. It is found in quite a number of manuscripts, but the epic's modern editors were convinced that it was an interpolation, and therefore relegated the whole thing to a footnote in the appendix of the critical

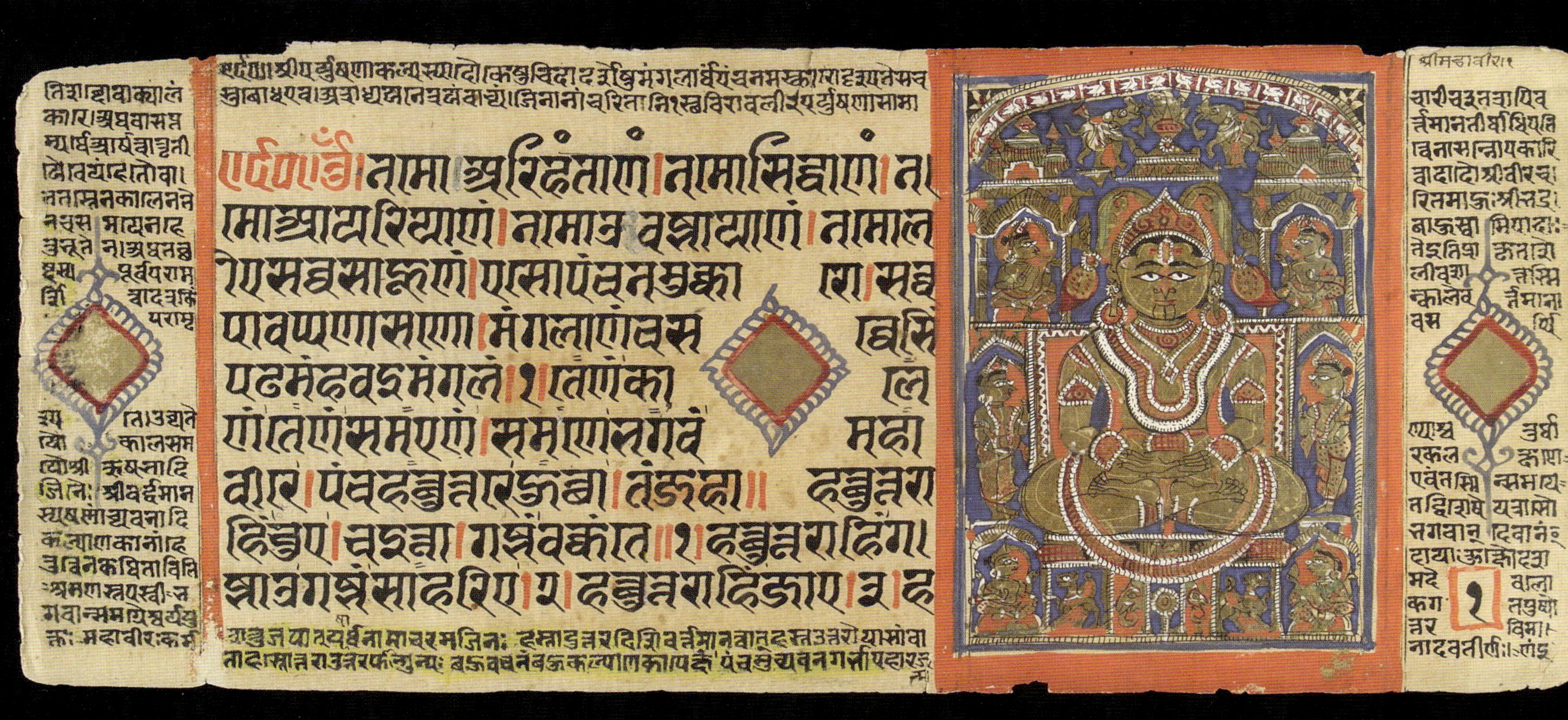

▲ **Jain illustrated paper manuscript in Devanāgarī script**
Western India • 1503
Ink on paper
11 × 26 cm
WELLCOME LIBRARY, LONDON, UK, SHELFMARK GAMMA 3, FOLIO 1, VERSO

The first folio from an illustrated paper copy of the Kalpasūtra *or "Manual of Ritual," one of the central canonical texts of the Śvetāmbara Jains of Western India. Composed in Ardhamāgadhī Prakrit, the* Kalpasūtra *is traditionally attributed to Bhadrabāhu, an ancient monk who is thought to have lived in the fourth century* BCE*. It provides detailed hagiographies of the twenty-four founders or* tīrthaṅkaras *(Ford-makers) of the Jain religious tradition. Pictured here is the twenty-fourth and final* tīrthaṅkara*, Vardhamāna Mahāvīra (599–527* BCE*), residing in the* puṣpottara vimāna*, a celestial palace where he is thought to have lived for many ages until taking on a human birth in order to gain liberation. This paper manuscript, produced in western India and dated 1503, not only exemplifies the artistic merits of Jain illustration, but also demonstrates the elaborate use of centre-hole decoration, rubrication, marginal commentary (in Sanskrit), and turmeric-based highlighting.*

edition of the epic. This would mean that it was not part of the original text, but had been inserted at a later date—perhaps by the year 500 CE, and in any case certainly before the early tenth century, when Rājaśekhara alludes to it. Still, even if it were a late addition, the story must have been added for a very good reason, for it remained a part of the epic tradition once it found its way in.

The Gaṇeśa story evokes, in striking mythological terms, the cultural power of Sanskrit manuscripts. For a text to truly exist, to be given public life, it has to be transformed from oral to written form. And if the manuscript is to be an effective conduit for the author's wisdom, the scribe must be the author's intellectual match, since the scribe is required to understand every single verse. In this way, the author maintains a scholastic primacy over the scribe—even if the latter happens to be a deity! Moreover, the anecdote authenticates whichever physical manuscript of the *Mahābhārata* a reader may happen to possess, even years later, assuring him or her that it faithfully represents the voice of the ancient author and the hand of his subordinate scribe.

Above all, the *Mahābhārata*'s Gaṇeśa anecdote acts as a mythological charter for the public reception of the written Sanskrit text. The idea that Vyāsa has intentionally interjected textual puzzles into his work means that any difficulties that readers might have in interpreting the manuscripts of the *Mahābhārata* are supposed to be part of the experience. It is not that Vyāsa had erred, or that his scribe had corrupted the text, but rather that the text was originally *meant* to contain enigmas. As readers, we can only struggle with such puzzles, inside our own heads, unless we seek the counsel of experts who can explain what the text means. In other words, while manuscripts were designed to be material vehicles for the original texts, they still required specially trained drivers—that is, scholastic commentators—who would orally generate the Sanskrit public culture around them.

A Scribe at Every Poet's Side: Rājaśekhara's Views on Writing (ca. 900 CE)

While the *Mahābhārata* yields a mythological reflection on the cultural value of written texts, a more practical perspective appears in the writings of Rājaśekhara, an illustrious Sanskrit poet who lived and worked at the onset of the tenth century in the North Indian city of Kannauj, the bustling imperial capital of the Gurjara-Pratihāras. Rājaśekhara's plays and poems abound with references to inscriptions, manuscripts, and other forms of writing, while his theoretical manual on poetics, the *Kāvyamīmāṃsā* (An investigation into poetry), details the place of scribes within Sanskrit courtly culture.

As one of the earliest examples of a theoretical work aimed at professional poets rather than critics or connoisseurs, the *Kāvyamīmāṃsā* is candid in its descriptions of what everyday life may have been like for the courtly literati of tenth-century India. Especially so is its tenth chapter, titled "The Life of a Poet and the Life of a King" (*kavicaryā rājacaryā ca*), which delineates how a good court poet ought to organize his home and establish a daily routine that would be most beneficial to his career. First, Rājaśekhara asserts that a poet should comport himself in a gentlemanly manner and make sure that his house and his gardens are well kept and accommodate the various natural settings, flora, and fauna that are conducive to Sanskrit poetry. Next, explaining that a poet should keep a retinue of attendants and friends who are skilled in the various registers of formal poetry, Rājaśekhara suggests that every good poet also ought to have a competent scribe (*lekhaka*) at his side. This scribe should be "adept in all languages, speak quickly, have pleasant handwriting, understand gestures, be conversant with many different scripts, and himself be a poet who understands the deeper meanings"—that is, the deeper meanings of poetry. Such an educated scribe is necessary, says Rājaśekhara, for the purpose of "polishing and editing one's work for the public." If no scribe is available, or if it happens to be late at night, he suggests the poet may get one of his servants or friends to do the job. But in all cases, he should be prepared to write down his compositions whenever inspiration strikes. The poet is therefore instructed always to keep close at hand "a box containing a slate and chalk, or another box filled with toddy palm leaves or birch bark, pens, pots of ink, or talipot leaves with an iron stylus, or well-wiped walls" onto which, one presumes, a desperate poet could scribble his new creations.[11]

Rājaśekhara also places strict regulations on a poet's daily routine, and here, too, writing plays a key role. After performing his morning rituals, a poet is instructed to engage in scholastic studies and compose new poetry. After lunch, he is to hold gatherings with fellow poets, solve riddles, or pursue other kinds of literary pastimes. For the rest of the afternoon, the poet should review and revise his morning compositions, and in the evening, finalize in writing (*abhilekhana*) everything that had passed his earlier inspection, before spending some time with his wife and retiring for the night.

Though the picture is assuredly an idealized one, Rājaśekhara's *Kāvyamīmāṃsā* speaks in highly practical terms about the importance of writing in the careers of Sanskrit poets and scholars in early medieval India. Handwritten documents were indispensable for the daily creation of poetry, and, as Rājaśekhara reminds us, they were the physical instruments through which a poet's work was presented within the *sadas*, or the public assembly, where they were to be recited aloud, perhaps by others besides the poet. Depending on how his work was received by the king, connoisseurs, and the other cognoscenti of the royal court, the poet would either succeed and achieve everlasting fame or fail and fall into ignominy. This is why Rājaśekhara sets such high standards for what constituted a good scribe—not only did he have to have a firm command of scripts and handwriting, he needed to be practically a poet himself.

The Written Gift: Donating Manuscripts in Ballālasena's *Dānasāgara* (1170 CE)[12]

As mentioned earlier, the vast majority of the Sanskrit manuscripts we now possess were *not* made in the way that Rājaśekhara described. That is, they are not, for the most part, the physical recordings of the original authors; rather, they are copies thereof, and copies of copies, which have been passed down through chains of scribal transmission for hundreds if not thousands of years. The reasons why manuscripts were copied are as diverse as the contexts in which the copying was done—in order to replace a worn-out manuscript in a temple, monastery, or royal court, or at the behest of a teacher or father, or perhaps for one's own personal edification. But it is clear that the world of Sanskrit copyists operated under quite a different set of rules and regulations than Rājaśekhara's world of Sanskrit poets did.

One especially fascinating motivation for copying a manuscript in the mainstream Hindu culture of the medieval period was to donate it to a temple, a spiritual guru, or a venerable Brahman scholar for the sake of earning merit, or *puṇya*. This process is described in great detail in the *Dānasāgara* (Ocean of gift-giving), a theoretical compendium composed at the court of the Bengali king Ballālasena in approximately 1170 CE. This encyclopedic text delineates the correct methods for all kinds of religious donations—everything from making rice and grain offerings to hosting large-scale sacrifices and festivals. In one chapter dedicated to the giving of knowledge (*Vidyādāna*, chapter 43), the *Dānasāgara* explains how and why manuscripts are to be copied and donated. First, the donor should select the appropriate text to be copied and gather together the right kind of paper (pure white, with a black or red border), pots of good black ink, gilded pens, and well-made wooden book covers. The *Dānasāgara* advocates the use of a special device for the copying process, called a *sarayantra* (spreading device) or *vidyādhara* (knowledge carrier). What this artifact looked like is unknown, but it was probably a kind of book stand, fashioned from gold, silver, ivory, or wood, that could simultaneously hold both the exemplar and the new copy in place. The scribe is instructed to face east; wear white garlands and clothing, a golden armband, and finger caps; and have at hand a set of pens and a nail cutter (for sharpening the pen). Then, as string music plays in the background, a sample of five or ten verses is to be copied and thoroughly scrutinized for writing mistakes as well as to check the content, consistency, and subject matter. In subsequent sessions, the copying is to proceed in this same, deliberate manner, and, upon completion, the manuscript should be nicely decorated, perfumed, tied, and wrapped in cloth, and if it was going to be donated to a temple, ceremoniously taken by palanquin, elephant, horse, or chariot to a temple, and offered to the presiding deity.

This procession is designed to be quite a public affair, and the *Dānasāgara* describes it with great pomp and circumstance. The vehicle should be brightly decorated with bells, garlands, and banners, and a large umbrella. It is accompanied by dancers, singers, and musicians, and the chanting of Vedic hymns. At the temple itself, elaborate ritual procedures are to be undertaken to honour the donor's ancestors and teachers, dignitaries, and devotees of the presiding deity, and an additional gratuity (*dakṣiṇā*) is to be offered to Brahman officiants to ensure the permanency of the gift. The donor then is asked to organize some festivities to celebrate the donation—a large-scale public festival if you are a king, and a simple house party for your relatives if you are a common citizen.

The *Dānasāgara* next instructs the donor to sponsor a formal public recitation of the text at the temple. A professional reader (*vācaka*) as well as a teacher (*guru*) are hired to read the text out loud and teach its contents to the general public assembled there. The *Dānasāgara* takes great pains to regulate this aspect of the public life of a manuscript. The reader must be highly educated in scripts as well as the Sanskrit language. The teacher must be well versed in all of the major branches of knowledge, such that his words act as rays of light dispelling the darkness of the audience's ignorance. And the audience must be ever attentive, respectful, and reflective. The recitation should not be rushed, should be in a tone that is appropriate to the content, should include pauses at the end of chapters or sections, and should close with auspicious benedictive utterances to ensure the well-being of the teacher and the audience.

Besides providing a detailed picture of the technicalities of Sanskrit manuscript production and how it continued to be fully couched within traditions of public oral performance well into the medieval period, the *Dānasāgara* also gives some clues about the religious and social motivations behind it. A manuscript donation was reckoned as having the equivalent merit of ten thousand Vedic

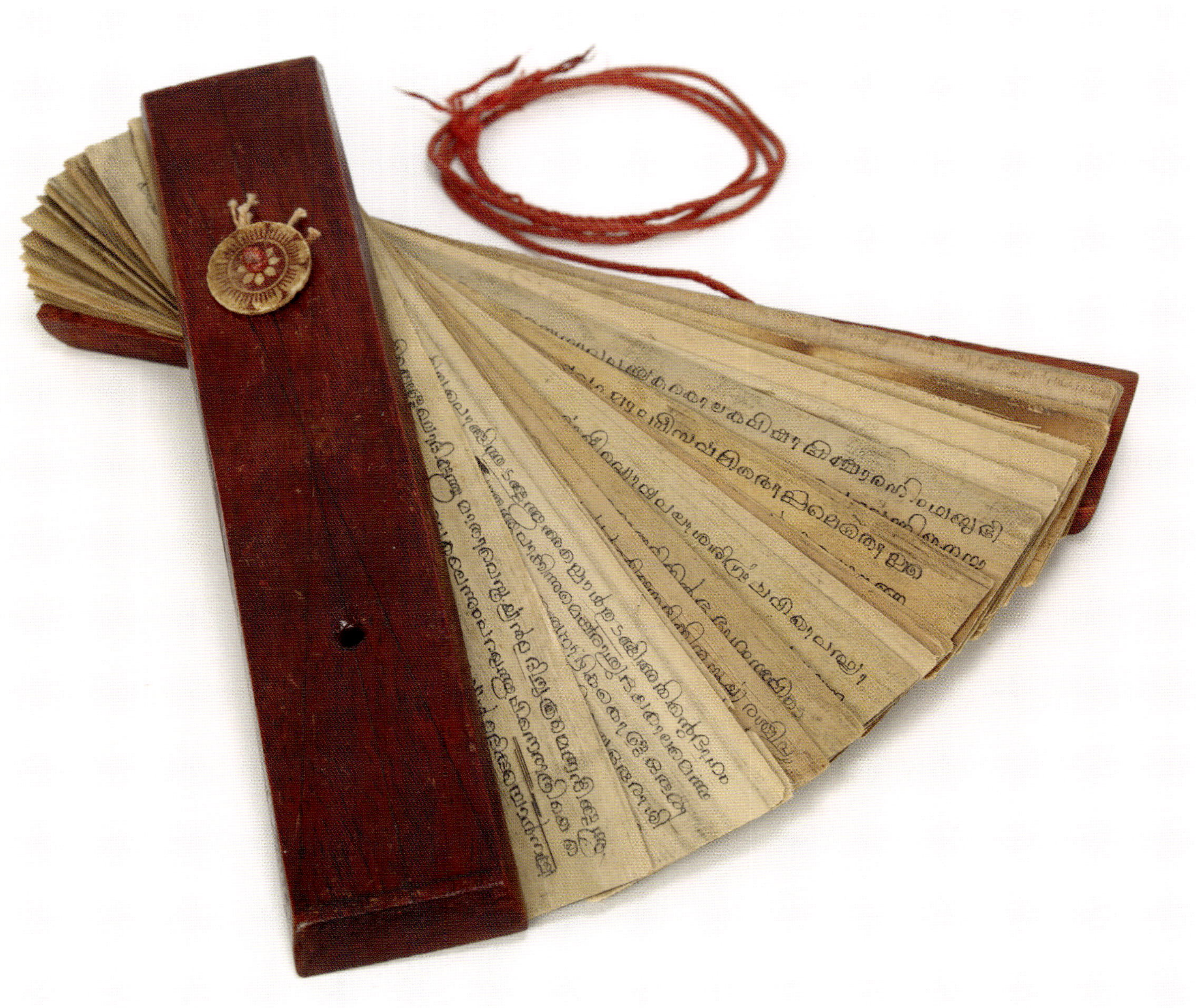

▲ **Palm leaf manuscript in Malayalam script**
Kerala, India • n.d.
Ink on palm leaf, and wood, fibre, and ivory
3.9 × 21.3 × 3.8 cm
MOA COLLECTION, B557

horse sacrifices, or a thousand royal consecrations. It would permit the donor to stay in heaven for as many thousands of years as there were syllables in the donated manuscript. And, perhaps most compelling of all, donating manuscripts in this ritually prescribed way was also thought to rescue one's ancestors from hell. Ballālasena's *Dānasāgara* provides a lucid, if idealized, impression of how copying certain kinds of Sanskrit writings generated a secondary cultural field—of merit-earning and public education at Hindu temples in medieval India.

The Pre-modern Public Culture of Sanskrit Manuscripts

Based on these brief explorations, how might we understand the public culture that developed around practices of writing Sanskrit texts onto palm leaf, birch bark, and paper in first-millennium India? The pre-modern world of Sanskrit manuscripts, it should be said, was quite unlike the modern notion of a "public sphere," which Jürgen Habermas has used to describe the new modes of civil life that emerged through print journalism, clubs, and coffeehouses in eighteenth-century Europe.[13] Rather, it bore a closer resemblance to the medieval European domains of elite cultural power and discipline that the bourgeois public sphere is said to have displaced. The world of Sanskrit, in general, was a domain of strict social regulation and control. There was a right way to do things, and complex hierarchies were put in place to self-circumscribe a refined "elite" society from the general public.

And so, in all three moments that we have considered, we find that great emphasis was placed on scribal competence, training, and procedure. The scribe needed to demonstrate proficiency in various writing systems, but also an ability to comprehend the Sanskrit text he was writing down. The copying of a manuscript was a methodical process in which the scribe's attire, his comportment, and even his background music were carefully spelled out. And throughout the process, a system of checks and balances enabled Sanskrit scholars to maintain authoritative command over the documents that scribes were creating. Gaṇeśa had to solve textual tangles before he could write down the *Mahābhārata*, Rājaśekhara's ideal scribe had to be good enough to be a poet himself, and the *Dānasāgara* stipulated that the scribe's work always be thoroughly double-checked and presented in public only under the guidance of professional scholars.

Finally, we should note that these are *idealized* depictions of scribes and their craft, written from the point of view of Sanskrit poets, pandits, and priests. We must keep in mind that their descriptions do not necessarily reflect the realities of how Sanskrit manuscripts were made. Still, they do give us valuable details about the cultural anxieties of Sanskrit authors regarding the technicians who made the manuscripts and how the public might receive them. The perspectives of the scribes are somewhat more difficult to locate, but they can be found either within the interstitial spaces of manuscripts—such as colophons, marginalia, or even scribblings on the covers—or in certain genres of Sanskrit literature that circulated more exclusively among scribal communities, such as verse anthologies, digests, and story collections. By studying more and more of the millions of existing Sanskrit manuscripts with a sensitivity to such scribal voices, we will undoubtedly gain a better appreciation of the public culture that formed around them, as well as the thoughts and inclinations of the copyists to whom we owe the manuscripts' survival.

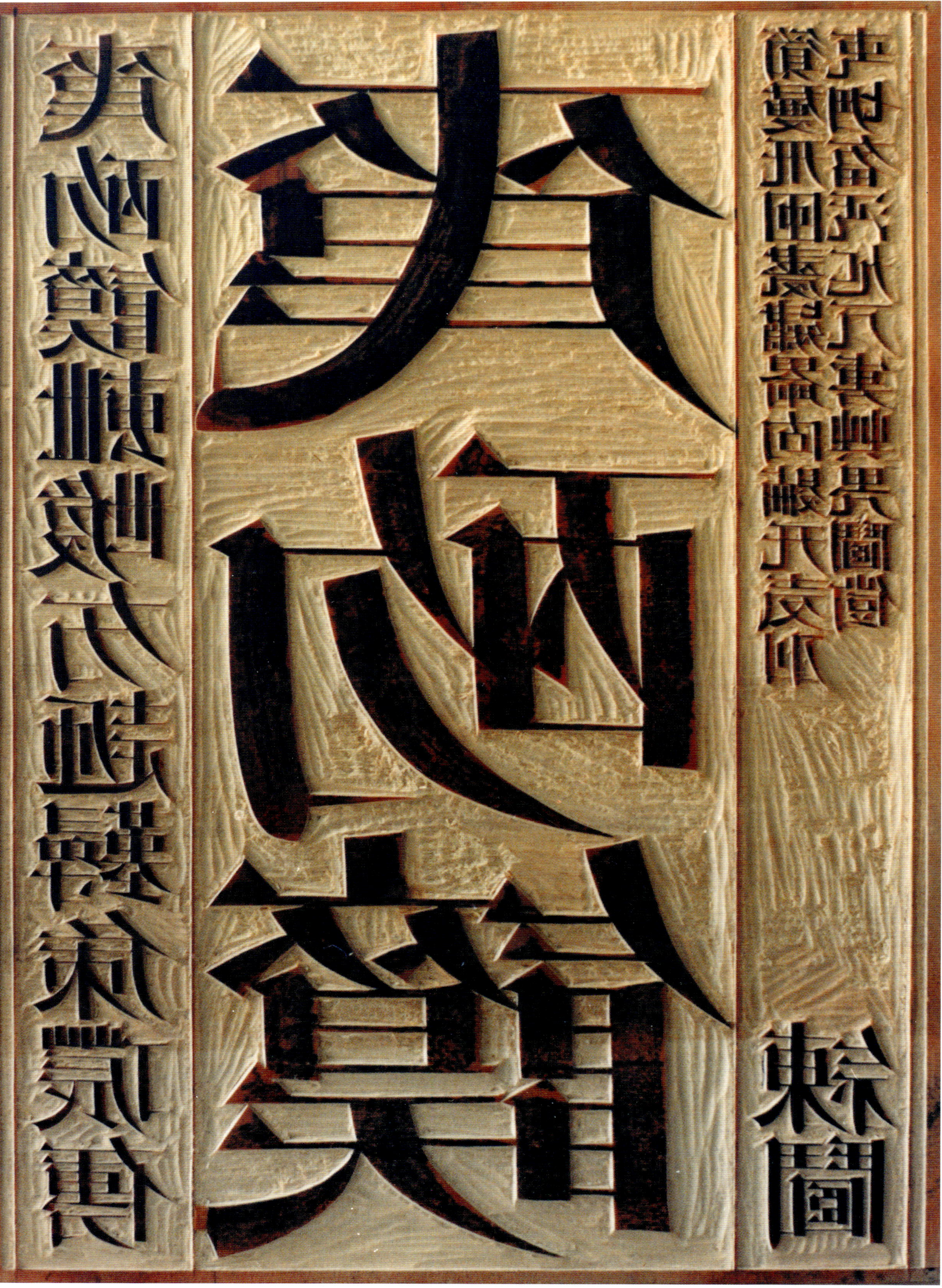

5

Beyond Words

Visual Poetics in the Contemporary Arts of Asia

APRIL LIU

FOR THE OPENING CEREMONY of the 2008 Beijing Summer Olympics, one of the most widely viewed events in human history, the filmmaker Zhang Yimou choreographed a high-tech stage performance based on the evolution of Chinese writing. In a climactic moment, over eight hundred performers coordinated their movements to form the character for harmony (*he* 和), a reference to state-sponsored slogans for a "harmonious society" and the official theme for the Olympics. Each performer was hidden inside a rectangular column, forming a sea of columns that rose and fell like a movable-type machine to form the character's three-dimensional shape. Broken down into its components, "harmony" is made up of the characters for "grain" or "rice" (*he* 禾, a character whose image is a plant with outstretched branches) and "mouth" (*kou* 口, an image of an open square-shaped mouth), suggesting nourishment and abundance. The image therefore resonates with the human performers, whose breathing bodies form the body of the character and, by extension, the body of the nation.

Zhang Yimou's performance demonstrates how Chinese script has profound layers of meaning that may be effectively augmented through visual and material means. In this case, the connotations of modernity, creativity, abundance, and unity are all folded into a grand spectacle of Chinese script, a glorified promotion of China's image on the world stage. Even for those unfamiliar with Chinese script, the performance provides a stunning image of a large human collective unified by a shared language and history. One could say it is the *visual poetics* of the word for *harmony* enlarged and animated on stage rather than its semantic meaning that leaves the deepest impression on the viewer.

In the context of contemporary Asian art, we can use the idea of visual poetry to describe a wide range of artistic and multimedia works that explore the realm of *script*, which can be loosely defined as any form of written language. I would like to draw attention to the many works of art that actively break down the boundaries between the visual and the textual, or between art and language to create new spaces of cultural encounter and exchange. As Asian artists share their works around the world, these experiments with script challenge viewers from different cultures to rethink their assumptions around language and the role it plays in the global arena.

I am particularly interested in those works that play at the very edge of what might be considered "writing" or "text." There are a number of artists who use pseudo-script or pseudo-writing that resembles a particular language but is in fact unreadable or nonsensical. There are also works that encompass various forms of performative writing, including acts

◂ **XU BING**
Detail of a carved woodblock used to print the nonsensical script for *Book from the Sky*, 1987–91
COURTESY OF XU BING STUDIO

that may or may not leave a tangible trace. I will look briefly at how artists from Asia are taking language and writing, the presumed building blocks of culture and identity, and deconstructing and reconfiguring them. I will argue that Asian artists are particularly well positioned to perform such interventions and to open up the world of visual poetry, given the rich diversity of Asian scripts, calligraphic arts, and the profound role of writing as a visual and textual culture in many parts of Asia.

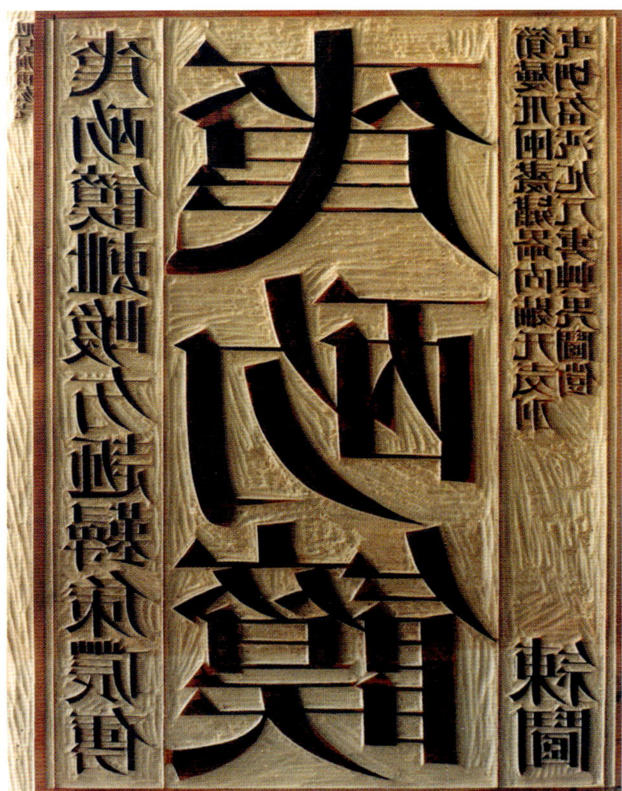

XU BING
Book from the Sky 1987–91
Mixed-media installation: hand-printed books and scrolls printed from blocks inscribed with false characters
COURTESY OF XU BING STUDIO

Pseudo-Script

The great divide between image and text that has profoundly shaped European art and poetry since the Renaissance era simply does not exist in many artistic traditions found in Asia. This is particularly true for the arts of East Asia, where painting, poetry, and calligraphy have a long history of being tightly integrated and revered as arts of the brush (see chapter 1). In China, Japan, and Korea, the brush has served as the basis of all three art forms, and many great works incorporate all "three perfections," a popular phrase that captures both the interconnected nature of painting, poetry, and calligraphy and their highly revered status in Chinese society.[1] In expressing his admiration of the legendary poet-painter Wang Wei, the Song dynasty poet Su Shi wrote, "There is painting in his poetry and poetry in his painting."[2] His praise suggests a seamless fusion between the two arts, a lofty achievement to be emulated.

In contemporary art from East Asia, the strategic collapse of text and image shows up as a prominent theme in works that incorporate written script. This is perhaps most vividly captured in the production of *pseudo-script*, loosely defined as false or unreadable script that resembles conventional forms of written language (see chapter 2 on the avant-garde Japanese calligraphers between the 1940s and 1960s). These works have had a ground-breaking effect, sparking wide-ranging debates and criticism in the world of contemporary art. By deconstructing the fundamental components of written language and disrupting the semantic meanings established within words and texts, these works play with the very limits of language to challenge the viewer's expectations about words, images, and meaning.

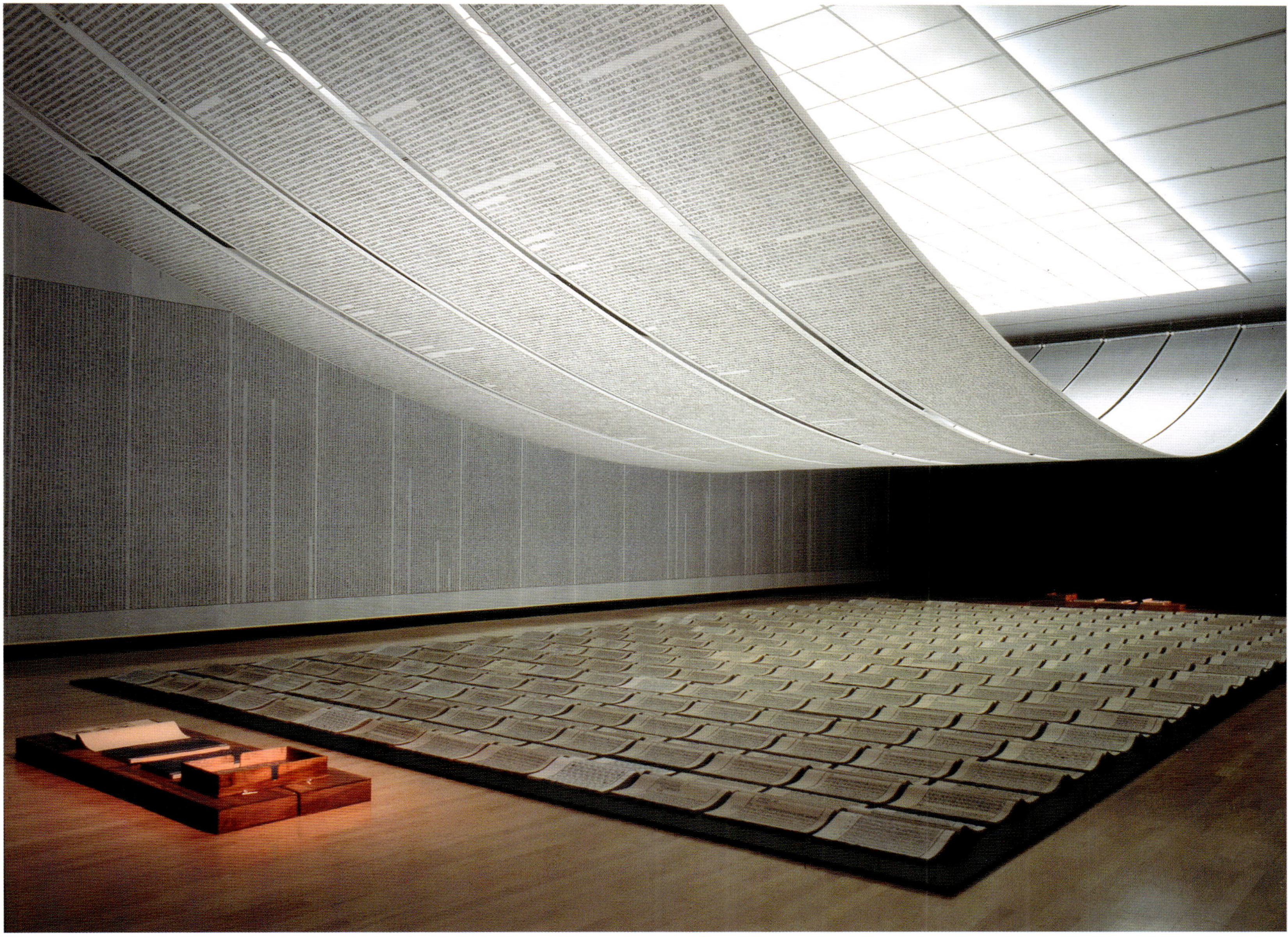

Xu Bing, one of the most prominent artists to emerge from China in the early 1980s, has devoted the bulk of his career to reconfiguring the written word using elements of both Chinese and English script. His pioneering work *Book from the Sky* (1987–91) involves an invented script that he painstakingly carved into some four thousand individual woodblocks over the course of several years (page 66 and 68). Xu Bing hand-printed his pseudo-characters onto elegant scrolls and traditionally bound books, re-creating the aura of classical texts. In this large-scale installation, scrolls are hung from the ceiling in billowing waves and books are arranged in a grid on the floor. Based on *songti,* a bureaucratic script popularized during the Song and Ming dynasties, the made-up characters are bold, crisp, and graphic on the page. They clearly reference a type of Chinese writing that was meant to be highly legible and thus suited for practical use in educational or official documents. This heightens the tension in the work, which feigns the familiarity of legible text but is in fact emptied of semantic meaning.

In contemporary parlance, it is as if Xu Bing "hacked" or "decoded" the Chinese language from the inside, robbing it of linguistic meaning to lay bare its fragile shell—the visual markers of authority conveyed in the elegant brush strokes, scrolls, and

GU WENDA
united nations—babel of the millennium 1999
Human hair–made screen tower with pseudo-Chinese, English, Hindi, and Arabic languages
2,287 × 1,037 cm
SAN FRANCISCO MUSEUM OF MODERN ART, COURTESY OF THE ARTIST

books. In an elaborate ruse, the work frustrates the viewers' expectations that they will be able to "read" the text in the work. As the artist says,

> The artwork itself is a contradiction because it makes a parody of culture while also placing culture in a temple to be taken seriously. *Book from the Sky* invites your desire to understand it and pushes you away at the same time. It treats everyone as equal—educated or uneducated, Chinese or non-Chinese—because no one can "read" it.[3]

This equalizing effect further underscores the role of language as a guardian of social hierarchies, as that which separates people as literate/illiterate or cultured/uncultured.

Xu Bing's deliberate denial of meaning seems to dismantle the illusion of cultural cohesion and national identity associated with Chinese script, an established trope that was played up in Zhang Yimou's stage act for the Beijing Olympics. It is no surprise that Xu Bing's work attracted harsh criticism from conservative art critics and practitioners at the time as a "meaningless work" or an instance of "irrational anti-art" that would do nothing to advance Chinese cultural discourse. At the same time, this deconstructive aspect of the work also earned praise from various avant-garde circles as a political and social critique of elite culture and its ideological use of the written word, especially in the wake of the 1989 Tiananmen Square incident and the ensuing harsh government crackdown on dissident voices. Many critics also saw the piece as an inevitable response to the simplification of Chinese script in the 1950s and the overwhelming bombardment of the senses through political slogans and posters during the Cultural Revolution of the 1960s and 70s.[4] As the work garnered attention from audiences outside of China, it sparked a flurry of global discussions about linguistics, philosophy, and postmodernism. Having transcended its immediate local context, it continues to serve as a touchstone work that exposes the blurry and socially constructed boundaries between language and art, or between text and image.

Chinese artist Gu Wenda, who also launched his subsequently illustrious career in the 1980s, was trained in classical Chinese ink painting and calligraphy before pushing these practices into radical new terrain as conceptual installation art. Like Xu Bing, he is interested in deconstructing written script to create new spaces of cultural encounter. Gu's most ambitious work to date is an ongoing project, launched in 1992, titled *united nations* (page 71). For this piece, he began creating a series of pseudo-scripts that resemble the major languages of the world. Lines of nonsensical text are woven out of massive quantities of real human hair that Gu collected from barbershops around the world. The woven "texts" are displayed on monumental hanging banners to form ceilings, columns, or curving walls of unreadable words. So far, the project has travelled to over twenty countries across five continents, inching towards Gu's ultimate goal to bring the project to every country in the world.

Gu's ongoing production of nonsensical script comes across as absurdist theatre, yet it sheds light on the divisive and laboriously constructed barriers erected between people from time immemorial. This is in contrast to the human hair that serves as the primary medium of all the pseudo-scripts, hair being one of the physiological traits that all people

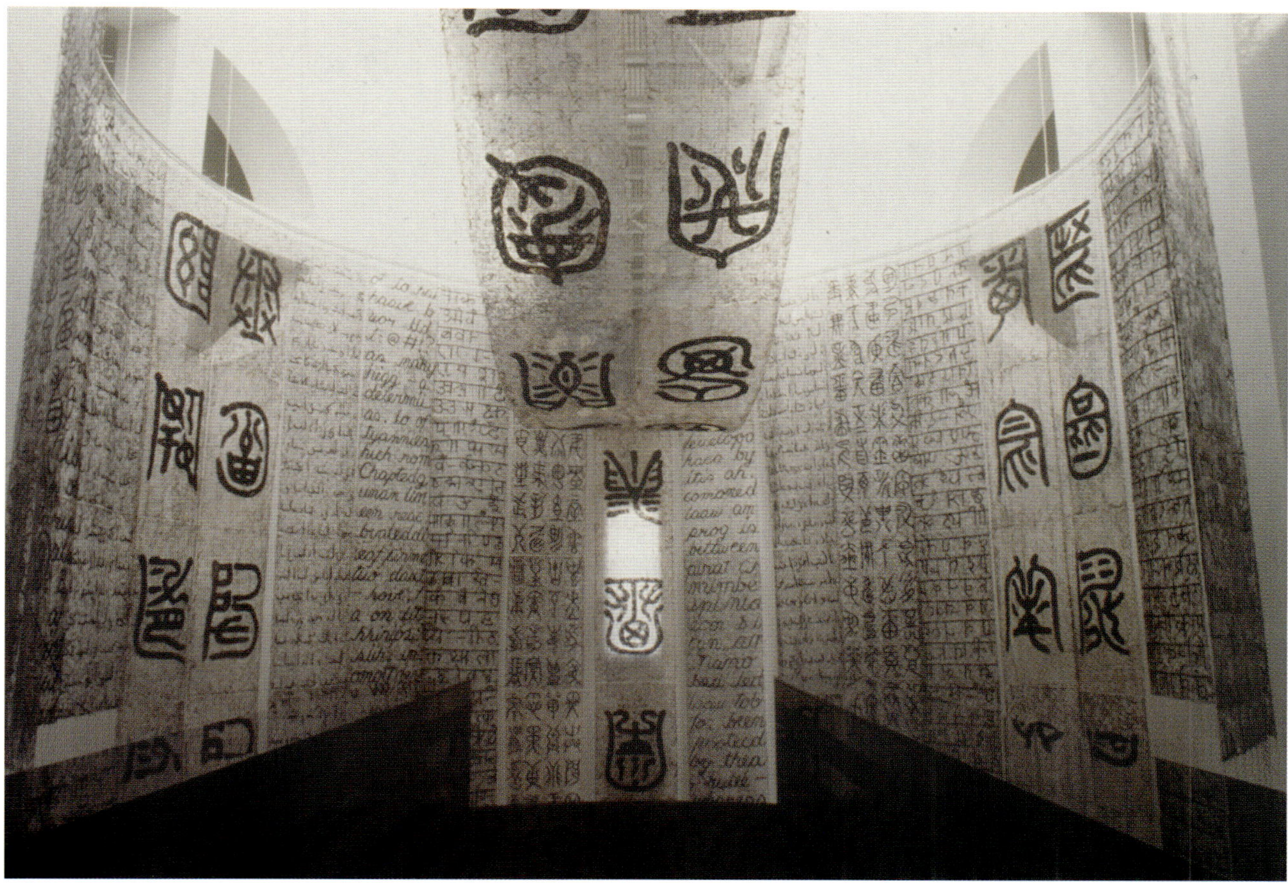

share. The piece seems to ask if we see ourselves as either the same or different, and how these perceptions come to shape the world of global politics as symbolized by the United Nations. The pseudo-scripts appear to stand in for the different nations, yet the denial of legibility satirizes the UN's efforts to facilitate global communication and collective action.

Whereas Xu Bing used the traditional methods of woodblock printing to create his nonsensical characters, Gu Wenda has invented an experimental method of weaving and sculpting human hair to produce pseudo-script. In doing so, Gu prompts his viewers to read the language of hair itself, to consider its colour, texture, length, or density. We are confronted by the sheer volume and materiality of human hair that has travelled around the world, effectively communicating meaning without using a single legible word. Gu describes the hair as "silent selves" that "make the viewer quickly think of the people from whom it comes. Moreover audiences can find their shared humanity in such common growths and bodily parts."[5] In this idealistic view of hair, it has the power to unite people in a way that neither language nor the United Nations can.

Both Xu Bing and Gu Wenda work with nonsensical script to deconstruct written language as a natural site of culture and identity. By removing the semantic meanings from the words, these artists push viewers to question the privileged status of script as cultural representation in the art world and in contemporary society at large. In doing so, they also draw attention to the visual and material qualities of the written word as powerful carriers of meaning in their own right.

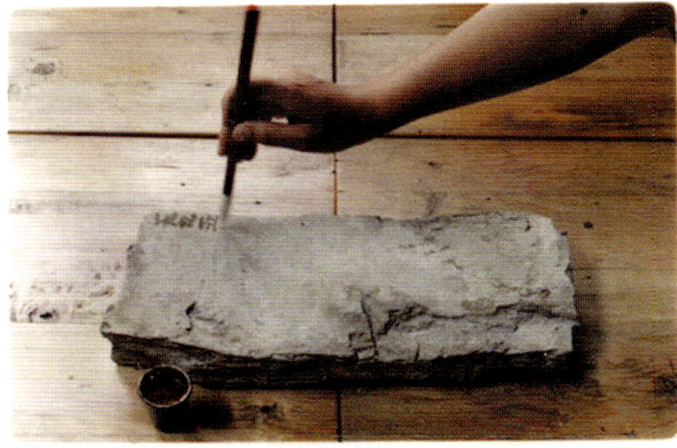

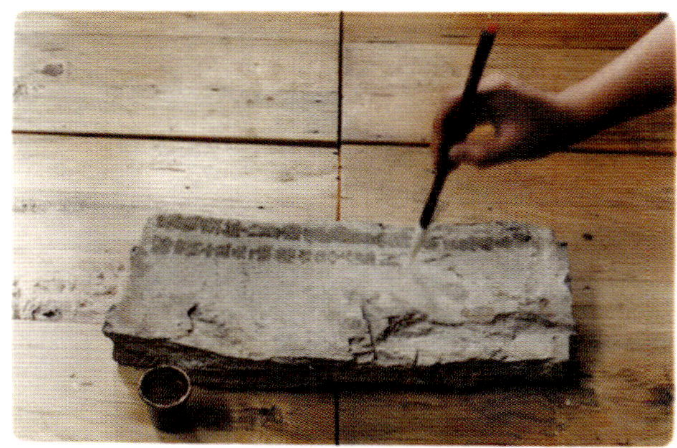

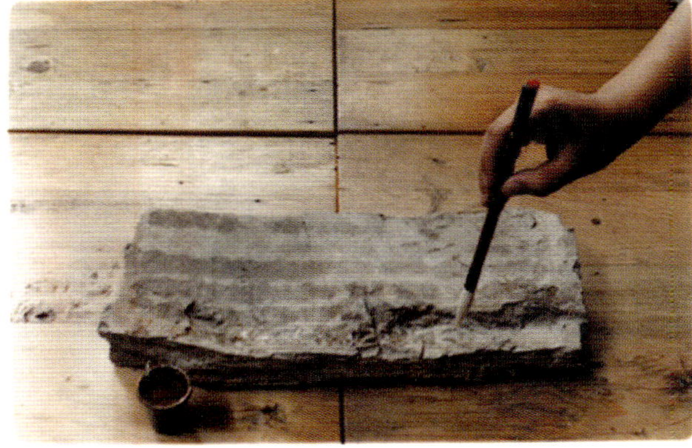

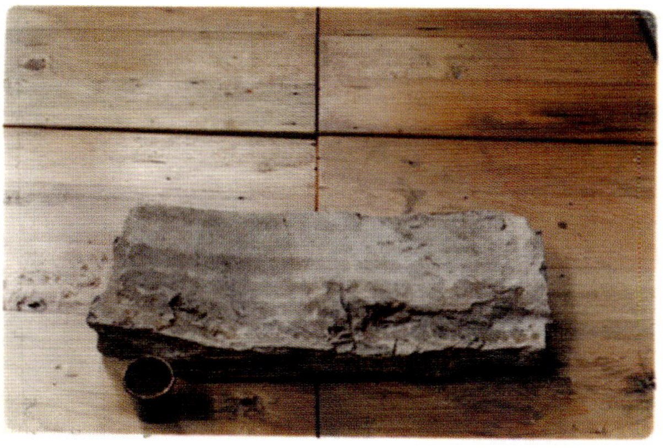

Writing as Body Mark

I would now like to look at some works that take a more intimate approach to writing and the representation of script. The extraordinary reverence expressed towards calligraphic works in various parts of East Asia is closely tied to the idea that a person's handwriting may capture their living presence. The art historian Birgit Mersmann, in her study of contemporary Chinese calligraphy, describes calligraphy as a form of bodily projection or "projected corporeality" rather than simply a form of aesthetic handwriting: "Calligraphy serves to register the internal and external body motions, and therefore it authorizes itself as body mark."[6] In other words, the act of writing is seen not only as a transmission or replication of linguistic meaning, but also, and more importantly, as a powerful projection of a real embodied self (see chapter 1). Contemporary artists from China, Taiwan, Hong Kong, and Japan have explored these ideas by approaching calligraphy as a form of live performance, where meaning lies in the transient act rather than the finished, tangible result.

This idea serves as a central theme in the art of Beijing-based artist Song Dong. During the mid-1990s, he began a daily exercise of writing with a brush dipped in water and traced on stone. This culminated in an ongoing series titled *Water Diary* (1995–), which focused on the repeated performance of ephemeral writing. In the photographs that capture this piece, we see a brush dipped in water and faint lines of text that quickly evaporate from the surface of the stone, leaving no trace. This transient form of writing, captured by the elemental materials of water and stone, resonates with the Chan Buddhist values of non-attachment and stillness. In contrast to the works that foreground

◂ **SONG DONG**
Writing Diary with Water 1995
from the series Water Diary 1995–
4 chromogenic prints, each 44 × 64 cm
COURTESY OF THE ARTIST AND ASIA ART ARCHIVE

the visual and material qualities of script, Song's work focuses on the meditative act of writing as a potentially transcendent ritual.

If we think about the idea of "projected corporeality" in relation to Song Dong's work, we can interpret his act of writing with water as an attempt to manifest his presence through a transient medium. He draws attention to the act of writing as a form of self-expression, but rejects any possibility of "fixing" or "freezing" the self in a tangible text. His work can thus be read as an act of defiant freedom that rejects any fixed definition or identity. As such, his ephemeral writing becomes like the source of water itself, wild and untameable as a river. The visual poetics of Song Dong's work can hardly be described as "calligraphy," as the work leaves no tangible traces of writing to speak of. However, the work directly deals with the time-honoured question, what is the essence or purpose of writing? Is it nothing more than a futile attempt to leave one's mark in the world, or does it ultimately serve as a medium of self-renewal and transformation?

A team of cutting-edge artists and designers from Japan are asking similar questions from the embodied standpoint of the viewer. Known as teamLab, the group is developing the interactive possibilities of calligraphic script through animated digital projections that respond to human movements. In a work titled *What a Loving, and Beautiful World* (2011), projections of calligraphic Japanese words written by the artist Sisyu float around a darkened room (pages 102–7). When a viewer's shadow touches a word, it transforms into the natural phenomenon it represents, such as a flower, a bird, falling snow, or a cloud. Many of the words seem to revert to the images in nature that inspired their earliest pictographic forms. As they disappear and reappear on the screen alongside the natural imagery, the words take on a living and unpredictable quality. This journey is further enhanced by an acoustic environment of bells, piano, flute, and natural sounds produced by Hideaki Takahashi, whose work lends an ethereal and otherworldly feel to the entire piece.

This is not writing in the conventional sense, but rather a performative and futuristic form of visual writing that blurs the boundaries between real and virtual worlds. The fleeting inscriptions, transformed by the movements and gestures of each viewer, speak to the infinite journeys one may take through any given language or environment. When multiple viewers engage with the piece at the same time, their spontaneous movements spark a shared authorship of the work as their shadows trigger an ever-shifting landscape of scripts, sounds, and images. In contrast to Song Dong's writings that focus on the projected body of the artist, teamLab's installation art creates spaces for viewers to project or "imprint" their own bodies into the work. In *What a Loving, and Beautiful World*, the viewer's shadow becomes a catalyst for the work by blocking out the light of the projections and thus activating the sensors. This sets up a poetic contrast between light and dark elements and between the preprogrammed images on the walls and the unpredictable movements of human agents. In this set-up, viewers gain a much more intimate relationship to Japanese script as a living and responsive entity rather than a static set of symbols.

Founded in 2001 by a group of Japanese engineers led by Toshiyuki Inoko, teamLab brings together an international team of some

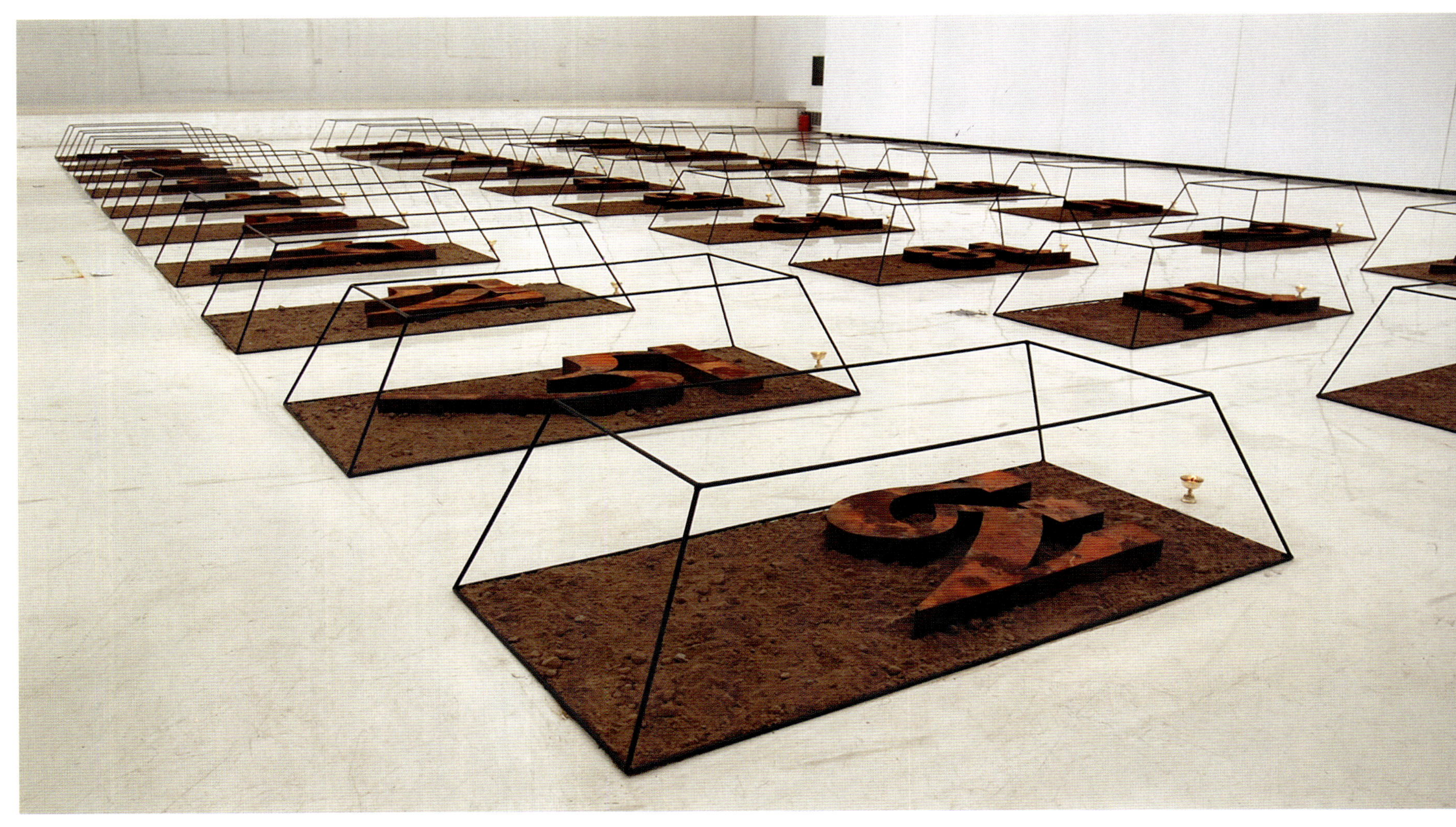

four hundred artists, programmers, engineers, CG animators, mathematicians, architects, designers, and video editors. While this collective is based in Japan, they represent a sophisticated and global network of creative professionals who collaborate on fusing art and technology. Their work is a prime example of how artists from Asia are now working in transnational contexts and communities to produce highly innovative works. Their presentation of Japanese script reflects this collaborative spirit, as the installation allows viewers from around the world to co-create the work. Most significantly, the viewers' passive gaze is instantly transformed into an active one. This is an important shift away from a framework of cultural consumption and towards one of cultural co-production and reflection.

Scripts of Loss and Survival

In contrast to works that deconstruct script to subvert the power of the written word, there are many Asian artists who deploy written script to address the marginalization or loss of language. This is a prevalent theme, for example, in the contemporary works of Tibetan artists such as Nortse, Gonkar Gyatso, and Ang Sang. Since the 1950 occupation of Tibet by the People's Republic of China and the subsequent Cultural Revolution (1966–76) that destroyed some 80 percent of Tibet's monasteries, the region has witnessed a steady decline of Tibetan-language education in state-run schools. Over the past decade, the rapid modernization of Tibet has accelerated the influx of Chinese-language media in all aspects of daily life and brought forth official language education policies designed to assimilate Tibetans into mainstream Chinese society.[7] These developments are further exacerbated by the mass resettlement

◂ **NORTSE**
30 Letters
Tibet • 2010
Iron, earth, and butter lamps installation
Each piece 60 × 80 × 190 cm
COURTESY OF THE ARTIST

of Han Chinese people to Tibetan areas, the restructuring of nomadic life through urbanization, and the transformation of sacred sites into tourist attractions. For a growing number of artists and activists, the use of Tibetan script has become a powerful means to critique these assaults on traditional culture.

In 2010, Nortse exhibited a large-scale installation titled *30 Letters*, which included thirty enormous iron-welded letters of the Tibetan alphabet (page 74). The letters were rusted, laid in rectangular plots of sand on the ground, and covered in an open metal frame. Each letter was accompanied by a butter lamp, commonly used in rituals to guide the spirits of the dead to heaven. Laid out in neat rows, the entire scene was reminiscent of a graveyard, with the heavy metal letters resembling industrial waste, tombstones, or fallen bodies. According to Nortse, the idea for the piece was inspired by a dream in which he was taking an exam in middle school and struggling to remember the Tibetan alphabet. In a fit of anger and frustration, he ran out of the classroom and buried his schoolwork in the sand.[8]

The anthropologist Clare Harris, who has written extensively on Tibetan artists, has compared *30 Letters* with Xu Bing's use of unreadable characters in *Book from the Sky* and noted Nortse's strong emphasis on legibility:

> Not only can the shapes of the alphabet be comprehended by Tibetans, they also inscribe something fundamental about the land of Tibet as a distinctive territory where the ancestors reside and are remembered. Rather than looking to the sky, Nortse suggests that Tibetans must root themselves in the ground and the language of their forefathers.[9]

Whereas Xu Bing's work disrupts the aura of power and authority tied to a classical Chinese script, Nortse's work seems to do the opposite by drawing our attention to both the legibility and enduring presence of the Tibetan script. Presented as a cohesive whole, Nortse's letters also point to the unifying power of the Tibetan script as the common written language for all dialects of spoken Tibetan.

This powerful work was exhibited in the 2010 *Scorching Sun of Tibet* exhibit at the Songzhuang Art Museum in Beijing, a groundbreaking show that marked an important milestone in the rise of contemporary Tibetan art in the Chinese and global art scenes. Curated by Li Xianting, a well-known Chinese critic and curator, the show openly addressed the social, cultural, and political tensions in the region. It was praised by influential Tibetan activists such as the poet Woeser, who emphasized its valuable contribution in "not expressing the views of the government but those of ordinary citizens."[10] The issue of language loomed large, and the exhibit was promoted in both Chinese and Tibetan. Li spoke directly of his decision to address the serious issue of declining Tibetan-language education, which he believes is "a form of control over Tibetans," and lamented the lack of young Tibetan artists who can read and write in Tibetan at an advanced level.[11] Yet as Harris has pointed out, it is ironic and problematic that such discussions are taking place in a "white cube-style institution" in Beijing while Tibetan artists face strict censorship in Lhasa and across the Tibetan Autonomous Region.[12]

Nortse has continued to tackle this issue through subsequent pieces titled *Ashes* (2014) and *Book of Ashes* (2015) (pages 94–97), which are made up of pieces of beech wood covered in illustrated Buddhist scriptures. Each piece is burnt to the point of near destruction, leaving blackened char and only fragmentary traces of the illustrated scriptures. The burnt pieces are laid out in neat rows and on rectangular plots of sand, just like the *30 Letters* installation. According to Nortse,

> The distorted shapes of the wooden books are evidence of their struggles within the fire. The 30 pieces of wood correlate to the 30 letters of the Tibetan alphabet. In *Ashes,* the 30 burnt books represent 30 lives destroyed by fire, however death cannot stop the process of rebirth and the liberation of the soul. Death is merely a stop in a cycle of life and death.

He also commented on his desire to

> highlight the situation of marginalised cultures and ask the viewer to directly address the crisis of identity faced by these cultures. I also wish to highlight the importance of cultural diversity while understanding the shared cultural heritage of all human beings.[13]

Nortse's mention of "30 lives destroyed by fire" likely refers to the spate of self-immolation incidents that have been spreading throughout Tibet since the 2008 protests that coincided with the Beijing Summer Olympics. In that pivotal year, viewers around the world witnessed both Zhang Yimou's celebratory performance of Chinese script as the unifying face of the nation and the Tibetan protests to express their wish for human rights, freedom of religion, and the right to Tibetan-language education. At the same time, we can observe a direct connection between the burnt pieces of wood in Nortse's work and the prevalent depiction of fiery flames in Tibetan Buddhist art. In the sacred paintings of Tibetan Buddhism, the image of fire is often depicted as a purifying entity that surrounds a mandala or a deity. This "purging fire" represents a difficult stage in a spiritual practitioner's journey towards enlightenment as he or she burns away ignorance, greed, or hatred.[14] Nortse's reference to fire therefore contains multiple layers of meaning, an effective strategy that invites viewers to explore the tensions between past and present, between religion and politics.

It should be noted that the depiction of religious scriptures as torn and burnt remnants may be offensive to Buddhist observers who consider the destruction of holy books a sacrilegious act. Despite presenting these scriptures in fragments, the work leaves the sacred figural images of the Buddha intact. Furthermore, these images are given a central placement on the pieces of wood, suggesting a reverence for tradition. Along with how the wood is placed in the rectangular frames of sand, the burnt scriptures seem to be framed as holy relics to be honoured and remembered.

Whereas Nortse re-creates a landscape through words, images, and objects, Shamsia Hassani uses various forms of script to transform real and imagined landscapes. Widely considered the first female street artist of Afghanistan, Hassani has gained international recognition for her site-specific murals, paintings, and digital prints. She began practising graffiti in 2010 when she attended a graffiti workshop in Kabul led by a UK-based graffiti artist named Chu. Like Tibet, Afghanistan has sustained a number of assaults from outside nations

▼ SHAMSIA HASSANI
The making of Secret 2014
Paint on wall in Kabul, Afghanistan
COURTESY OF THE ARTIST

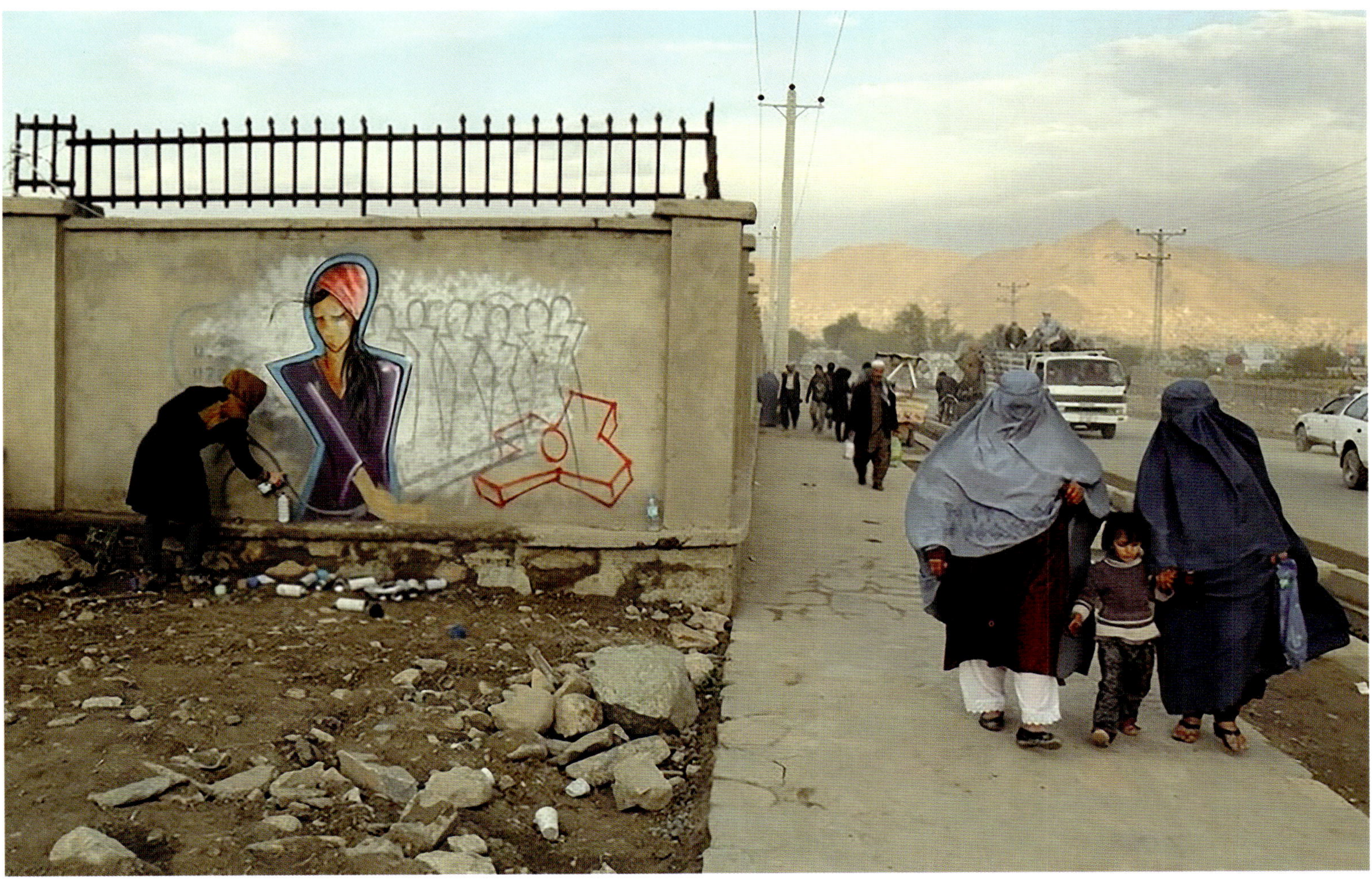

given its strategic geographic position between powerful empires. Afghanistan has been gripped by three decades of warfare: the Soviet-Afghan War (1979–89), the Afghan Civil War (1979–2001), and the US War in Afghanistan (2001–14). Hassani's public murals have been painted onto the urban ruins of Kabul, transforming the sites of war or decay into colourful works of art. In one of her earlier murals (pages 88–89), we see a figure of a woman in a blue burqa who is strategically placed to appear as if she is sitting on the steps that are part of the space. She is hunched in a contemplative posture.

A blue swirl, suggestive of smoke or water, rises up from below her feet. In white text, we see a poetic verse in Dari script that Hassani translated as "The water can come back to a dried-up river, but what about the fish that died?" The shades of blue underscore the reference to water, as do the swirling bubble-like shapes that echo the cracks and holes in the wall. The rounded forms of the outlined words appear to float on the wall, as if borne in air or water. In interviews, Hassani has linked this poetic line to her thoughts about the ongoing war at the time: "When I heard this poem, I thought how it was about the situation in Afghanistan. A lot of people died in the war; now the situation is better, but those people cannot come back."[15]

The mural combines evocative words and images to produce a powerful commentary on war, gender, and the transformative power of artistic expression in public spaces. As in Nortse's work, language is used here to give voice to a marginalized identity in a hostile environment, in this case a woman artist working in wartime Afghanistan. As a site-specific piece, the words and images recast the meaning of an actual site in Kabul. Hassani's sitting figure and poetic quote imprint a human presence upon the wall, inviting viewers to pause and contemplate the metaphor of a dried-up river with no fish. As with many graffiti works, we see the signature of the artist here, simply represented by her initials, SH, in blue letters. The use of Roman letters for her name serves as an interesting contrast to the Dari script, a subtle reference perhaps to her growing international audience and recognition of her name in English.

While graffiti is not illegal in Afghanistan, many of Hassani's projects have gone unfinished because her safety was threatened. Shamsia has documented the process of creating these works through photographs that show her working in the streets, often in public view and with signs of war-related destruction around her (page 77). According to Hassani, while there is actual warfare happening in the streets, her status as a woman may also be putting her in danger. She has described occasions when local observers have verbally abused her and attempted to stop her from working. Instead of letting this slow her down, she has developed a method of working that involves writing and painting on digital photographs or altering digital images through Photoshop. In her series *Dreaming Graffiti,* Hassani alters photographs of public spaces by inserting her mural designs onto the architectural surfaces (pages 87 and 92–93). Viewers are prompted to imagine the transformation of public sites as well as the social conflicts and barriers that prevent their realization.

Whereas Nortse combines Tibetan script with elements of a natural landscape (sand, wood, etc.) to convey the presence of his homeland, Hassani uses script to transform the significance of both real and imagined architectural spaces. Both artists use legible forms of written language to lay claim to a particular locality and identity. In other words, legibility is aligned with visibility, survival, and agency. In contrast to artists such as Xu Bing or Gu Wenda, who intentionally deconstruct a script to destabilize its associations with culture and identity, these works exploit such associations to assert the voices of a particular community.

IN THINKING THROUGH THESE different experiments with the written word, it is evident that artists from Asia are pushing calligraphic practices in radical and unexpected directions. In terms of visual formats, they are going far beyond the arts of aesthetic handwriting to engage in performance, installation, interactive digital media, and site-specific projects. Conceptually, the works are also pushing the limits of what we consider "writing" or "script" to challenge viewer expectations and to open up new forms of art making. From the production of pseudo-scripts to various performative and interactive forms of writing, these works are opening up the fundamental structures of language and script for critical examination. By disrupting the semantic meaning of a word, removing its trace, or inviting a viewer to co-create the meaning, artists from Asia are creating new spaces of cultural encounters that resist easy definition or translation.

As contemporary artists transform the realm of script as we know it, we can think of visual poetry as a broad, multimedia phenomenon that encompasses diverse forms of calligraphy and other, constantly emerging experimental practices. Instead of framing this as a break with the past, I see it as an exciting continuation of calligraphic practices that were always innovative in form and content. The magic of any living script and its artistic expression lies in its intimate connections to the past and the present, and to its region of origin and its continual movement around the world. Given the infinite possibilities of visual poetry, and the profound impact it has already had on the world of contemporary art, it is surely a realm that will continue to grow and to transform our thinking about self and society.

Traces of Words

Phaptawan Suwannakudt **ภาพตะวัน สุวรรณกูฏ** (b. Thailand, 1959) was trained as a mural painter by her father and led a team of painters who worked in Buddhist temples throughout Thailand. She was also involved in the women artists' group Womanifesto. She relocated to Australia in 1996 and creates contemporary art in Sydney. She has exhibited internationally, including the solo exhibition *Retold-Untold Stories* (Chiang Mai, 2014; and Sydney, 2016) and the group exhibitions *Thresholds: Contemporary Thai Art* (New York, 2013) and the 18th Biennale of Sydney, *All Our Relations* (2012). Her works are in public collections, including the Art Gallery of New South Wales in Sydney and the Thai Embassy in Paris.

CAST-OFF SERIES AND THREE WORLDS SERIES

My work is involved with objects of memory and conversations and based on lived experience, the intertwined nature of different cultures, and how all of this applies to the Buddhist precept and practice of "awakening mind." Thai script first appeared in my work in 2002 and continues to appear in my later works. I use the language to which I am emotionally connected as a vehicle to make sense of this unfamiliar place in which I live and to create a space for me to fit in. The *Cast-Off* series features text from *Traiphum Phra Ruang (Three Worlds of King Ruang)*, written by King Lithai (King Ruang) from the fourteenth century. The images of any motif that came to my mind at the moment I touched my brush on paper were drawn freehand. The sculptures were made from fabric I wove on a handloom under the guidance of the late Mae Pan during my Womanifesto residency in 2008 in Sisaket, Thailand. The work is a Buddhist metaphorical gesture. It contains the mind I observed while I wove each thread. *Three Worlds 9* from the *Three Worlds* series also incorporates the same text, interwoven with images using both Australian and Thai icons.

ฉันใช้แนวคิดเชิงสัญญะแห่งวัฒนธรรมต่างด้วยวัสดุรูปทรงแห่งความทรงจำกับชีวิตที่ประสบมาโดยอ้างอิงปรัชญาพุทธทางเจริญสติตื่นรู้ อักษรไทยปรากฏในเนื้องานจากปี ๒๕๔๕ เรื่อยมา ภาษาแม่คือความยึดเหนี่ยวทางใจ แม้โดยรูปลักษณ์อาจดูแปลกแยก แต่มันเป็นกลไกที่ฉันใช้สร้างเนื้อที่ทางอารมณ์กับสังคมใหม่ที่ไม่คุ้นเคย

งาน *ถอดคราบ ความทรงจำ* ลายเส้นดินสอตัวอักษรไทยบนกระดาษ คัดลอกจากหนังสือไตรภูมิกถา หรือไตรภูมิพระร่วง วรรณคดีสมัยพุทธศตวรรษที่ ๑๘ วาดทับด้วยลายเส้นรูปทรงของสรรพสิ่งที่ใจนึก ณ ช่วงขณะที่จรดปลายพู่กันลงบนเนื้อกระดาษ ส่วนวัสดุทรงสามเหลี่ยมทำจากใยฝ้ายที่ฉันฝึกทอกับแม่ปานเมื่อครั้งเป็นศิลปินในพำนักอยู่ที่ไร่ในจังหวัดศรีสะเกษ เมื่อปี ๒๕๕๑ เปรียบเป็นภาชนะหีบห่ออารมณ์หรือจิตที่เป็นไปกับเส้นฝ้ายทุกเส้นที่ถักทอ ในงาน *ไตรภูมิ ๙* คัดลอกจากไตรภูมิกถา เนื้อหาลายเส้นนั้นมีทั้งไทยและออสเตรเลียนประสานสอดคล้องกันอยู่

PHAPTAWAN SUWANNAKUDT
Cast-Off series 2007–10
Pencil and dye on handmade paper, handwoven fabric
42 pieces, each 15 × 10 × 5 cm
COURTESY OF THE ARTIST AND 100 TONSON GALLERY, BANGKOK

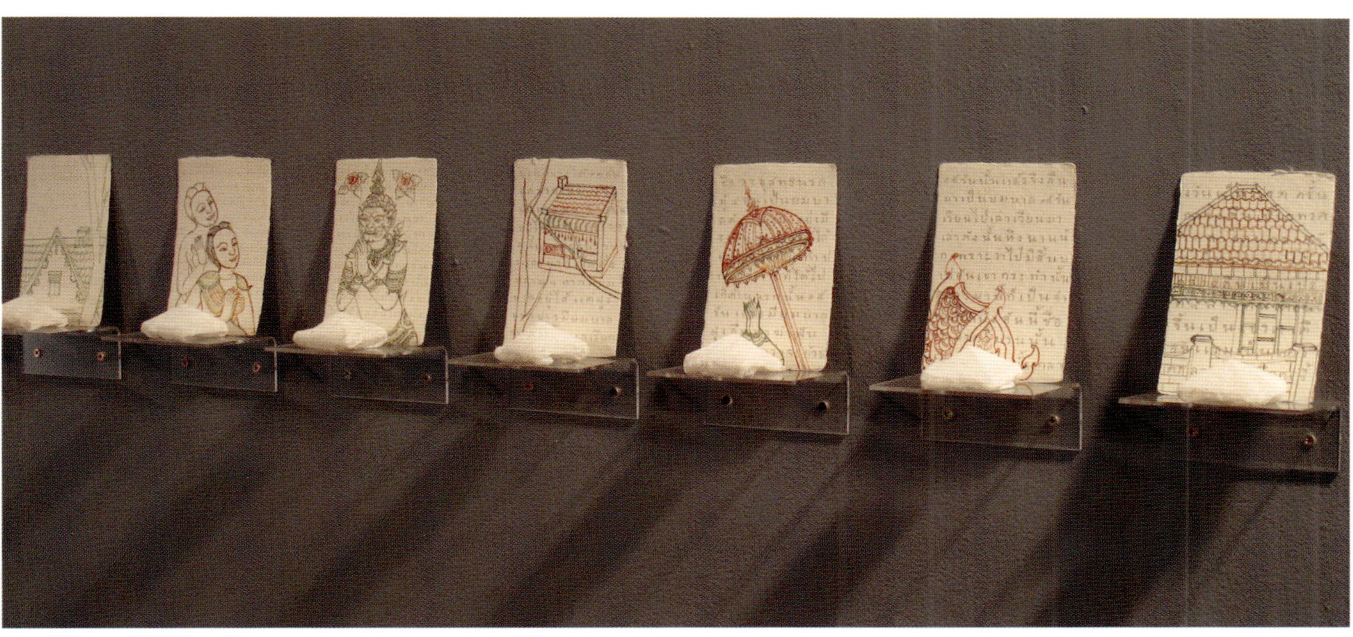

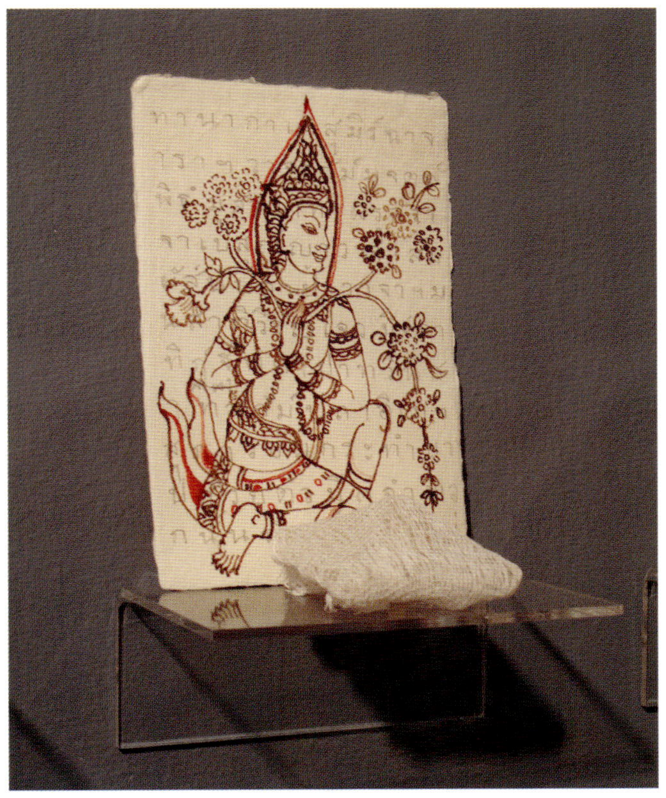

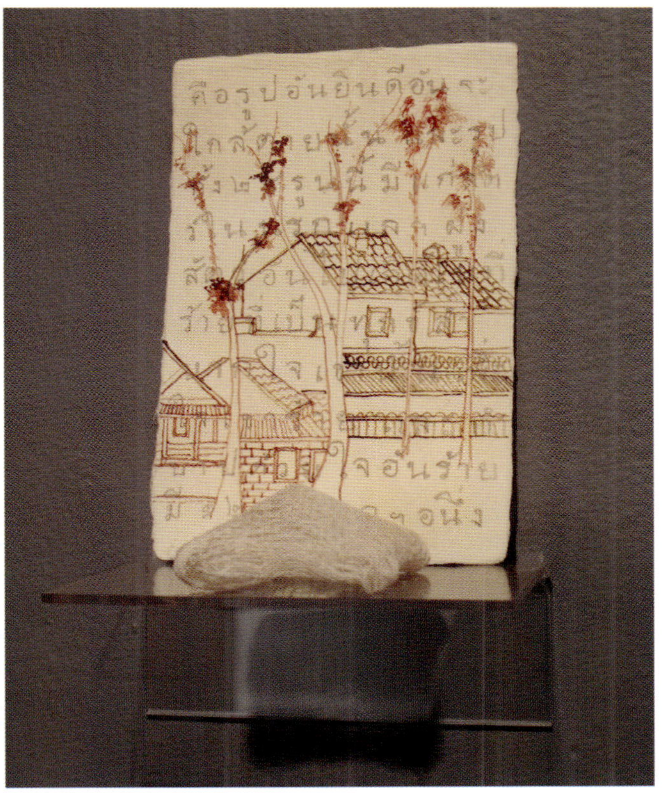

▸ **PHAPTAWAN SUWANNAKUDT**
Three Worlds 9 2009
Acrylic on canvas
135 × 65 cm
PRIVATE COLLECTION: COURTESY OF THE ARTIST

เนตรและในโลกันตนรกนั้นมืดนักหนาผู้สัตว์ซึ่งได้ไปเกิดในโลกันนรกนั้น
นั้นดังหลับตาอยู่เมื่อเดือนดับนั้นแลเมื่อดาวเดือนแลตะวันอันไป
ส่องให้คนทั้งหลาย ๔ แผ่นดินนี้ให้เห็นหนทุกแห่งดังนั้นก็มิอา
จส่องให้เห็นหนในโลกันตนรกนั้นได้เพราะว่าเดือนและตะวันอั
นเป็นไฟและส่องให้คนทั้งหลาย ๔ แผ่นดินนี้ไปส่องสว่างกลาง
หาวแต่เพียงปลายเขายุคนธรไส้และส่องสว่างไปแต่ในกำแพ
งจักรวาฬ และโลกันตนรกนั้นอยู่นอกกำแพงจักรวาฬไส้อยู่หว่าง
เขาจักรวาฬภายนอกเรานี้จึงบ่มิได้เห็นหนไส้เพื่อดังนั้นแล ฯ
เพราะว่าเดือนและตะวันมิได้ส่องไปได้เพราะว่าปลายเขายุคนธร
อันเห็นหนทางเดือนตะวันส่องไปนั้นแหละถ้าและว่าต่อเมื่อใ
ดโพธิสัตว์ผู้จะลงมาอบัติตรัสต่อสัพพัญญูตญาณนั้นและเมื่อ
ท่านเสด็จลงเอาปฏิสนธิในครรภ์พระมารดานั้นก็ดี และเมื่อท่านสม
ภพจาตุโกรธรนั้นก็ดี แลเมื่อพระพุทธเจ้าตรัสแก่สัพพัญญูตญาณ
นั้นก็ดีแล เมื่อพระพุทธเจ้าตรัสเทศนาพระธรรมจักรนั้นก็ดีแลเมื่อ
พระพุทธเจ้าเสด็จเข้าสู่นิพพานนั้นก็ดีในกาล ๕ ทีนี้ในโลกันตนรก
จึงได้เห็นหนแท้นักหนา คนซึ่งอยู่ในนรกนั้นจึงได้เห็นกันแลส
[illegible] กันตนรกก็คิดว่าฉันนี้เดียวว่าแต่กูมาอยู่ที่นี่คนเดียวด
[illegible] ทั้งหลาย [illegible] มาอยู่ในนรก [illegible] ว่าร้ายนี้ดจเดียว
[illegible] นั้น [illegible] บ่มิได้เห็นอยู่ [illegible]
[illegible] นปรนดังสายฟ้าแล [illegible] เดียวไ
สั้เมื่อ [illegible] ว่าอันใด [illegible] นั้
นแล้วโลกก [illegible] ผิเมื่อ [illegible] ตรัส ๔ ทศ
นาธรรมจัก [illegible] อยู่เริ่น [illegible] แล้ว
นส่ายจึงวายเรื่องคนผู้ใดอนกระทำว่า [illegible] แม่และสม
ณพราหมณาจารย์ผู้มีศีลและยยงพระสงฆ์ให้ผิดกันครั้นว่
ตายไปเกิดในนรกอันชื่อว่าโลกันตนรกนั้นและตนเขาใหญ่
นักหนาโดยสูงได้ ๖๐๐๐ วาเล็บมือเล็บตีนเขานั้นดังค้างคาวแล
ะใหญ่ยาวนักหนาสมควรด้วยตัวอันใหญ่นั้น เล็บนั้นสมนักหน
าผิและเกาะแห่งใดก็ติดอยู่แห่งนั้นเขาเอาเล็บเขานั้นเกาะกำ
แพงจักรวาฬมั่นหน่วงอยู่และเขาห้อยตนอยู่เขาอยู่ดังค้างคา
วนั้นแล เมื่อเขาอยากอาหารไส้เขามิไปเพื่อจะหากิน ครั้นได้ตั้
งมือกันเข้าไส้จ เขานึกว่า เขากินก็จับกุมกันกินคนผู้หนึ่งก็นึก
ว่าเขากินจึงคนทั้งสองนั้นก็จับกุมกันกินต่างคนต่างตระครุบกัน
กินก็รัดเอาด้วยกันทั้งสองคนในน้ำอันชื่อแผ่นดินแดดบ่ห้อย
จะไปต้องน้ำนั้นได้สักคาบหนึ่งเลยและน้ำนั้นเย็นนักหนาครั้น
ว่าตกลงมาในน้ำนั้นบัดเดียวใจไส้เห็นปานนี้ตนเขาก็เปื่อยแหล
กออกไปสิ้นดังก้อนอาจมซึ่งตกลงในน้ำนั้นก็ตายบัดใจแล้วจึงกลั
ยเป็นตนเขาขึ้นอีกเล่าไส้คุเขาจึงปีนขึ้นไปเกาะกำแพงจักรวาฬ
ภายนอกนั้นอยู่ดังก่อนเล่าแลแต่เขาทนทุกขเวทนาอยู่ที่นั้น
ช้าหิงนานนักชั่วพุทธันดรกัลปหนึ่งแท้วก [illegible] ภูมิซึ่งว่
าสิ่งอันดีนั้นคือราชสีห์อันว่าราชสีห์นั้นมี ๔ สิ่ง ฯ สิ่งหนึ่งชื่อ
ติณะสิงหะ สิ่งหนึ่งชื่อกาละสิงหะ สิ่งหนึ่งชื่อบัณฑุระสิงหะสิ่
งหนึ่งชื่อไกรสร สีหะ ๓ อันว่าติณสิงหะนั้นมีตนมันดังปีกนก
กเขาย่อมกินแต่หญ้าเป็นอาหาร กาลสีหะนั้นดำดังวัวดำย่
อมกินหญ้าเป็นอาหาร บัณฑุรสีหะนั้นมีตนเหลืองดังใบย่
อมกินเนื้อเป็นอาหารไกรสรสีหะนั้นมีฝีปากแลปลายตีน
ทั้ง ๔ นั้นแดงดั่งนั้นไส้ดวงน้ำครั่งละลายด้วยน้ำชาดหรดา
ทาทั้งปากทั้งท้องแดงดั่งนั้นไส้เป็นแนวแดงแต่หัว
ตลอดรอบบนหลังอ้อมละในแต่งซาบสอดหลังแดง
ดังรสเอวนั้นงามดังท่านแลสร้างแต่งตนราชสีห์นั้นมี
สร้อยอันอ่อนดังนั้นงามดังท่านเอาผ้าแดงอันมีค่าได้
แสนตำลึงทองแลเอามาพาดเหนือตนไกรสรสิงห
ะนั้นที่ขาวก็ขาวนักดังหอยสังข์อันงามท่านฝนใหม่เ
ผิเมื่อไกรสรสิงหะนั้นออกจากคูหาทองก็ดีเงินก็ดี คูห
าแก้วก็ดีอันเป็นที่อยู่แห่งไกรสรสิงหะนั้นตนจึงไปยืนอยู่
เหนือแผ่นดินศิลาเหลืองอันเรืองงามดังทอง สีตีน ๒ ตีน
หลังเหยียบเพียงกันและเหยียบสองตีนเบื้องหน้าจึงฟ
บสองตีนหลังลงและยืนตัว [illegible] แล้วจึงกระทำเสียงออก
ดังเสียงฟ้าลั่นแล้วจึงสั่นขนพึงในตนเสียแล้วจึงแต่ง
ตนไปเดินเล่นไปมาดังลูกวัวแล่นนั้น เมื่อไกรสรสิงหะนั้น
เดินไปเดินมาครั้นดูพลันงามนักดังผู้มีกำลังและถือดังไ [illegible]

Shamsia Hassani شمسیا حسنی (b. Iran, 1988) is regarded as the first female graffiti artist from Afghanistan. Through her art, she aims to colour over the sad memories of wars and to bring positive changes to society. Her work often depicts women in burqas, and fish. When she cannot work on the street, she creates a "dreaming graffiti" by painting on photographic images of her city. She has held solo and group exhibitions in Afghanistan and internationally and was selected as one of the top ten artists for the second Afghan Contemporary Art Prize in 2009. She teaches at the Faculty of Fine Arts, Kabul University, and is one of the founders of the Berang Arts organization.

CALLIGRAPHY IN MY ART

I translate my ideas into images and those images into words. I use different types of calligraphy, both legible and symbolic, in my work. Calligraphy may appear as a visual image, but in my work, calligraphy is inseparable from words. I often use texts in my own Dari alphabet and language. In my works, most of the shapes and images are drawn from my own mental alphabet as that could be considered as a kind of writing. Some of these "words" are there just to be seen, not to be spoken or read. The meaning of a word is different from the shape of a word, yet an artist can use images to reveal meaning more directly. Artworks are able to speak to people in different languages—that is the magic of art. When people find an artwork difficult to understand, it is because they have a different mental alphabet. They just need to translate it into their own mental language and alphabet.

خط در هنر من

من ایده هایم را با تصاویر ترجمه میکنم و آن تصاویر را به کلمه ها. من نوع های مختلف خطاطی را، به شکل واضح، خوانا و سمبولیك به کار می گیرم . بیشتر اشکال و تصاویر در آثارم از طراحي های الفبای ذهنی ام هستند که میتوان گفت نوعی از نوشتن است . بعضی از این کلمات فقط برای دیدن هستند، نه برای صحبت کردن ویا خواندن. معناي يك کلمه متفاوت از شکل اش است. يك هنرمند میتواند از تصاویر برای آشکار کردن معنی به طور مستقیم استفاده کند .
آثار هنری توانایی دارند که با مردم به زبان های مختلف صحبت کنند و این جادوی هنر است .
وقتی مردم نمیتوانند يك اثر هنری را درك کنند به این خاطر است که آنها الفباي ذهنی دیگري دارند و فقط نیاز دارند که اثر هنری به زبان و الفبای ذهنی آنها ترجمه شود .

SHAMSIA HASSANI
Dreaming Graffiti 2012
Paint on a digital print of photograph taken in Kabul, Afghanistan
The text reads, "Like me (looking like me)."
COURTESY OF THE ARTIST

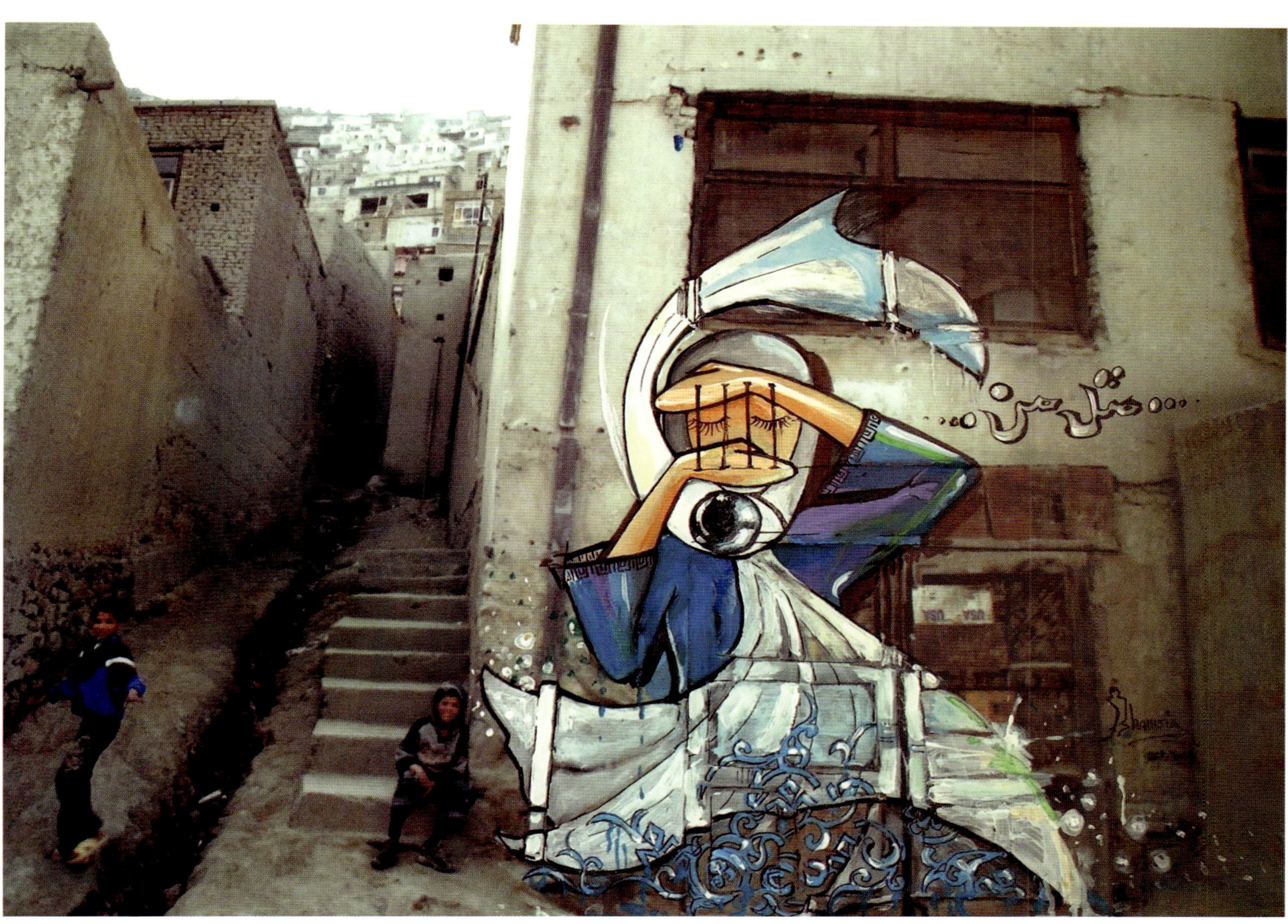

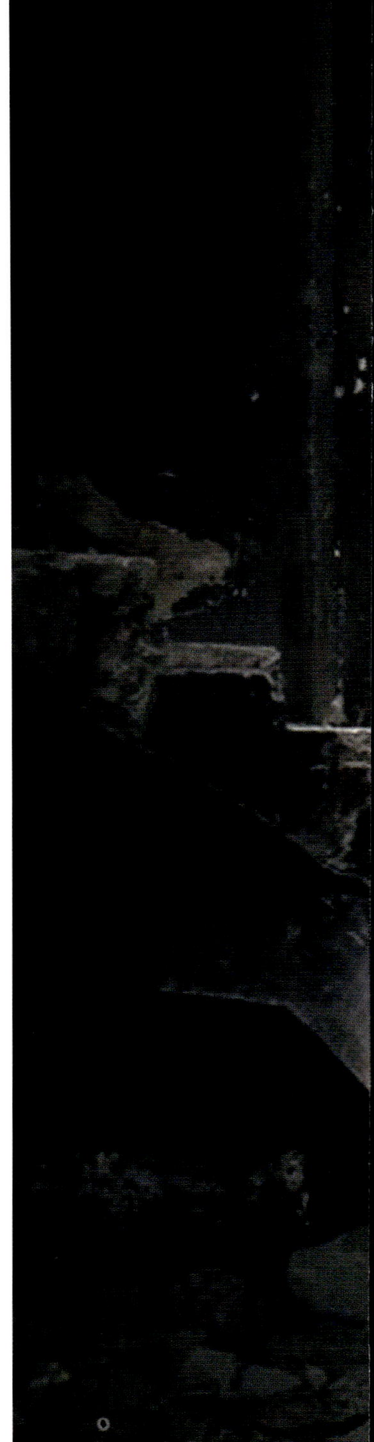

▸ **SHAMSIA HASSANI**
What about the Dead Fish? 2011
Paint on the ruins of the Russian Cultural Centre, Kabul
The text reads, "The water can come back to a dried-up river, but what about the fish that died?"
COURTESY OF THE ARTIST

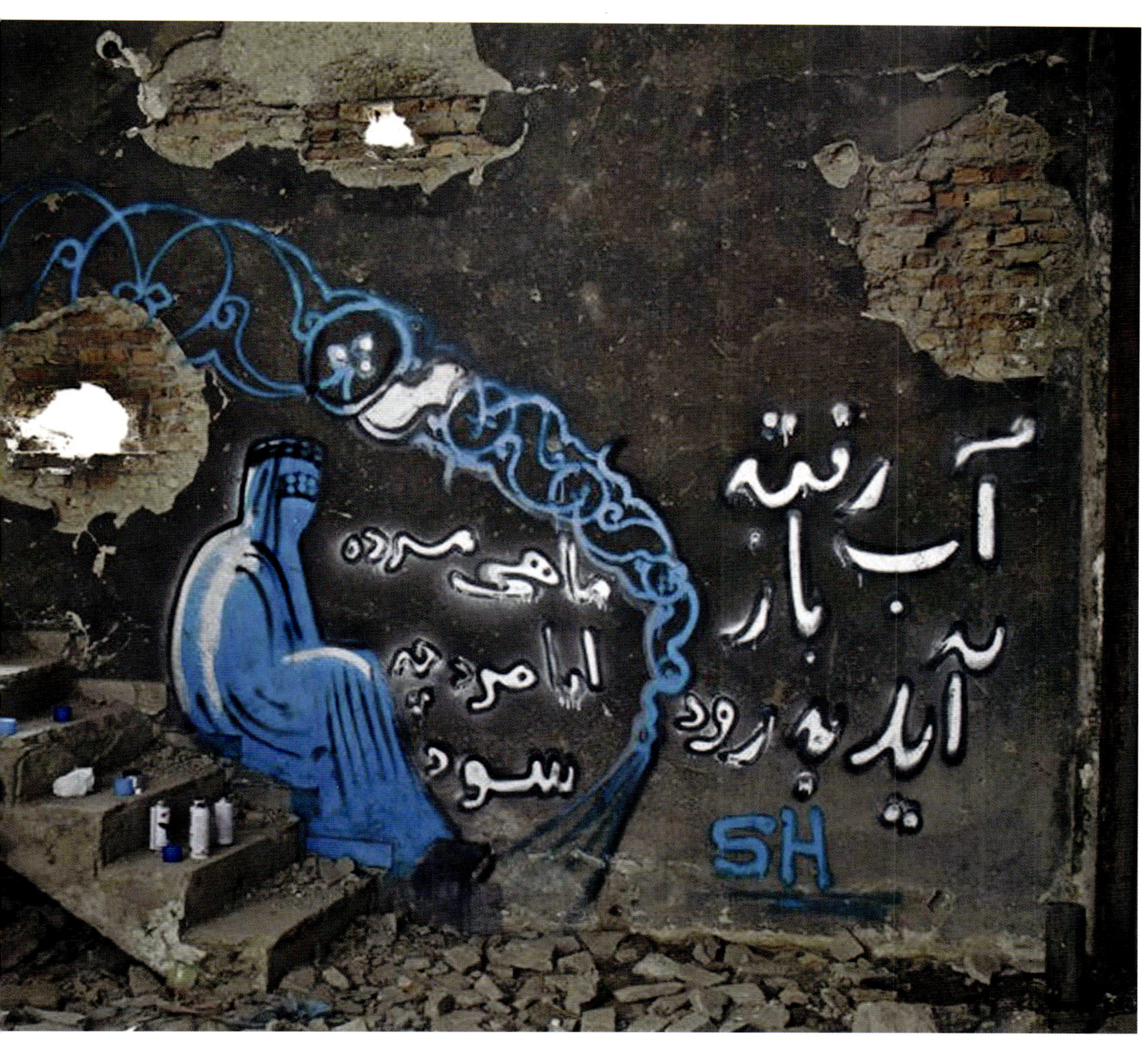

آب رفته
باز
آید به رود
ماهی مرده
اما مرده
سود
SH

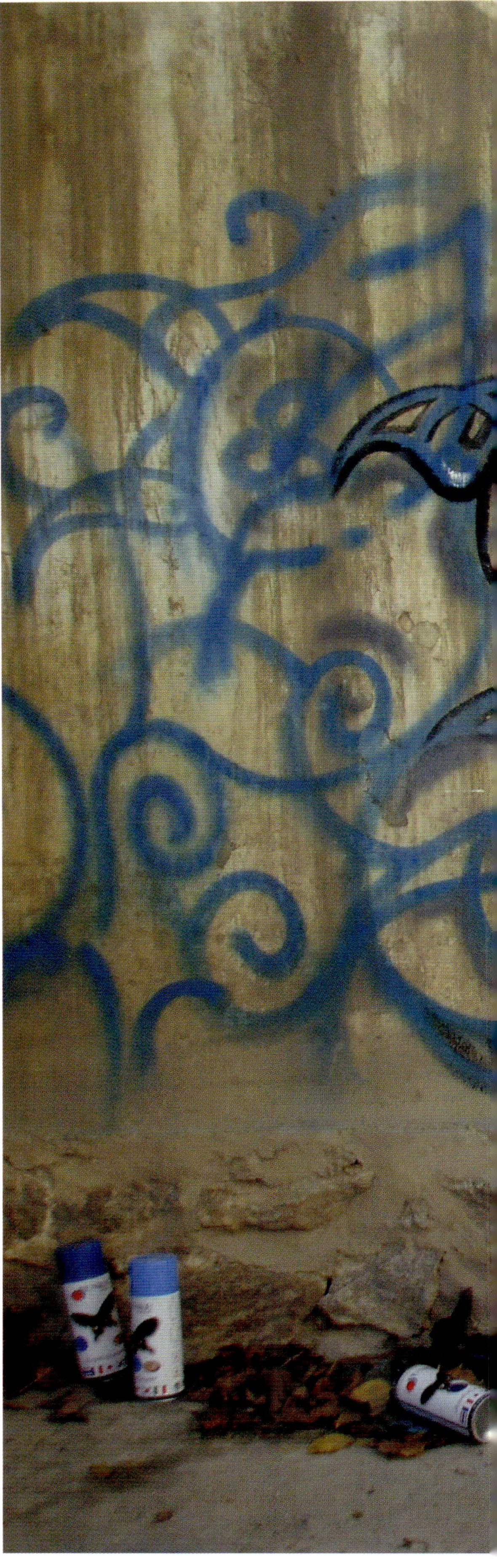

SHAMSIA HASSANI
Words 2012
Paint on wall in Kabul, Afghanistan
COURTESY OF THE ARTIST

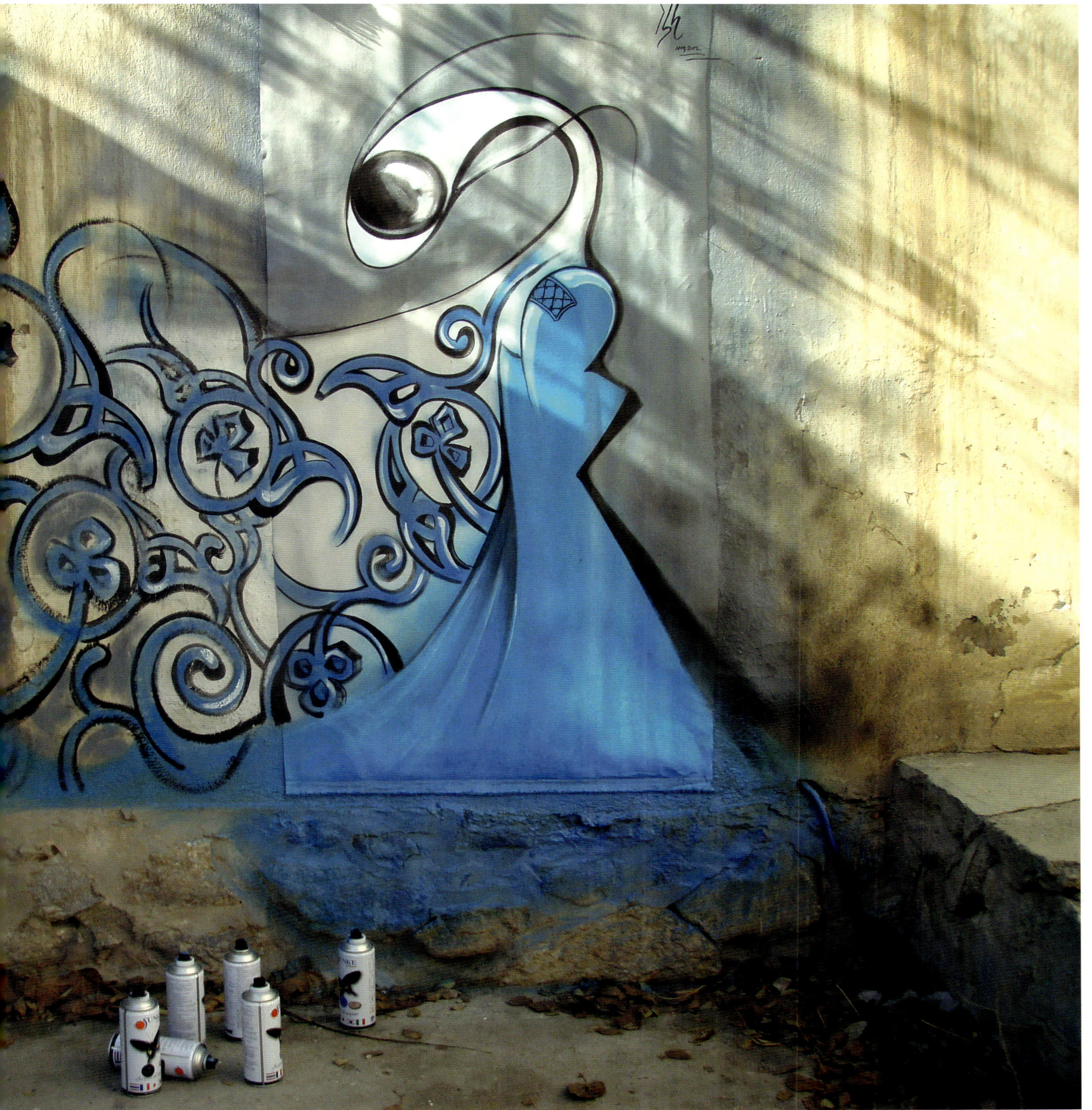

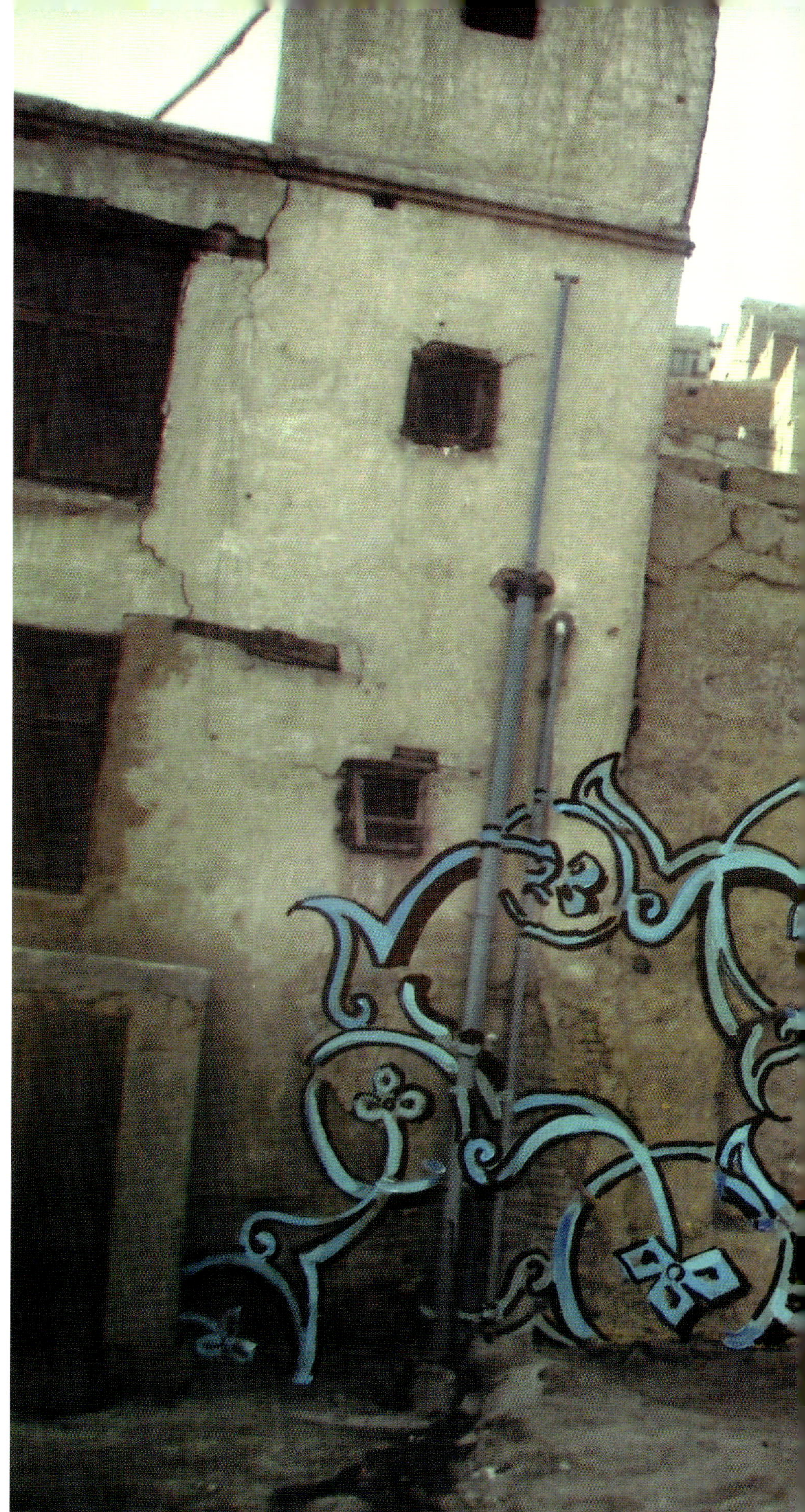

SHAMSIA HASSANI
Dreaming Graffiti—Words 2012
Paint on a digital print of a photograph taken in Kabul, Afghanistan
COURTESY OF THE ARTIST

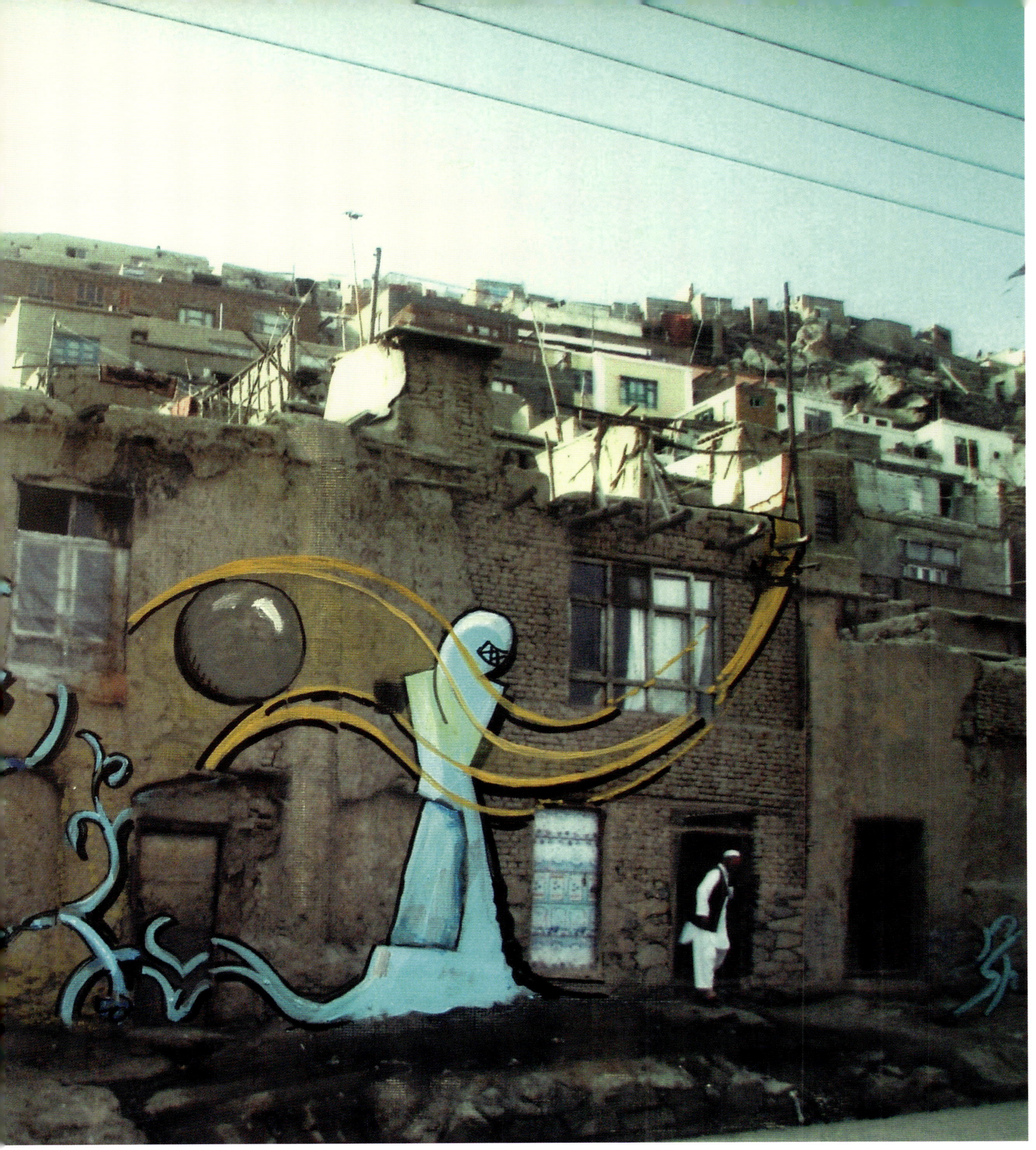

Nortse ནོར་ཚེ། (b. Norbu Tsering, Lhasa, 1963) studied at Tibet University in Lhasa, the Central Academy of Fine Arts in Beijing, and art academies in Guangzhou and Tianjin. He creates striking mixed-media works that experiment with forms and imagery from traditional Tibetan art and culture while addressing universal concerns: global warming; environmental degradation; overpopulation; and the erosion of culture, tradition, and language and its impact on the construction of identity. Given the recent history of Tibet, the artist addresses these issues with an added urgency and poignancy. Nortse's works have been exhibited in Asia, Europe, and the United States and are held in public and private collections worldwide.

BOOK OF ASHES

There have been several disasters inflicted upon Tibetan Buddhism during its long history of development. Especially during the 1960s, Buddhism was badly destroyed in the "mass cultural movement" (the Cultural Revolution). A memory from my childhood is a scene with burnt books and broken Buddhist statues abandoned everywhere on the ground. *Book of Ashes* is an artistic reproduction, representing the fragments/cultural remains that had long been burnt into ashes. The sands beneath the books symbolize the ashes, and they are the ultimate destination/home of the destroyed books.

སོལ་ཐལ་གྱི་དཔེ་ཆ།

༄༅།། བོད་ལ་ནང་པ་སངས་རྒྱས་ཀྱི་ཆོས་ལུགས་རིག་གནས་དར་ཁྱབ་བྱུང་ནས་ལོ་ངོ་སྟོང་ཕྲག་གི་ལོ་རྒྱུས་ལྡན་ཡོད། དེའི་རིང་ལ་སྔར་གྱི་ལོ་རྒྱུས་ལ་ཐེངས་མང་གི་གཡོ་འགུལ་ཚབས་ཆེན་བྱུང་བ་དང་ལོ་རབས་༦༠ནང་ཀྲུང་གོར་ཚ་རླབས་འཕྱུར་བའི་རིག་གནས་ཀྱི་ལས་འགུལ་བྱེད་སྒོ་སྤེལ་བས་ནང་བསྟན་རིག་གནས་ལ་ཡ་ང་བའི་རྡུང་རྡེག་དང་གོད་ཆག་ཚབས་ཆེན་བྱུང་ཡོད། དེ་ཡང་ཁོ་བོའི་དྲན་གསལ་ལ། བོད་ལྗོངས་ཁུལ་དུ་རྒྱུན་དུ་མཐོང་ཆོས་སུ་གྱུར་པ་ནི་གང་སར་སྤྱུངས་པའི་ཐལ་རྡུལ་ཁྲོད་ཀྱི་དཔེ་ཆ་དང་སྐུ་འདྲ་འདི་རྣམས་ལགས། ད་ཐེངས་ཁོ་བོས་སོལ་ཐལ་གྱི་དཔེ་ཆ་ཟེར་བའི་གྲིག་ཆས་ཀྱི་སྒྱུ་རྩལ་བརྒྱུད་ནས་སྔར་ཡང་སྐྱོན་ཆག་བྱུང་བའི་ཐལ་རྡུལ་གྱི་དཔེ་ཆ་རེ་རེ་བཞིན་ཀུན་གྱི་མཐོང་ལམ་དུ་གྱུར་ཡོད།

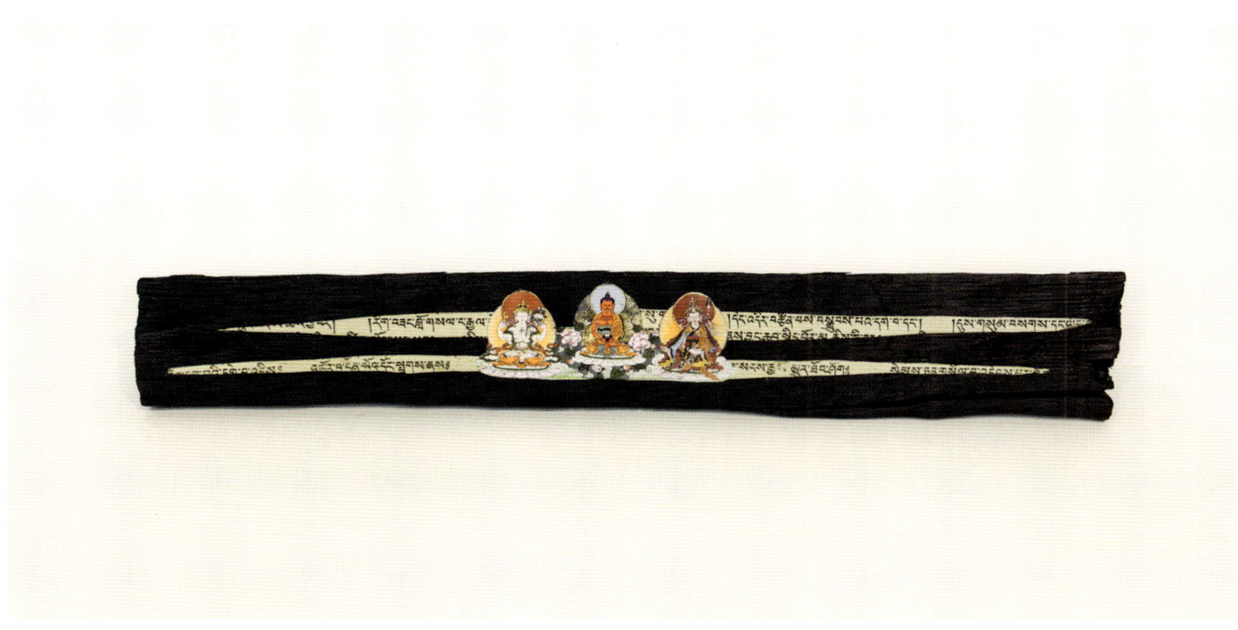

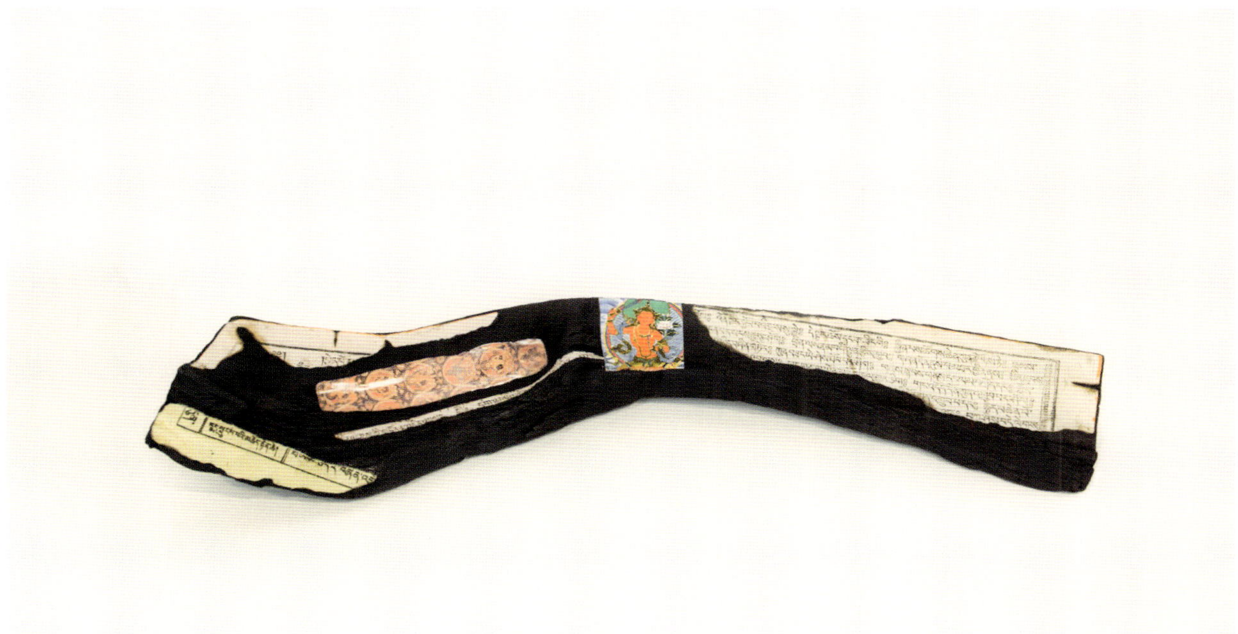

▲ **NORTSE**
Book of Ashes (detail)
Tibet • 2015
Beech wood, acrylic, and paper, soil and metal
40 pieces, each approx. 11 × 70 cm;
40 frames, each 30 × 90 cm
THE GENE AND BRIAN SHERMAN COLLECTION, SYDNEY; COURTESY OF THE ARTIST

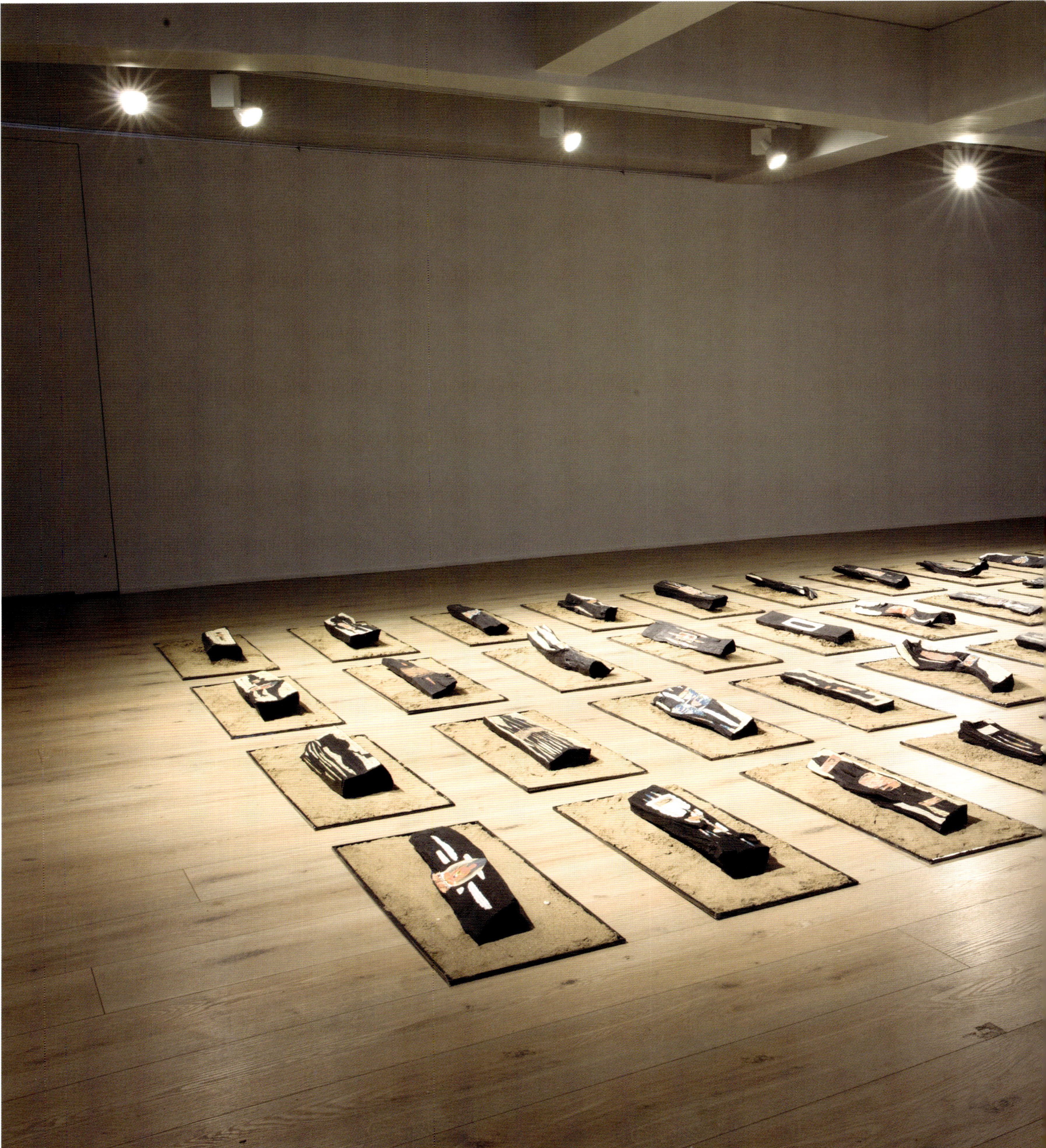

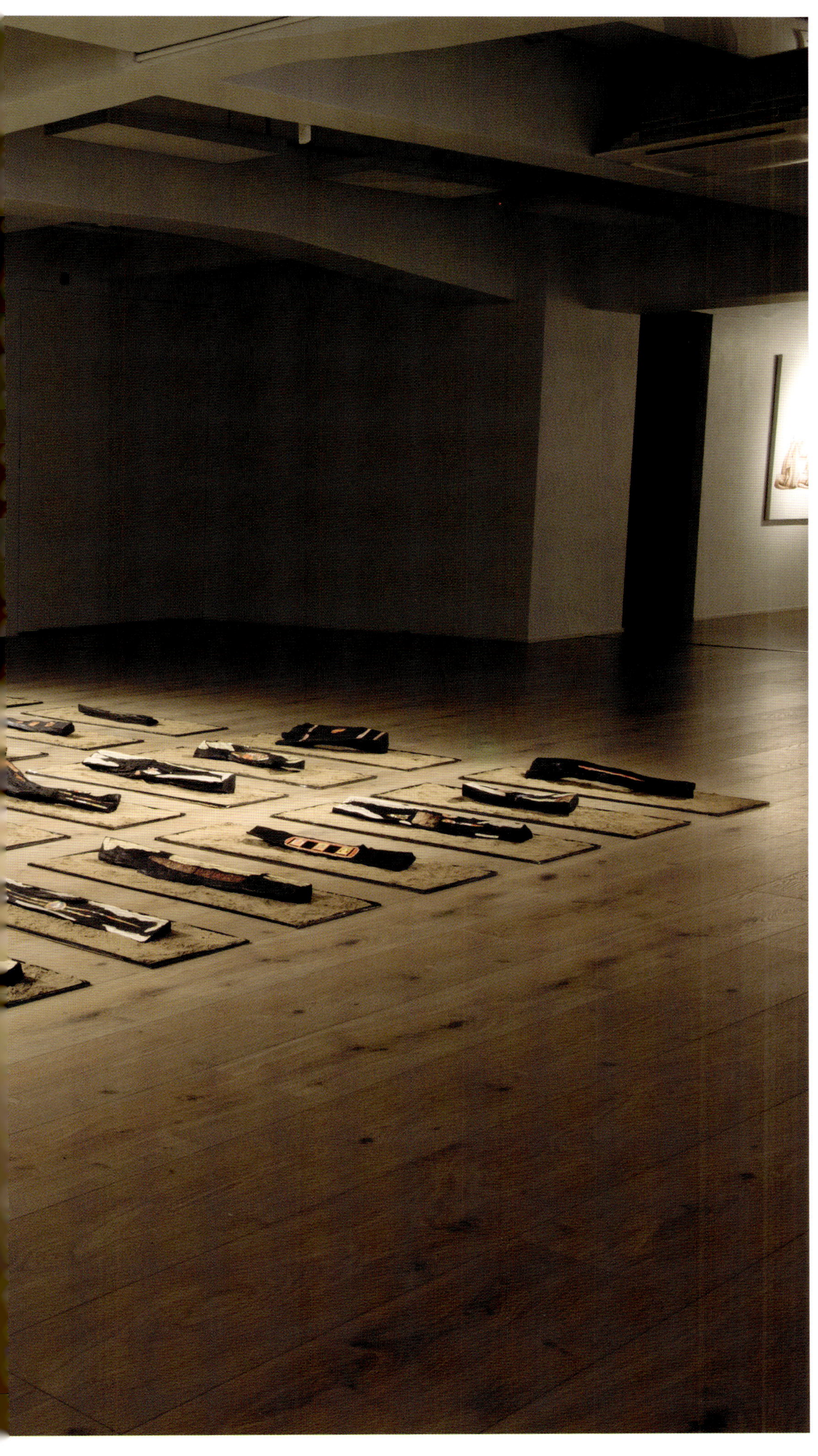

NORTSE
Book of Ashes
Tibet • 2015
Beech wood, acrylic, and paper; soil and metal
40 pieces, each approx. 11 × 70 cm; 40 frames, each 30 × 90 cm
THE GENE AND BRIAN SHERMAN COLLECTION, SYDNEY; COURTESY OF THE ARTIST

Kimura Tsubasa 木村翼沙 (b. Osaka, 1978) has been trained in the traditional style of calligraphy since the age of seven and has won a number of prestigious awards. Kimura began experimenting with a variety of new calligraphic forms in 1998. She majored in Buddhist studies for her bachelor of arts at Ryūkoku University in Kyoto and studied *bokuseki*, or the calligraphy of Buddhist monks, during her postgraduate years at Kyoto University of Education. She has held a number of solo and group shows both in Japan and internationally, including a solo exhibition at the Hyogo Prefectural Museum of Art in 2008, where she showcased a massive installation *Forest of Calligraphy* and performed live calligraphy.

ABOUT THE WORK

Written in this work are my own words or poems—often meaningless, rambling words, which are just for myself to write when creating calligraphy. I wanted to remove anything emotional that we often attach to words and writings, and instead focus on the act of writing itself. These poems are fragments of writings from my diary or random thoughts, which I kept on the computer. By repeatedly cutting and pasting bits and pieces from the writings, I made meaningless sentences and modified them, and presented them as if they were a proper piece of Japanese writing.

作品に関して

作品には私自身の言葉を書いていますが、それは意味のない言葉で、ただ、私が書くためだけにある言葉です。言葉や文字に込める感情的なものを排除したかった。文字を書くということだけを取り上げたかった。詩は自分の日記や思いをパソコンの中でカット＆ペーストを繰り返し、意味のないものにして、日本語として文章を整えたものです。

▼ **KIMURA TSUBASA**
Outline 2007
Sumi ink on faille fabric
12 sheets: 4 sheets each 110 × 700 cm;
2 sheets each 114 × 1.000 cm; 3 sheets each
110 × 285 cm; 3 sheets each 114 × 355 cm
COURTESY OF THE ARTIST

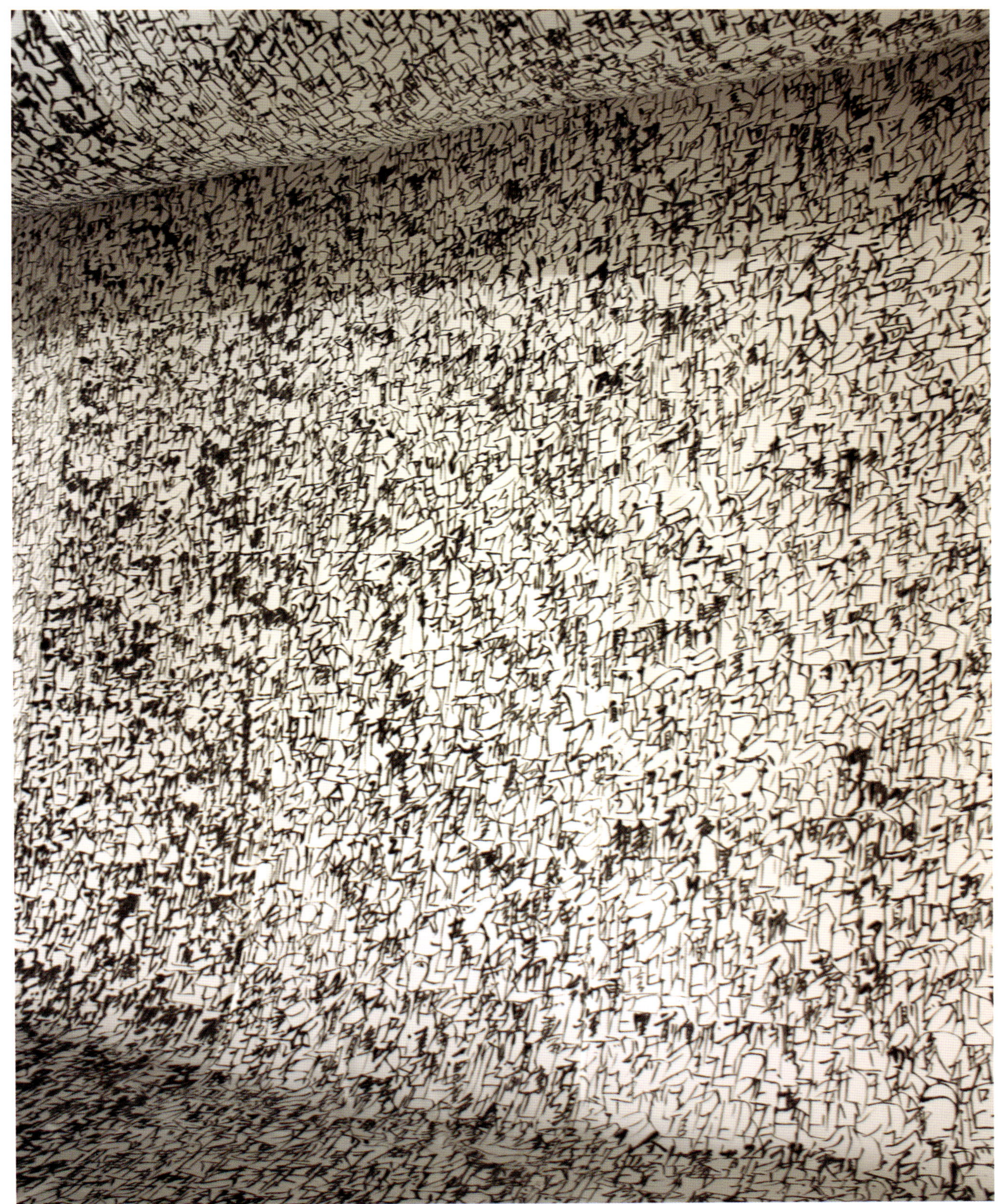

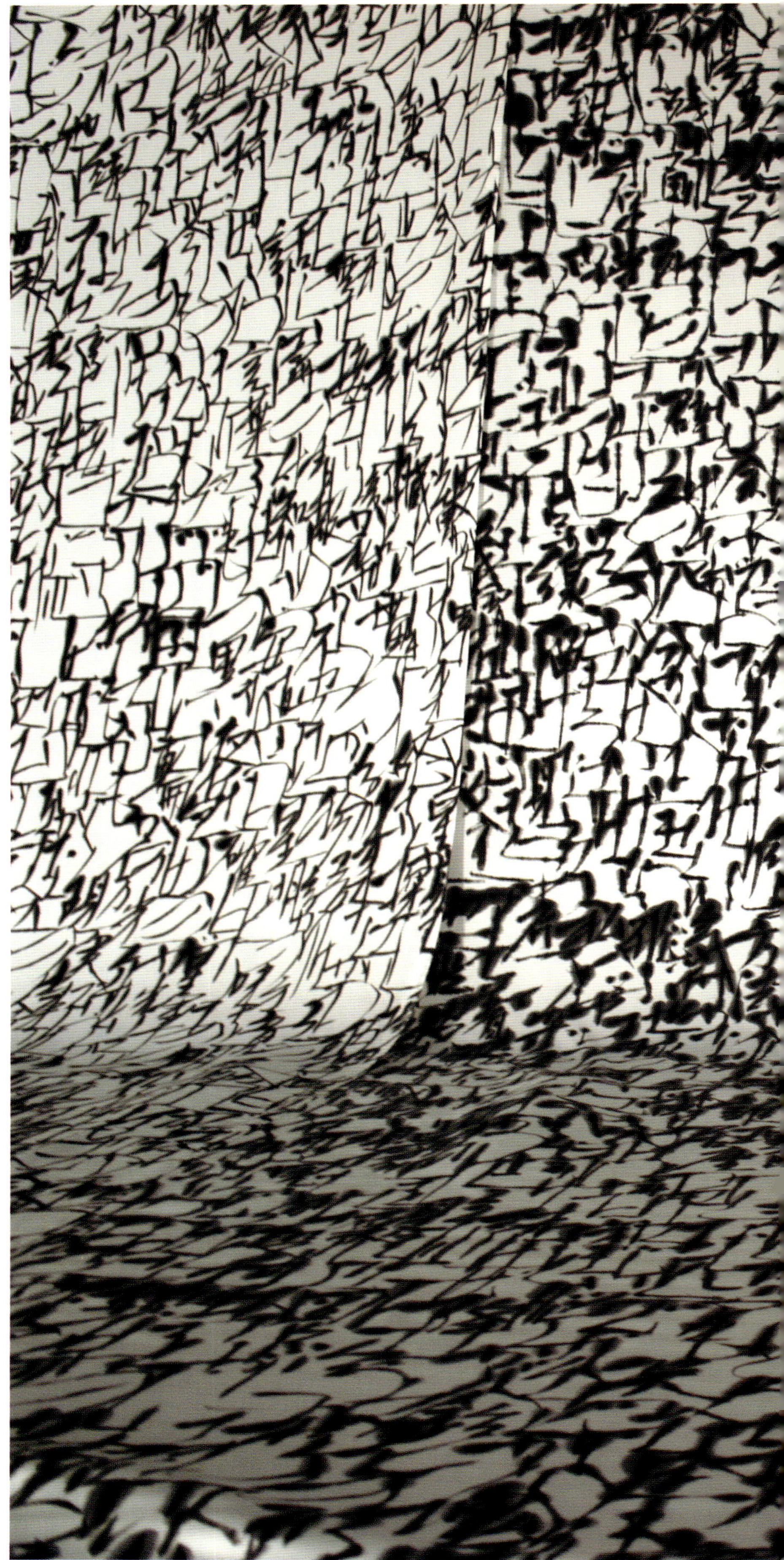

KIMURA TSUBASA
Outline 2007
Sumi ink on faille fabric
12 sheets. 4 sheets each 110 × 700 cm;
2 sheets each 114 × 1,000 cm; 3 sheets each
110 × 285 cm; 3 sheets each 114 × 355 cm
COURTESY OF THE ARTIST

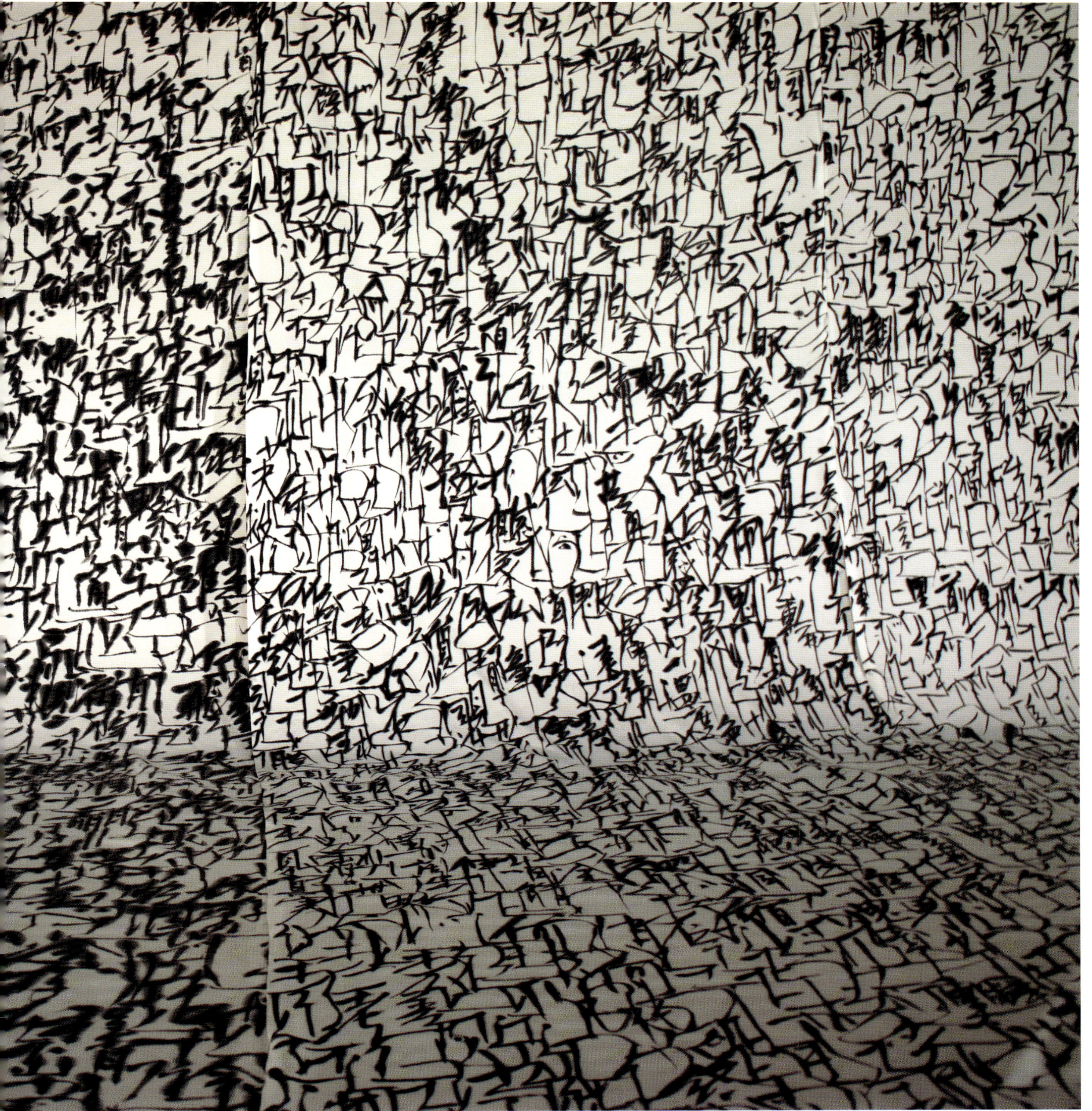

teamLab チームラボ (co-founded by Toshiyuki Inoko in 2001) is an interdisciplinary group of ultra technologists whose collaborative practice seeks to navigate the confluence of art, technology, design, and the natural world. Rooted in the tradition of ancient Japanese art and in contemporary forms of anime, teamLab operates from a distinctly Japanese sense of spatial recognition and investigates human behaviour in the information era and proposes innovative models for societal development. teamLab's works are in the permanent collection of Borusan Contemporary in Istanbul, the Asian Art Museum in San Francisco, and the Art Gallery of New South Wales in Sydney. They have participated in numerous exhibitions worldwide, including a projection-mapping work on the façade of the Grand Palais in Paris (2015).

WHAT A LOVING, AND BEAUTIFUL WORLD

When your shadow touches a character, the world that character embodies will appear, and a new world will be created. The objects that are released from the characters go on to influence each other in the new world.

This projected world is a 360-degree computer-generated space. The objects that are born from the characters appear at various positions within that space, and the physical influences and connections between objects is calculated in real time, producing a complex and natural world. For example, if you see a wind blowing, the objects react to the physical influence of the wind; butterflies are frightened by fire but attracted to flowers. Just as in nature, no two moments are repeated; they are just passing moments of the world, and new visual worlds are constantly being created. Chinese characters were first carved in turtle shell and in ox or deer bones, and were engraved in bronzeware. It can be said that each character contained its own world. With characters, there is the world that you call up and the worlds that the people around you call up, and they all connect with and influence each other to create a new world.

世界はこんなにもやさしく、うつくしい

鑑賞者の影が文字に触れると、その文字がもつ世界が表れ、世界を創っていく。そして文字から生まれたものたちは、世界の中で互いに影響し合う。

投影された世界の裏側には、360度広がる空間があり、文字から生まれたものたちは、空間上のそれぞれの位置や、それぞれが持つ知能や関係性、物理的な影響などによって、互いに影響を受け合いながら、空間上でリアルタイムに計算され、複雑かつ自然な世界をつくっていく。風が吹けば、風の物理的な影響を受け、蝶は火が嫌いだけれども、花が好きで、花に近づいていく。自然の景色に同じ瞬間がないように、同じ瞬間は二度となく、常に初めて見る景色を創り出す。漢字が亀の甲羅や牛や鹿の骨、青銅器に刻まれていたころ、漢字の一文字は、ひとつの世界の部分を持っていた。漢字を通して鑑賞者どうしが呼び出した世界は、連続し、互いに相互作用を与えながら、世界は創られていく。

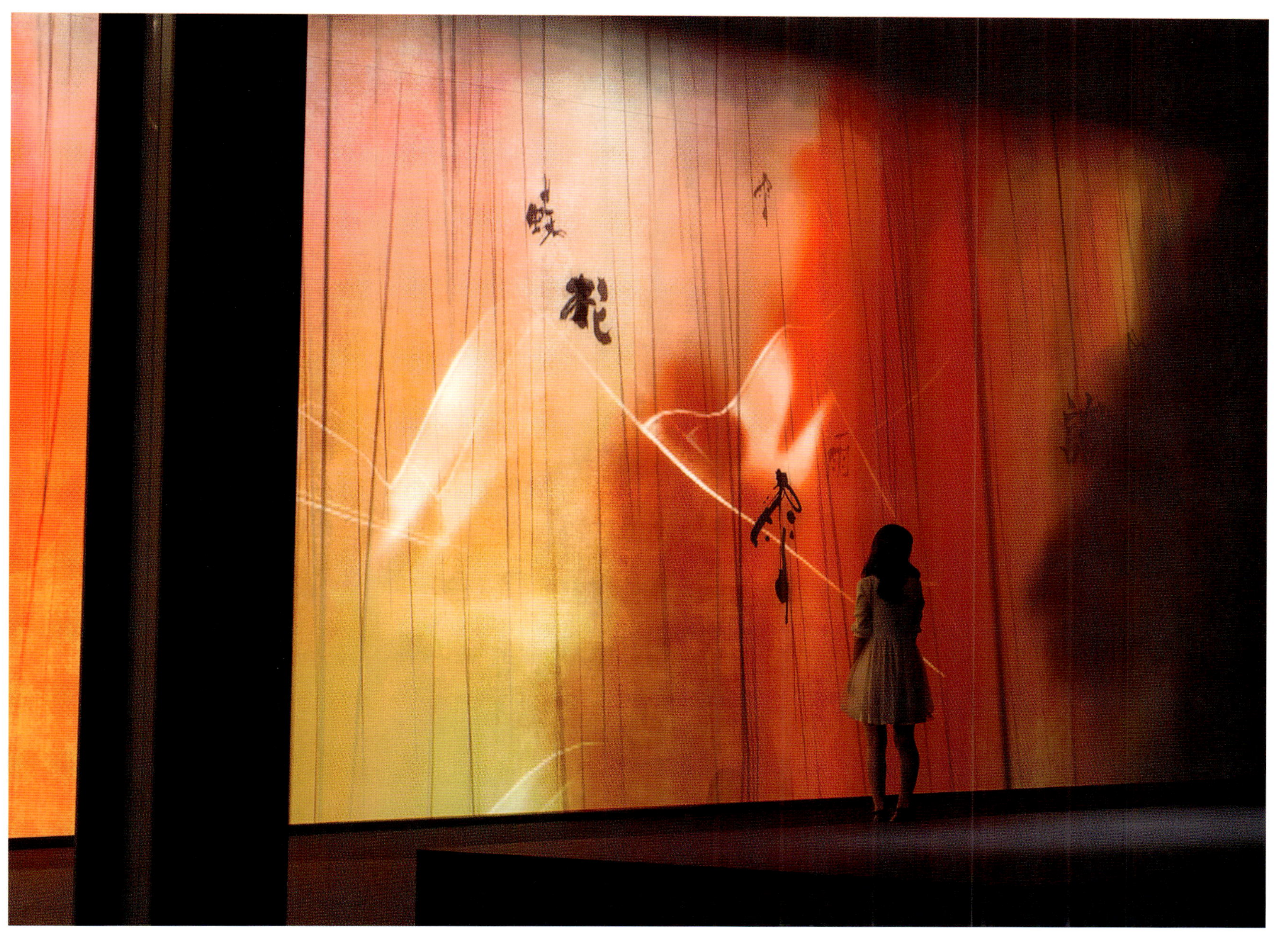

▲ **SISYU + TEAMLAB**
What a Loving, and Beautiful World 2011
Interactive digital installation
Calligraphy by Sisyu, sound by
Hideaki Takahashi
COURTESY OF THE ARTISTS AND PACE GALLERY

▸ **SISYU + TEAMLAB**
What a Loving, and Beautiful World 2011
Interactive digital installation
Calligraphy by Sisyu, sound by
Hideaki Takahashi
COURTESY OF THE ARTISTS AND PACE GALLERY

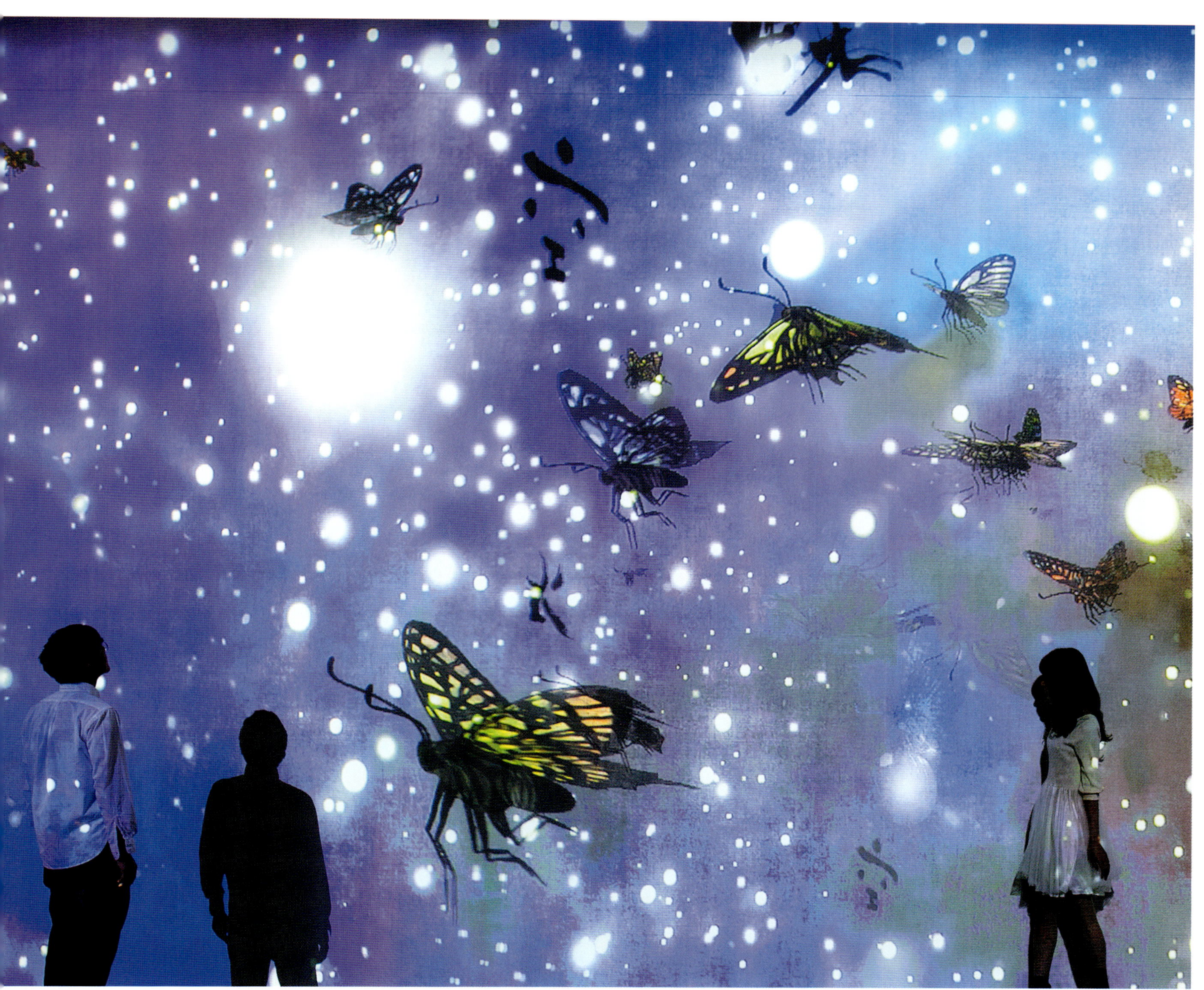

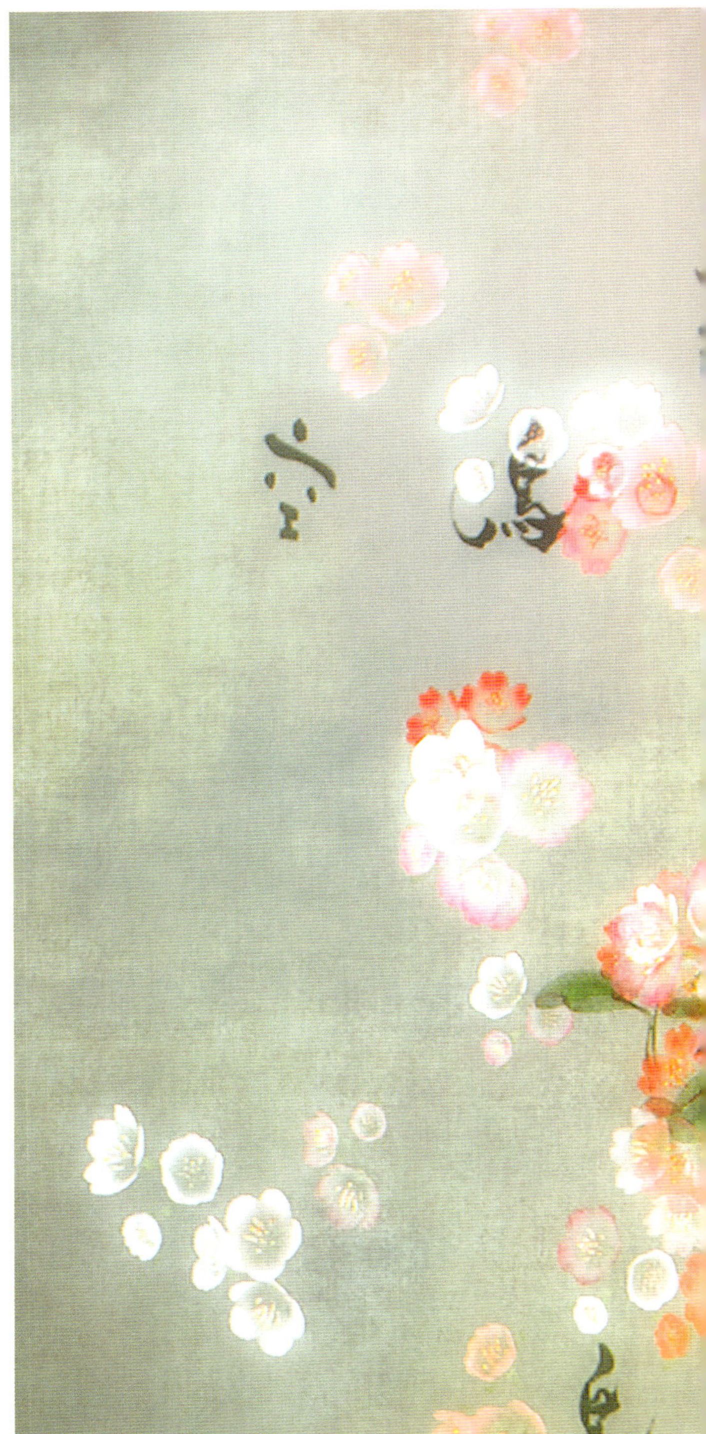

SISYU + TEAMLAB
What a Loving, and Beautiful World 2011
Interactive digital installation
Calligraphy by Sisyu, sound by
Hideaki Takahashi
COURTESY OF THE ARTISTS AND PACE GALLERY

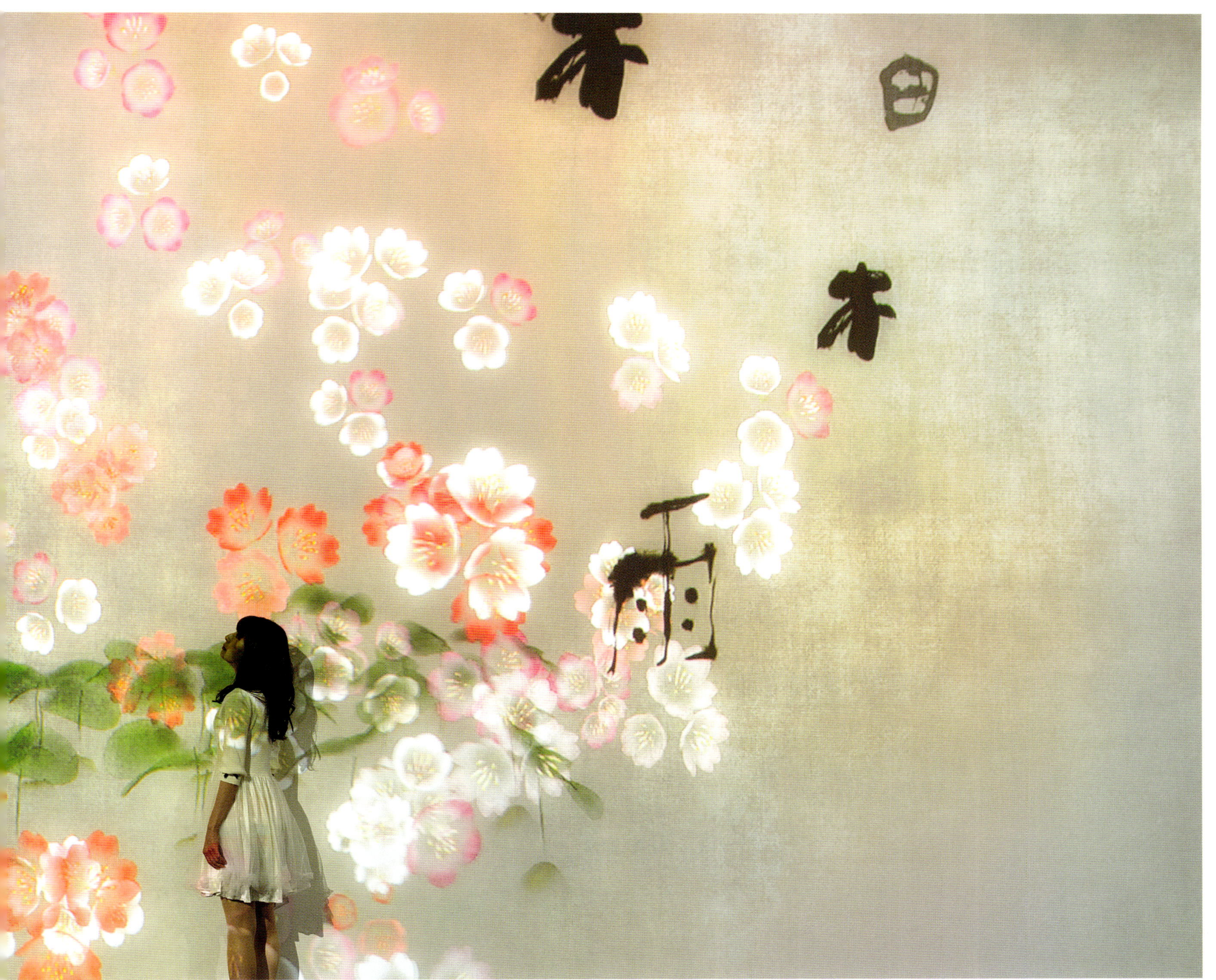

Yugami Hisao 湯上久雄 (1976–) is a calligrapher from Kyoto, Japan, known for his innovative work. With a strong background in traditional Japanese calligraphy, Yugami seeks new approaches and expressions in calligraphy. He is a recipient of a number of calligraphy prizes. His solo exhibitions include *The Stains of Words* (Kyoto, 2002) and *The Distance between White and Black* (Kyoto, 1998); his group shows include the International Impact Art Festival in Kyoto (2002–11), the Sweden-Japan International Exhibition (Osaka, 2002), and *Traces of Words, Traces of Time* (Buenos Aires, 2011).

ABOUT MY WORK

"Writing *moji* (letter/character)" is crucial in creating my work. Because it is so important, I contradictorily depart and deviate from writing *moji* from time to time, but always naturally come back to *moji*. When there are a brush, paper and ink, the first thing I would do is to write *moji* or words.

There is black space and white space in *sho* (Japanese calligraphy) and there is "*ma*" (space/a consciousness of place) between these two. This distance between the white and the black is very important in my work. Some of my works are without the *urauchi*—a technique of lining or backing a piece of paper by pasting another stronger piece of paper over the backside of the main paper to straighten it with minimal shrinkage. I avoided this commonly used technique intentionally because I wanted to leave the traces of *moji* and words visible to indicate the process of how these words were created amid the friction between the paper and the ink with various densities, which scratches, sometimes strokes or rubs the paper.

作品に関して

僕の制作にとって「文字を書くこと」はとても重要です。あまりに大切過ぎて時に文字から離れ逸脱することもありますが、まず自ずと文字に戻ってきます。筆と紙、そして墨があれば僕は先ず、「文字」（言葉）を書きます。

書には「黒場」と「白場」、そしてその「間」があります。僕の書にはこの「白と黒の距離」がとても重要です。僕の作品の中には「裏打ち」という作品の後ろにもう一枚紙を貼り、作品をまっすぐ平らにする作業を敢えてしていないものがあります。様々な濃度をもった墨で時に引っ掻き、時に撫で、時にこすりつけられた紙との軋轢の中、文字言葉が沁みついていく様を残しておきたいと思ったからです。

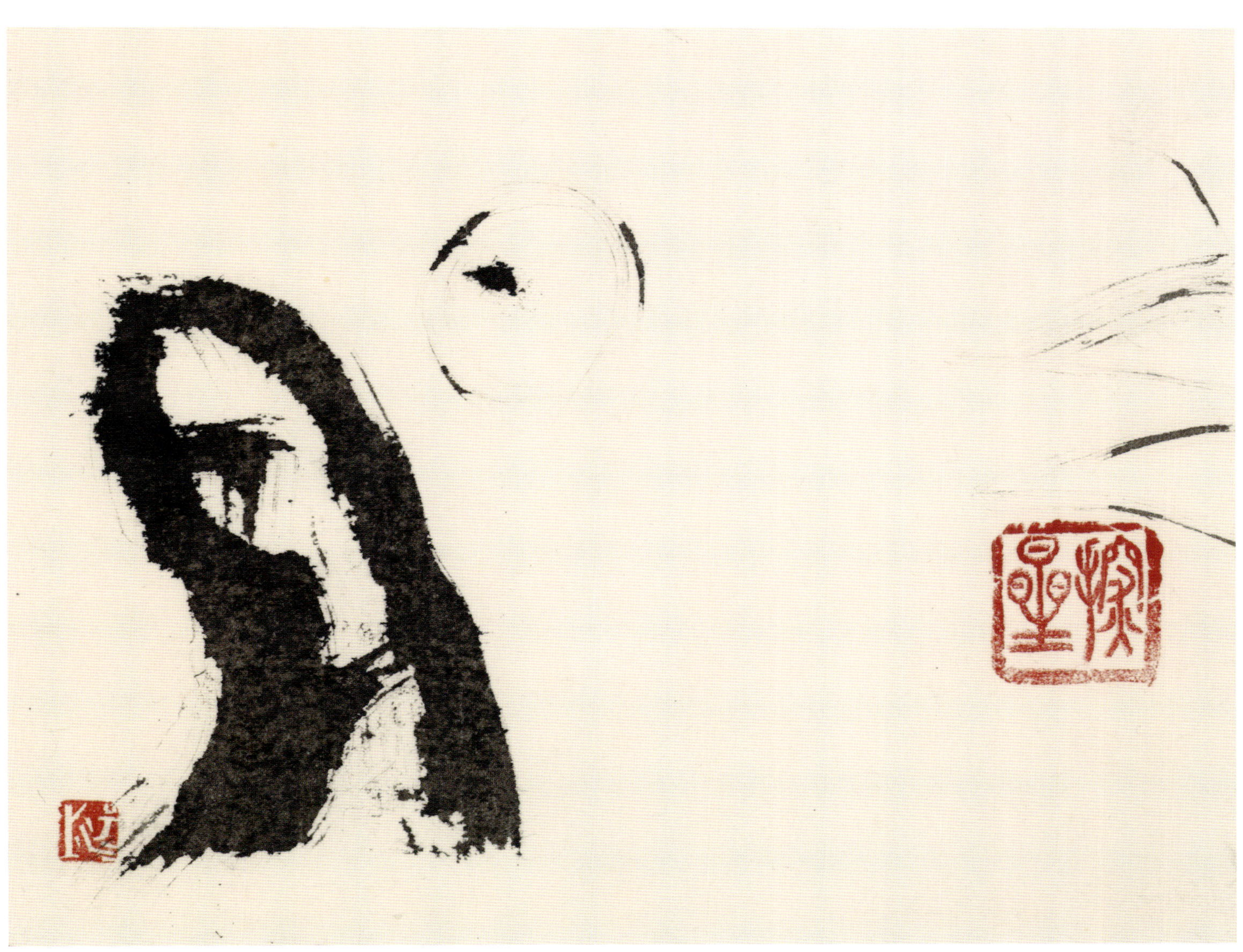

▲ **YUGAMI HISAO**
***Mikazuki* 三日月 (Crescent)** 2015
Sumi ink on *gasen* paper mounted on wood panel
14 × 18 cm
MOA COLLECTION, 3186/4

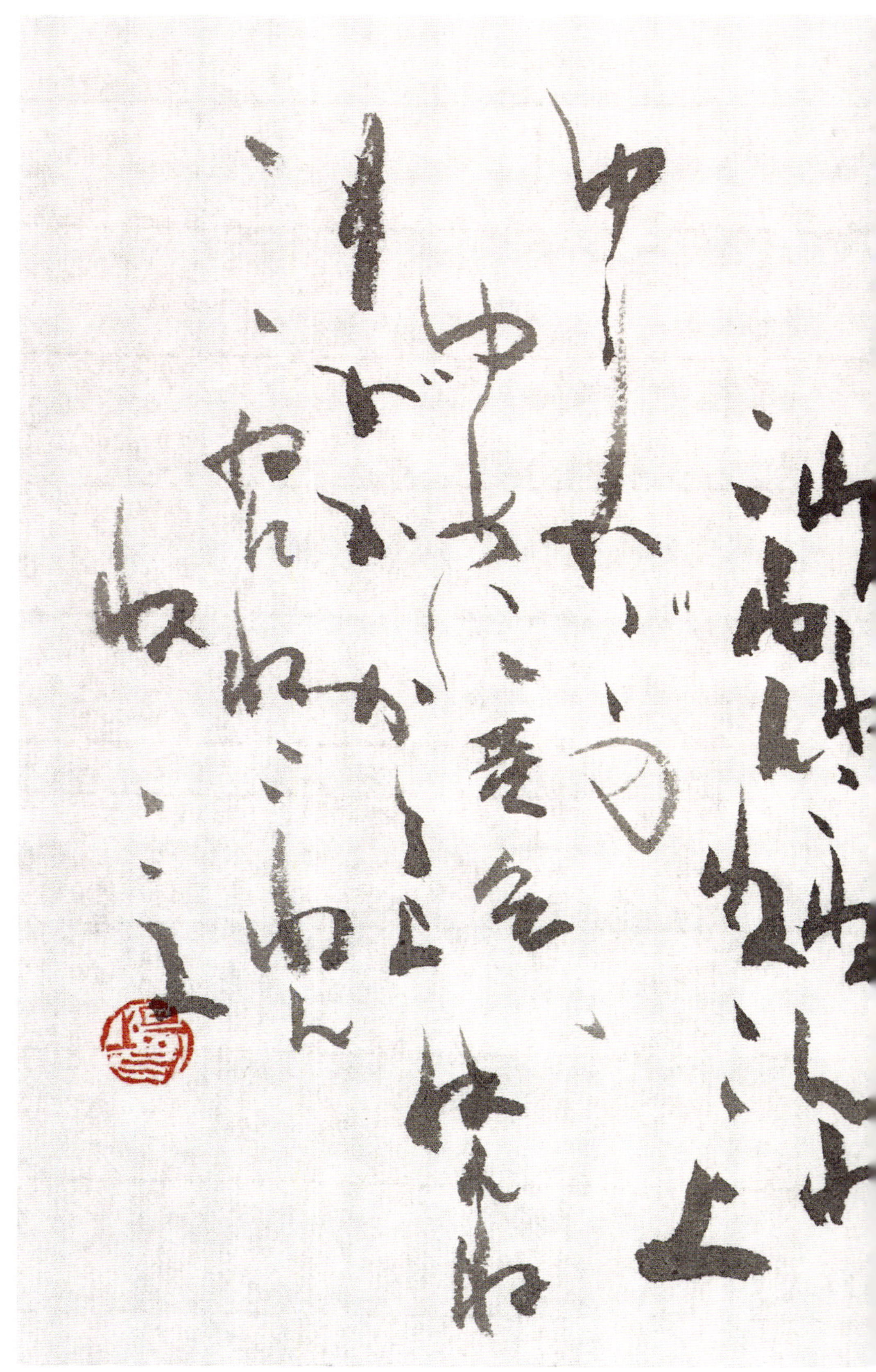

YUGAMI HISAO
***Yurikago no uta* ゆりかごの歌**
(Lullaby) 2009
Sumi ink on *gasen* paper
19.7 × 34 cm
MOA COLLECTION, 3186/5

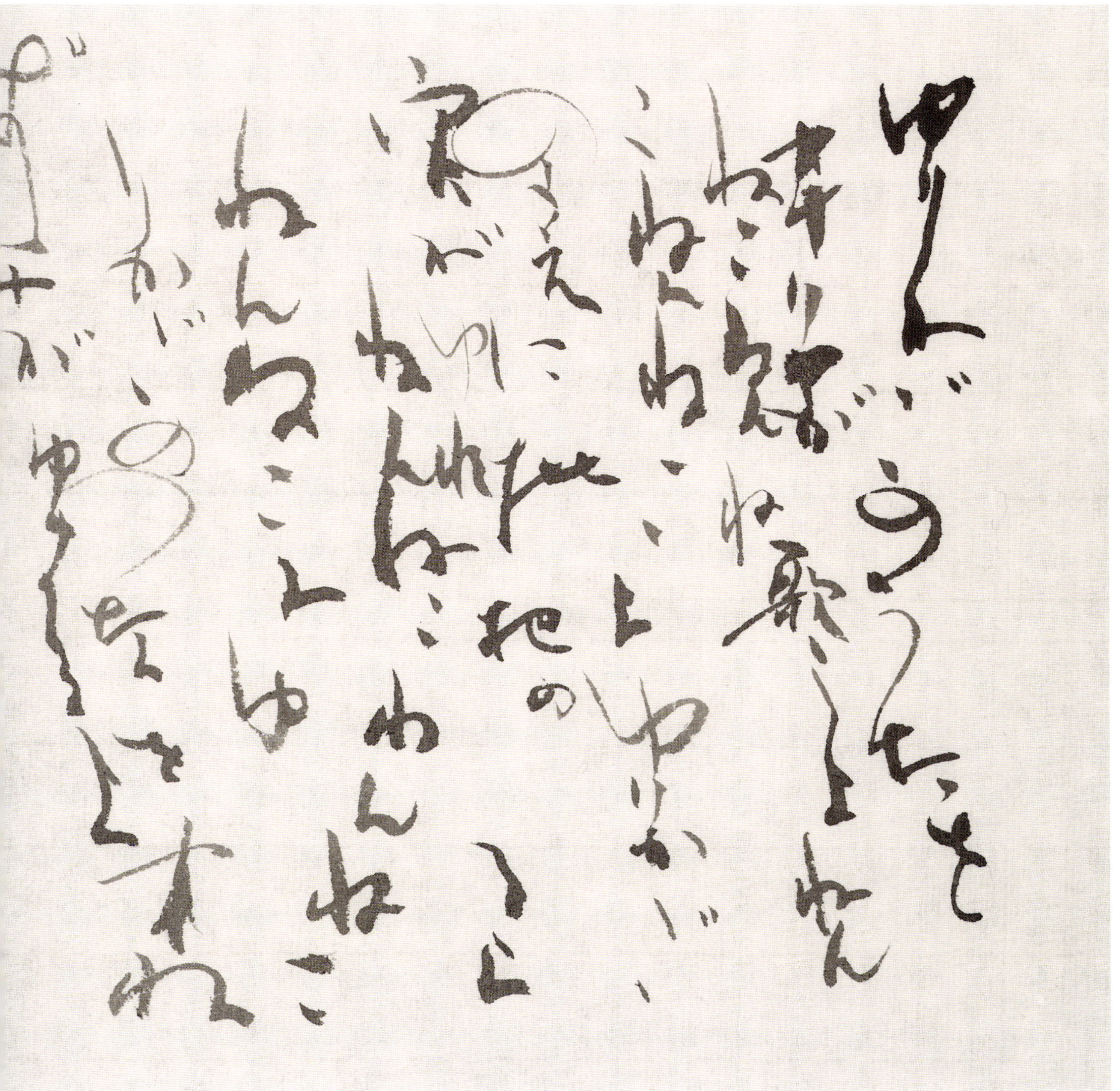

The Museum of Anthropology Asian Collections

FUYUBI NAKAMURA

THE MUSEUM OF ANTHROPOLOGY (MOA) at the University of British Columbia (UBC) is located on the traditional, ancestral, unceded territory of the Musqueam First Nation, one of Canada's indigenous peoples. MOA is internationally renowned for its Pacific Northwest Coast First Nations collection, but is perhaps less known as a museum of world arts and cultures. The ethnographic collections consist of about forty-five thousand items from around the world (as of 2016). The Asian collection contains over eighteen thousand items, about 40 percent of the total holdings, and is the largest collection at the museum. Highlights of this rich, eclectic Asian collection include one of the world's largest collections of Cantonese opera costumes, Japanese woodblock ukiyo-e, Indian calendar prints, and an extensive collection of textiles, including magnificent Tibetan robes. The collection also contains a wide range of ceramics, masks, and puppets. Additionally, MOA has a large collection of historical photographs in its archives, including photographs taken in Tibet in the early twentieth century.

About two hundred and fifty items from Southeast Asia were part of the Frank Burnett Pacific collection donated to UBC in 1927, which marks the beginnings of the museum. Audrey Hawthorn, MOA's first curator, was interested in acquiring items from East Asia for the museum. The objects from Okinawa, collected in the 1950s by Wayne Suttles, a former UBC professor of anthropology, served as the foundation for the Asian collection after the museum was established in 1947. This was followed by a collection of over two hundred Japanese objects collected by Ronald Dore, another former UBC professor and a Japan specialist. The early Chinese collection was developed thanks to Ping-Ti Ho, who used to teach Chinese history at UBC, and includes fine pieces of calligraphy and paintings. MOA's second director, Michael Ames, was a specialist of the region and the South Asian collection grew during his time there.

Among the Asian collections, there is a little known collection of Chinese, Japanese, and Persian calligraphy, as well as various manuscripts such as Southeast Asian palm leaf manuscripts, woodblocks for printing, and objects with inscriptions. The items featured in this publication are the highlights of this collection of approximately two hundred and fifty items.

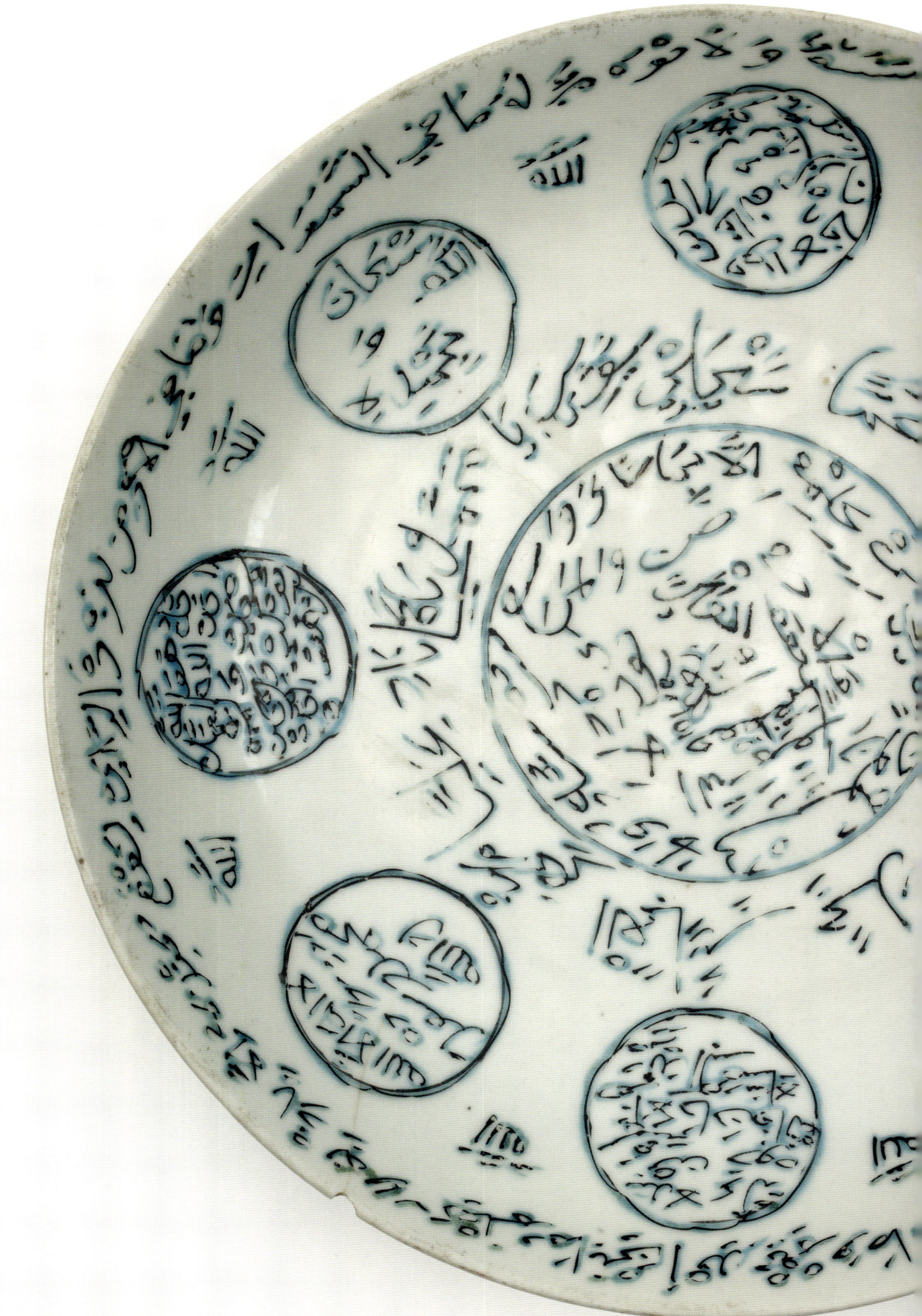

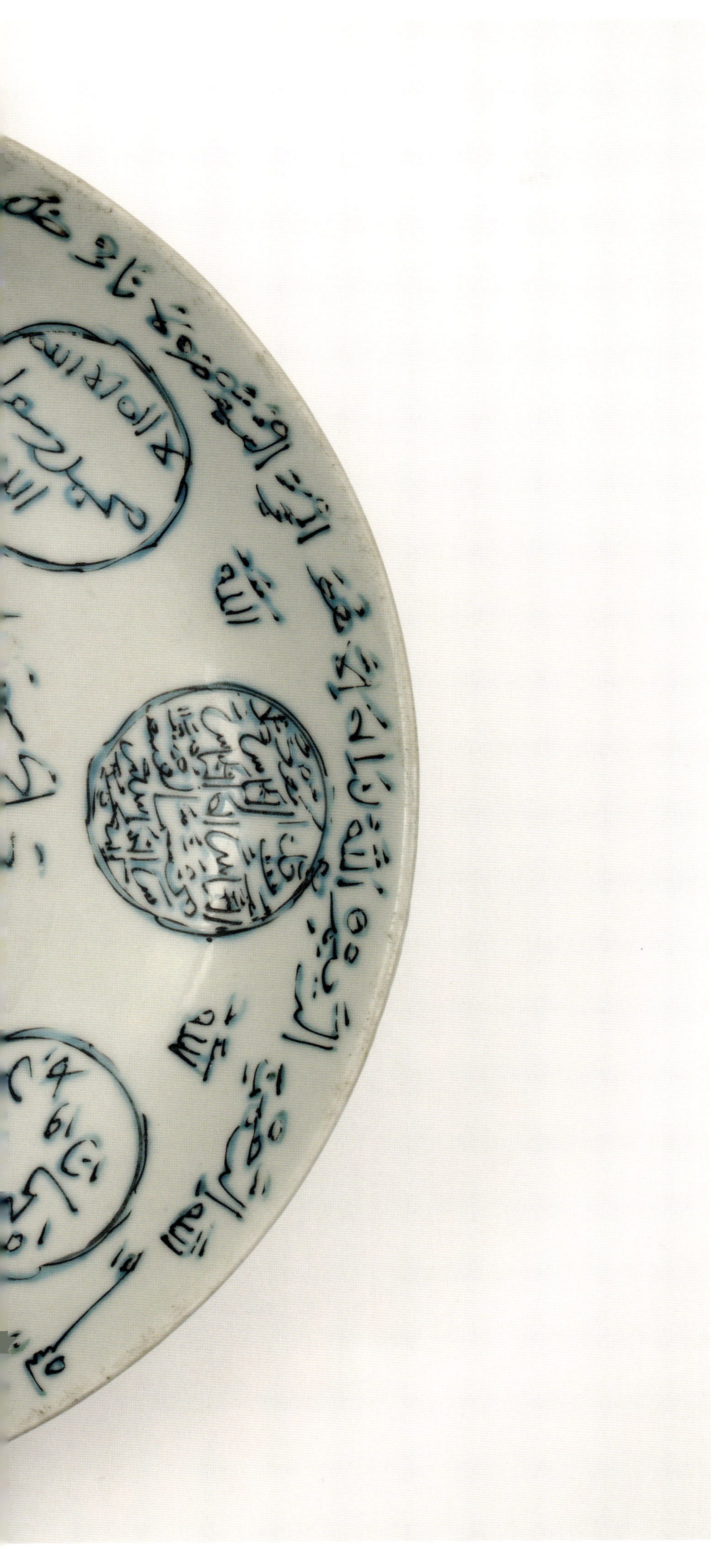

Chinese "Swatow" dish with Arabic scripts
Zhangzhou, Fujian, China •
late 16th to mid-17th century
Clay, glaze, and paint
8.0 × 35.5 cm
MOA COLLECTION, 2988/2

Coarsely potted and glazed dishes like this belong to a group of Chinese export porcelain known as "Swatow ware" or "Zhangzhou ware." The name Swatow *derives from Shantou, a coastal town in Guangdong Province where these wares were allegedly shipped, but recent archaeological research has proved such wares were actually made in Zhangzhou, Fujian Province. Mass-produced in the late Ming dynasty (circa 1550–1644), they were exported to Japan, Europe, and especially Southeast Asia. Decorated with Arabic inscriptions, dishes similar to this one are believed to have been ordered by the sultans of Aceh in the northwest of Sumatra. The inscriptions are written in cursive Arabic script and include invocations of God and verses from the Qur'an; the word* Allah *is repeated in between the eight roundels along the cavetto of the dish.*

Illustrated manuscript
China • undated
reproduction of the
1696 edition
Hand-painted woodblock
prints in ink on paper;
two accordion albums
29 × 26.5 × 5 cm
MOA COLLECTION, N1.553
AND N1.554

This book is a reproduction of an illustrated manuscript titled Yuzhi gengzhi tu 御製耕織圖 *(Imperially commissioned illustrations of agriculture and sericulture), using hand-painted woodblock prints. The original 1696 edition was commissioned in the early Qing dynasty by the Kangxi emperor (r. 1661–1722) and produced by his court painter Jiao Bingzhen* 焦秉貞*. It is based on an earlier version compiled by Lou Shou* 樓璹 *(1090–1162). Distributed nationwide, this set of two accordion-style books served as a guide to rice cultivation and silk production. Each part contains twenty-three woodblock prints meticulously hand-painted in colour and paired with poems in semi-cursive calligraphy on the facing pages. During the Qing period, the Manchu leaders commissioned this text to promote themselves as the legitimate heirs to the Confucian social order. The images and poems depict the ideal of a harmonious society in which ordinary men and women carry out their tasks with diligence and reap the rewards of their labour.*

御製耕織圖序

朕早夜勤毖研求治理念生民之本以衣食為天嘗讀豳風無逸諸篇其言稼穡蠶桑纖悉具備昔人以此被之管弦列於典誥有天下國家者洵不可不留連三復於其際也西漢詔令最為近古其言曰農事傷則飢之本也女紅害則寒之原也又曰老耆以壽終幼孤得遂長欲臻斯理者舍本務其曷以哉

朕每巡省風謠樂觀農事於南北土疆之性黍稌播種之宜節候早晚之殊蝗蝻捕治之法素愛咨詢知此甚悉聽政時恆與諸臣工言之於豐澤園之側治田數畦環以溪水阡陌井然在目桔槔之聲盈耳歲收稉稻數十鍾隴畔樹桑傍列蠶舍浴蠶繅絲恍然如茅簷蔀屋因構知稼軒秋雲亭以臨觀之古

東皋力穡慮偏周
晝夜扶犁未肯休
更駕烏犍施耖耨
好乘春水滿平疇

耖耨

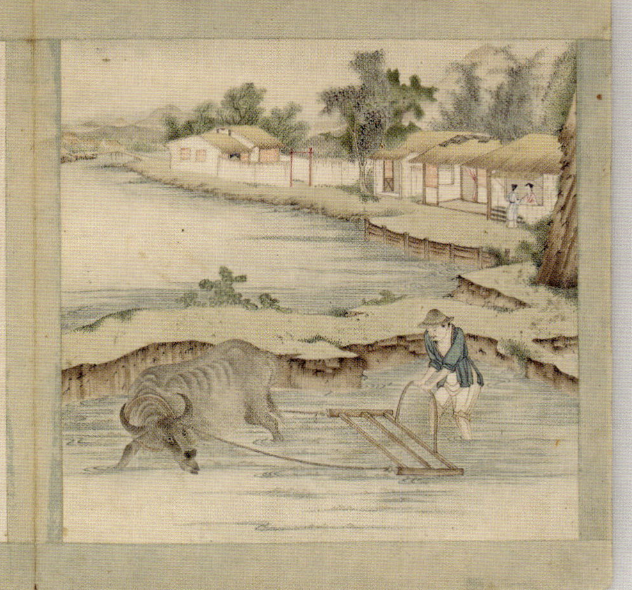

豳風曾著授衣篇
蠶事初興穀雨天
更考工桑傳禮
制先宜浴種向晴
川

浴蠶

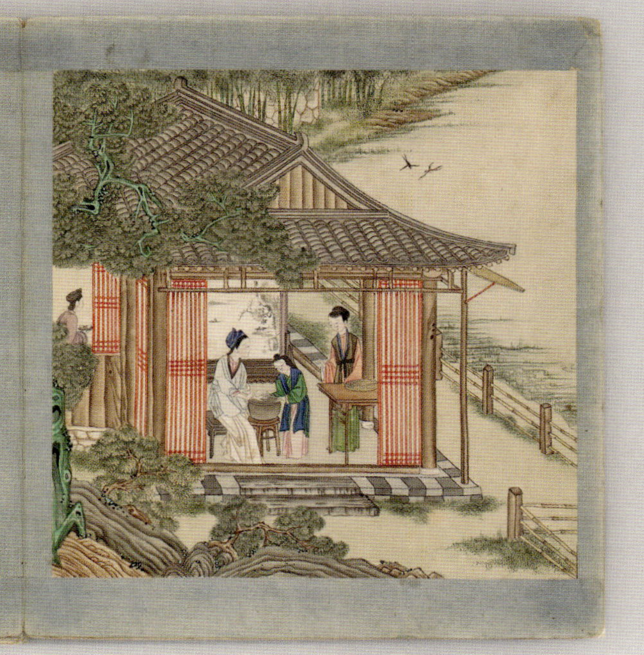

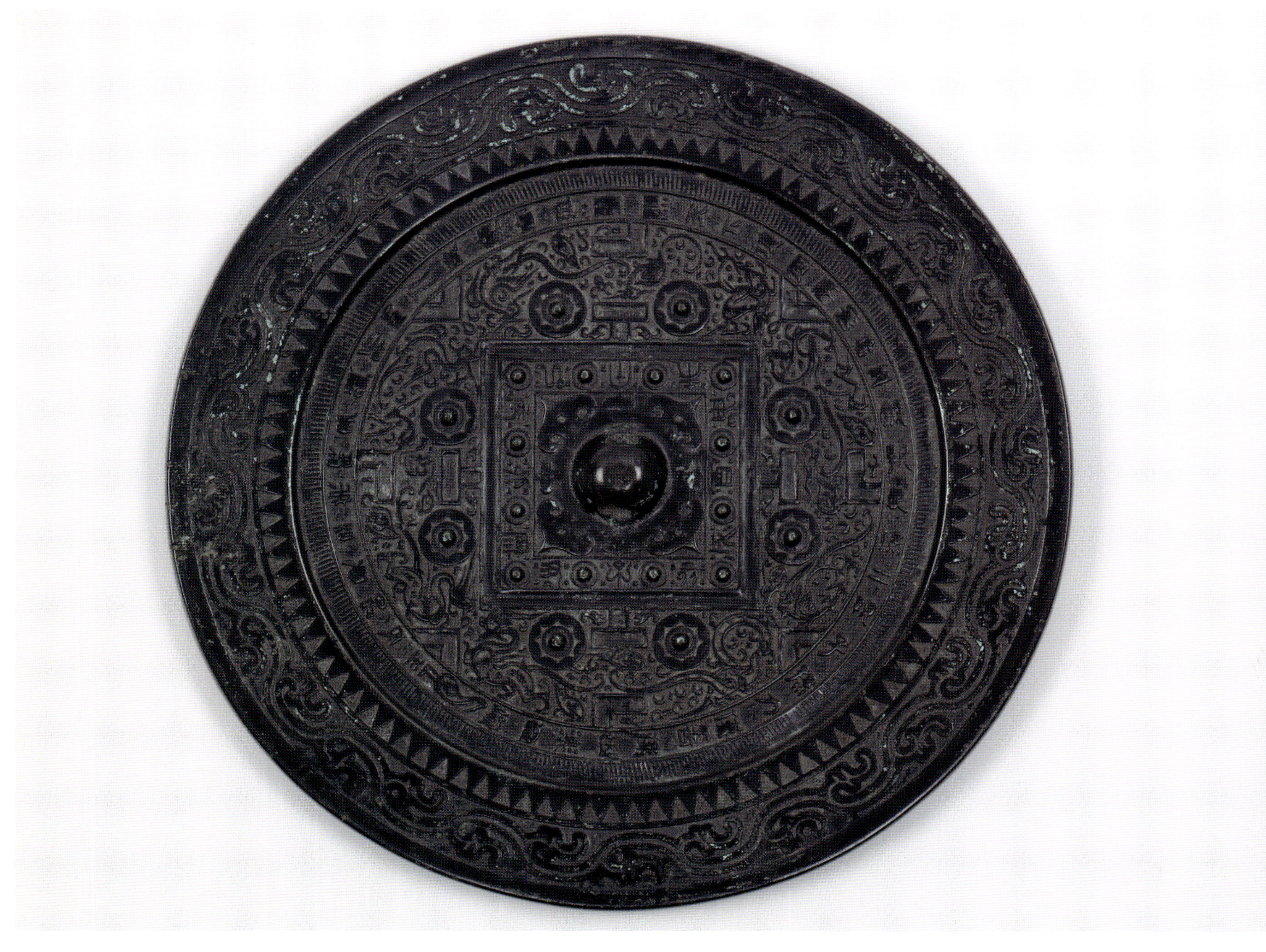

▲ **Mirror with the *liubo* chessboard pattern and inscriptional bands**
China • Xin interregnum (9–23 CE)
High-tin bronze
19.9 × 1.5 cm
MOA COLLECTION, N1.207

The mirrors of early imperial China could be used in daily life as part of one's toiletries, but they were also prized as objects to be buried in tombs. Most mirrors of this period are bronze discs, with a smooth reflective surface on one side and designs on the other side that appear almost identical if you rotate the mirrors clockwise or counter-clockwise. In this mirror, there are six concentric bands, four decorative and two inscriptional. The inner circle of inscriptions is framed in a square and lists the names of the twelve earthly branches, which correlate with the twelve intervals of the day, the twelve months, and the twelve zodiac animals. The outer inscriptional band begins with "Mr. Wang" and "new family," possibly a reference to Wang Mang (r. 9–23 CE), founder of the short-lived Xin dynasty that briefly overthrew the Han. The characters are in an ornamental seal script rather than the bureaucratic clerical style, a feature that underscores the auspicious and luxurious significance of the mirror itself. The three sets of T-, L-, and V-shaped marks symbolize the popular game of liubo *chess and reference the sundial, a device for measuring solar time. The reflective surface on the other side is now black from oxidation.*

Calligraphy scroll by Dr. Sun Yat-sen
China • ca. 1900–1911 and 1955
Ink on a paper hanging scroll
235 × 45 cm
MOA COLLECTION, N1.246

Dr. Sun Yat-sen 孫中山 *(1866–1925) is known as the father of modern China for his role in overthrowing the last dynasty and for serving as the first president of the Republic of China (1911–12). After China's defeat in the Sino-Japanese War (1894–95), Sun built a revolutionary movement that spanned East Asia, Europe, and North America. Sun's calligraphy, situated in the centre, is a couplet that reads, "Knowledge should not stray from honesty / actions should not stray from courage." This phrase references his philosophical doctrine on the integration of knowledge and action, where one arises from the other. The calligraphic colophon above Sun's verse was added in 1955 and signed by his supporter Lin Jin* 林近, *who praises Sun's calligraphic expression of knowledge, action, and leadership. The colophon below is another congratulatory note that lauds Sun's distinctive calligraphy and brilliant mind.*

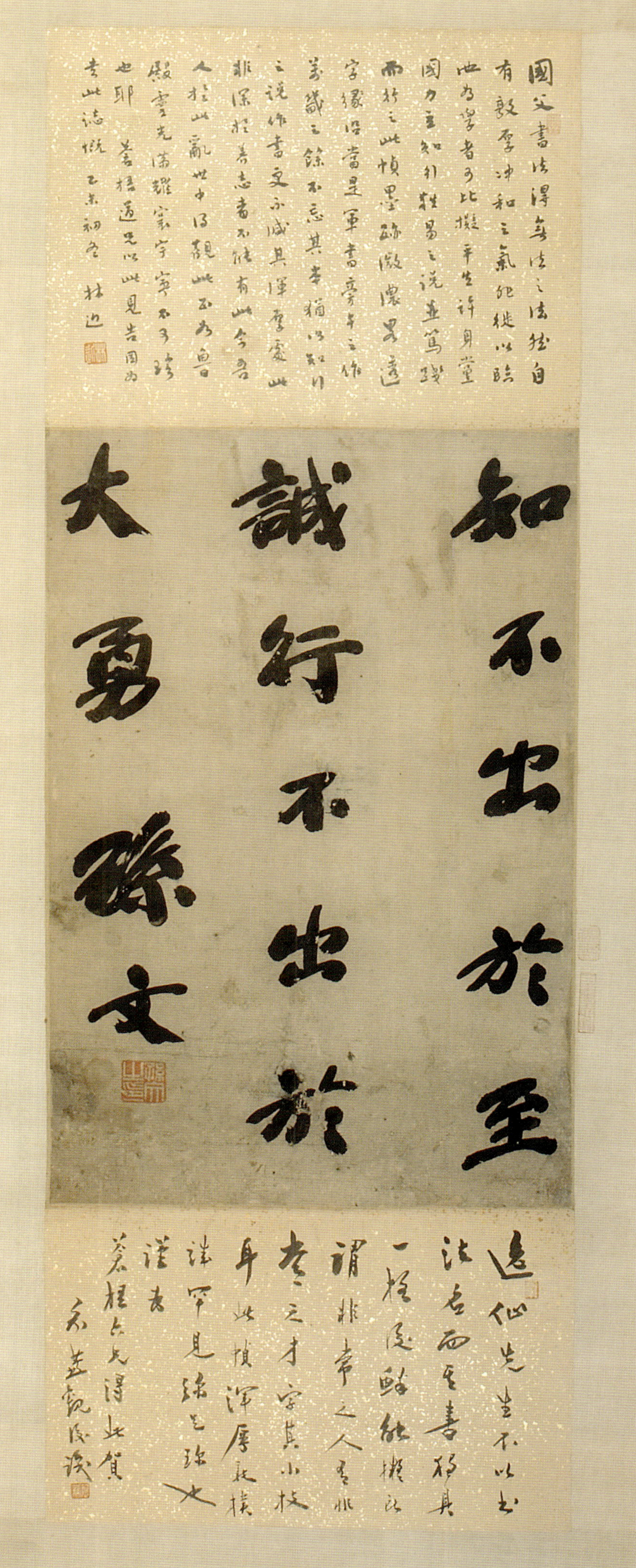

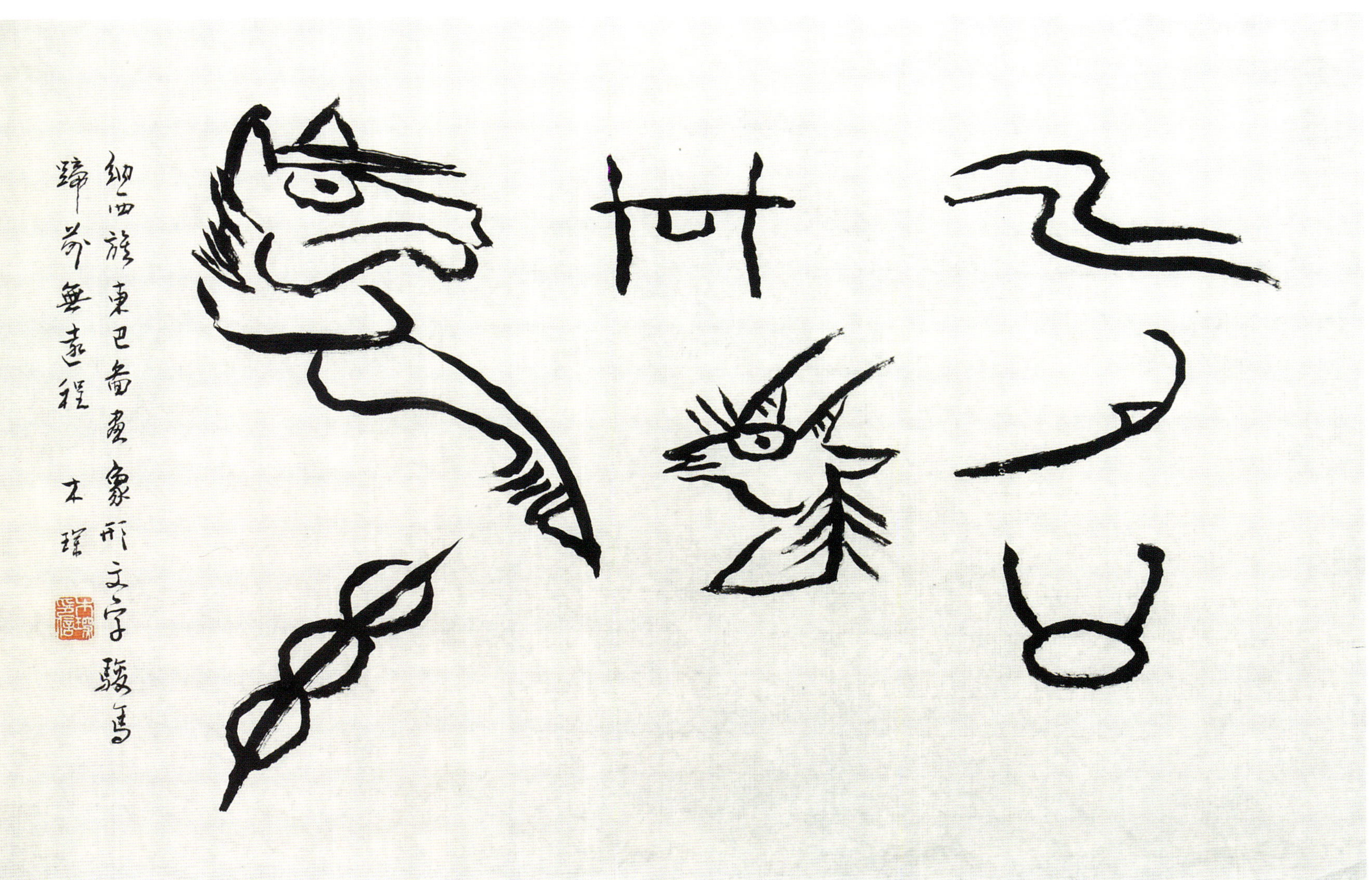

Naxi Dongba calligraphy
Yunnan, China • late 20th century
Ink on handmade paper
43.2 × 67.7 cm
MOA COLLECTION, 2636/2

This calligraphic work shows seven Dongba pictographs, written with a stylus (likely a bamboo pen or modern fountain pen) using black ink on handmade paper. In contrast to the ritual texts that were arranged in horizontal registers, this work reflects a modern approach to Dongba writing that evolved during the 1980s and onwards, a time of cultural revival for economic development and tourism. This is evident from the vertical lines of Chinese calligraphy on the left that offer explanatory notes regarding the "Dongba pictographs of the Naxi nationality." The Naxi (or Nakhi) people of China's Yunnan and Sichuan Provinces are known for their distinctive Dongba shamanism and mainly pictographic writing system. Dongba is one of two systems used by the Naxi people to write their language, which is part of the Tibeto-Burman family. It is named for the shamans who used it to facilitate ritual ceremonies in their religion, which is related to the Tibetan Bön tradition. The writing was in use by the seventh century and grew to encompass over two thousand characters. Since the Communist Revolution of 1949, thousands of Dongba texts have been destroyed in various ideological campaigns. Today there are about sixty Dongba shamans who can still read and write the script.

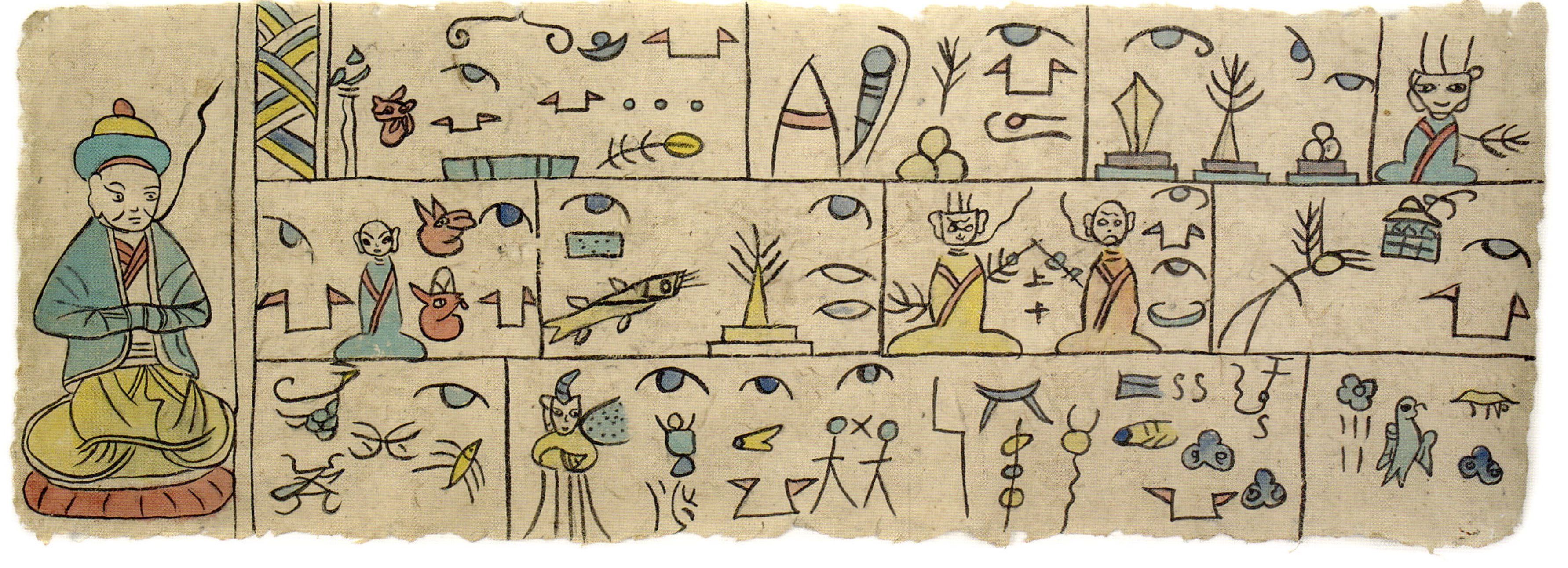

▲ **Naxi Dongba manuscript leaf**
Yunnan, China • late 20th century
Paint and crayon on handmade paper
22.5 × 61.2 cm
MOA COLLECTION, 2636/3

The manuscript leaf is likely a modern reproduction of part of an older manuscript document that was used in ritual recitations. By the Song dynasty (960–1279), the Naxi had mastered papermaking and shifted away from writing on bark, leaves, and animal skin. Since then, ritual texts have been written on narrow strips of handmade paper, with the characters arranged in horizontal registers.

On the left side of this work, we see a seated figure on a round mat with folded arms and a slight turn of the head in the direction of the text. He wears the simple robe and hat of a devotee rather than the five-pronged crown of a shaman. To his right, we see three rows of registers containing Dongba glyphs or images, including animals, plants, and several robed figures in seated meditation postures.

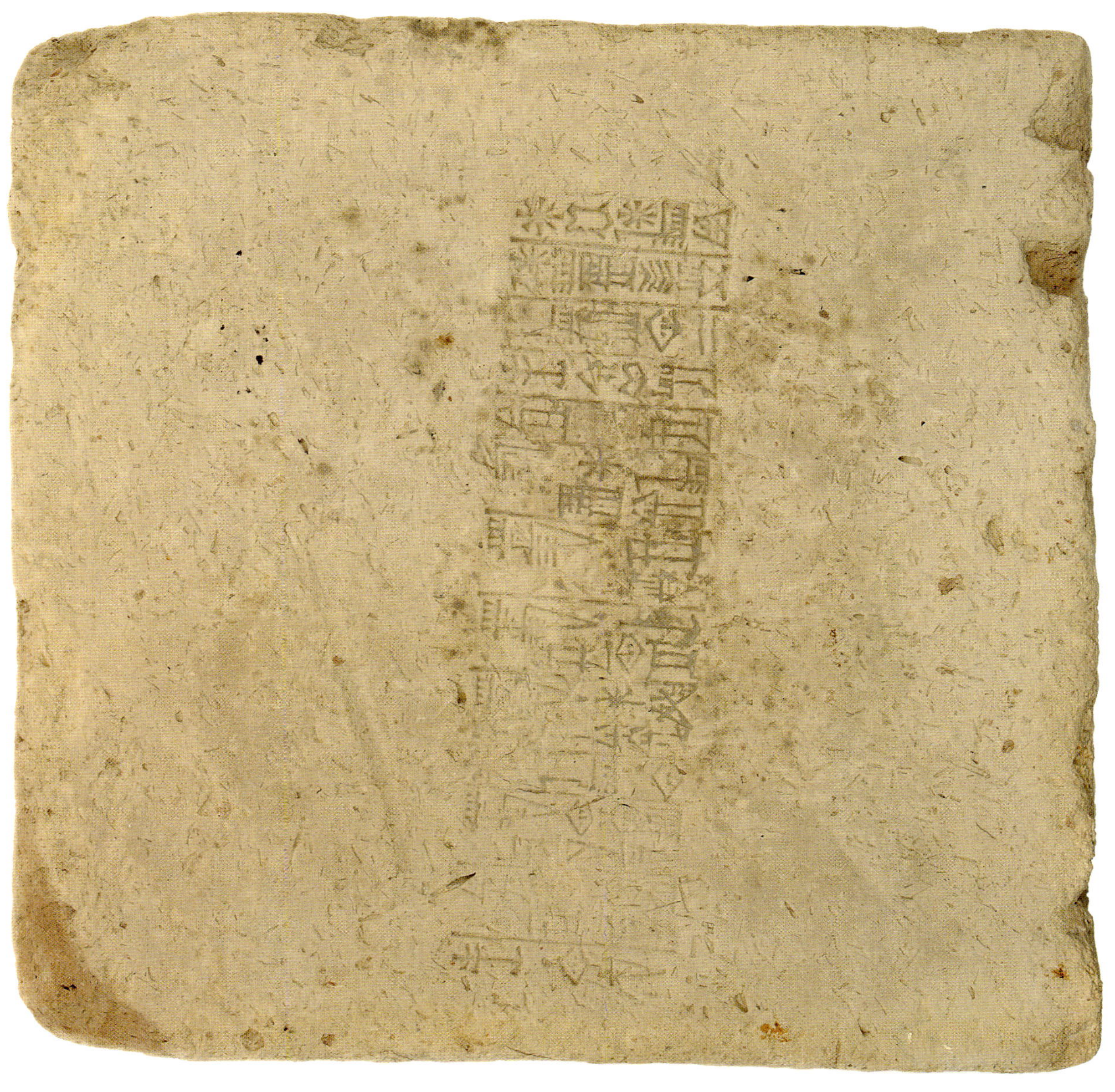

▲ **Stamped Brick**
Eridu, Iraq • 2112–2004 BCE
Clay brick
6.9 × 26.6 × 26.1 cm
MOA COLLECTION: M4.29

This brick shows a stamped cuneiform inscription of King Amar-Suena of the Third Dynasty of Ur (2112–2004 BCE), the last Sumerian dynasty in ancient Mesopotamia. Mesopotamia—a vast region around the Tigris and Euphrates Rivers, located mostly in today's Iraq—developed civilizations over six thousand years ago, and it was where one of the earliest writing systems evolved. Cuneiform signs were used for writing Sumerian and other ancient languages of Mesopotamia. This brick, one of thousands used to construct the temple of the god Enki in the city of Eridu (now Tell Abu Shahrain) in southern Mesopotamia, was intended to glorify the king, and to preserve for posterity the memory of the builder. The inscription on the face and right edge of the brick translates as "Amar-Suena, (the one) chosen by the god Enlil in Nippur, the constant (supporter) of the temple of the god Enlil, mighty king, king of Ur, king of the four quarters, for the god Enki, his beloved lord, built his beloved Apzû (temple) for him."

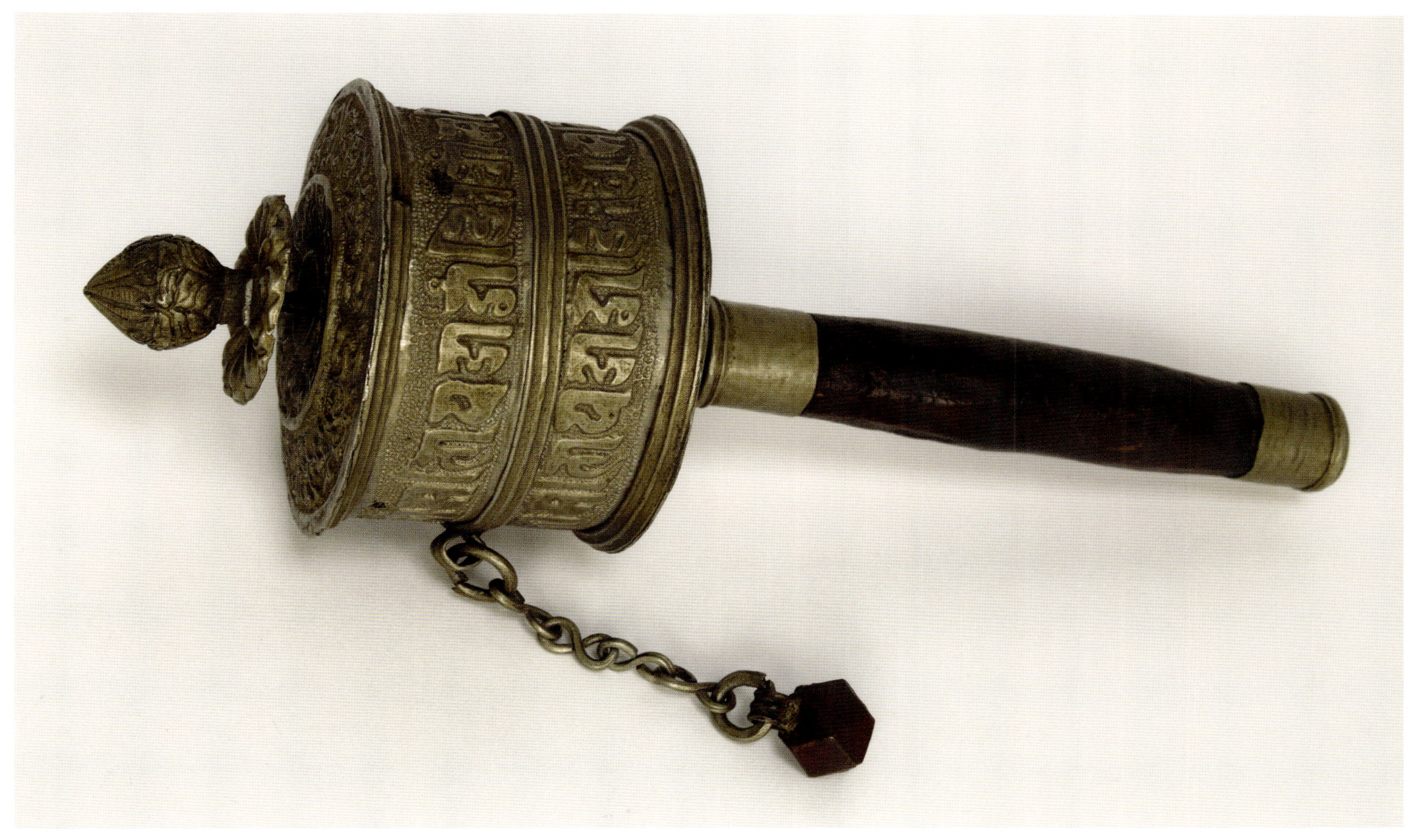

▲ **Prayer wheel**
Tibet • 1890–1900
Metal, wood, and stone
29 × 9 cm
MOA COLLECTION, EE4.42

This handheld prayer wheel, or "mani wheel" (mani khorlo), *comprises a metal cylinder mounted on a wooden handle. The wheel spins with the movement of the wrist, while the stone on the short chain sustains the momentum. The cylinder is covered in repoussage metalwork, with two bands of Sanskrit text inscribed in Lantsa script conveying iterations of* **|| Oṃ maṇipadme hūṃ |, *the sacred six-syllable mantra for Avalokiteśvara. The same mantra is printed on thin paper and rolled around the cylinder's core spindle, where it is hidden from view. This wrapped spindle is known as the "life tree." The top and bottom of the cylinder are adorned with stylized lotus blossoms, an auspicious symbol of one's progression from delusion to enlightenment. In spinning the wheel, the practitioner reaps the same benefits of having read the countless prayers coiled inside, a useful means for illiterate Buddhists to attain merit. The wheel should be spun clockwise to coincide with the sun's movement and the direction of the writing on the wheel to facilitate the release of the blessings into the world.*

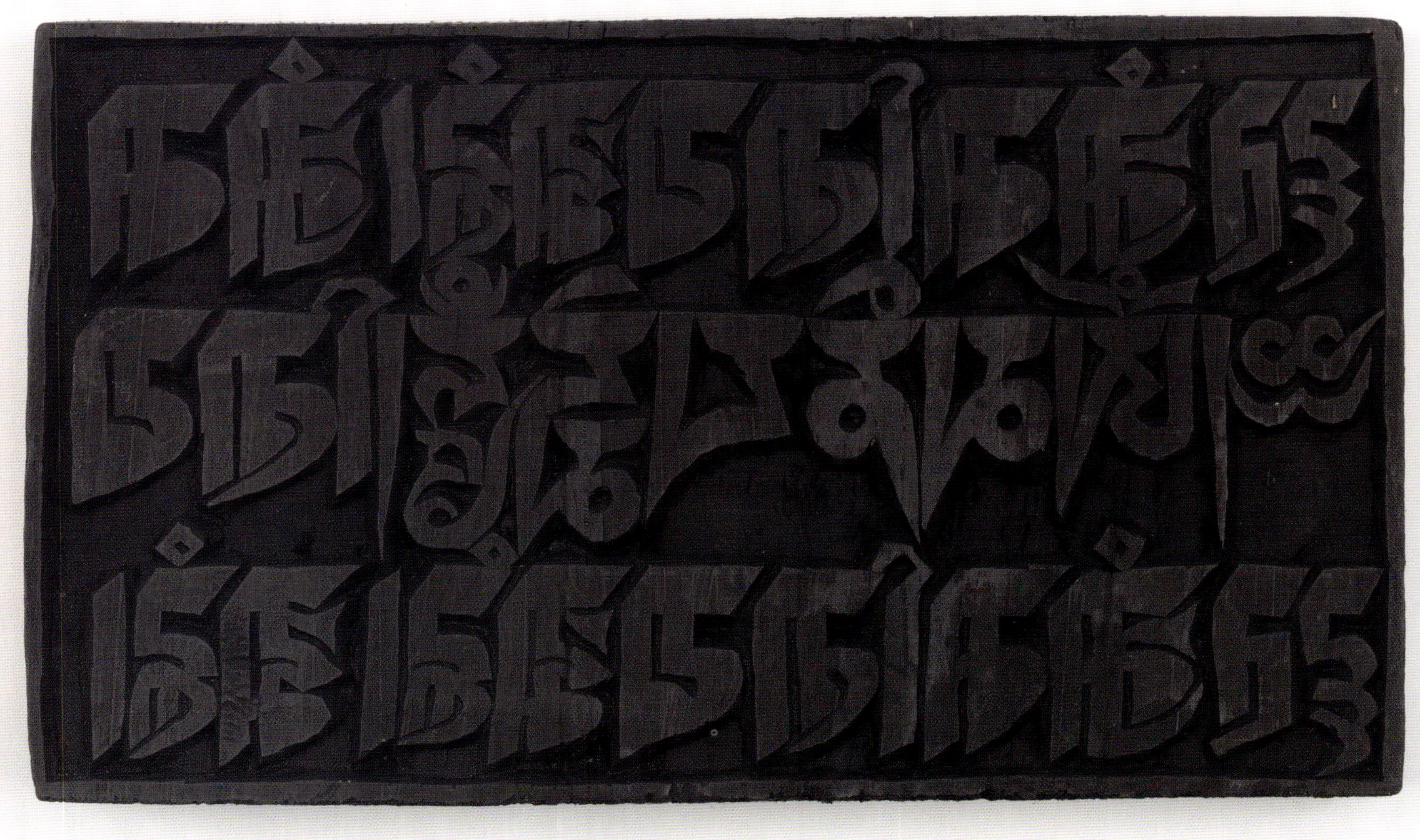

▲ **Woodblock**
Himalayan region • n.d.
Wood and paint
2.8 × 20.7 × 12.2 cm
MOA COLLECTION, 1431/15

This carved woodblock was used for hand-printing on paper or textile surfaces. A printed image from this block would have three lines of text that would be read left to right, with each line conveying the six-syllable mantra for Avalokiteśvara, the bodhisattva of compassion of Mahayana Buddhism. The top and bottom lines are in the Lantsa Sanskrit script that became popular in eleventh-century Tibet for transcribing Sanskrit scriptures and for adorning temples, prayer wheels, and other sacred objects. The middle line bears the mantra in Tibetan script, which may be transliterated as **|| Oṃ maṇipadme hūṃ |*. Each line ends with two syllables in Lantsa script that belong to a fourth iteration of the mantra. All three lines also open with a different silent symbol that marks the beginning of a text, which is known in Tibetan as the* mgo-yig, *or "head letter" and transliterated as* **||*. This mantra is repeated as a daily prayer to summon Avalokiteśvara and may be loosely translated as "Om, praise to the jewel in the lotus!" However, the deeper meaning lies in each syllable and their many layers of mystical significance.*

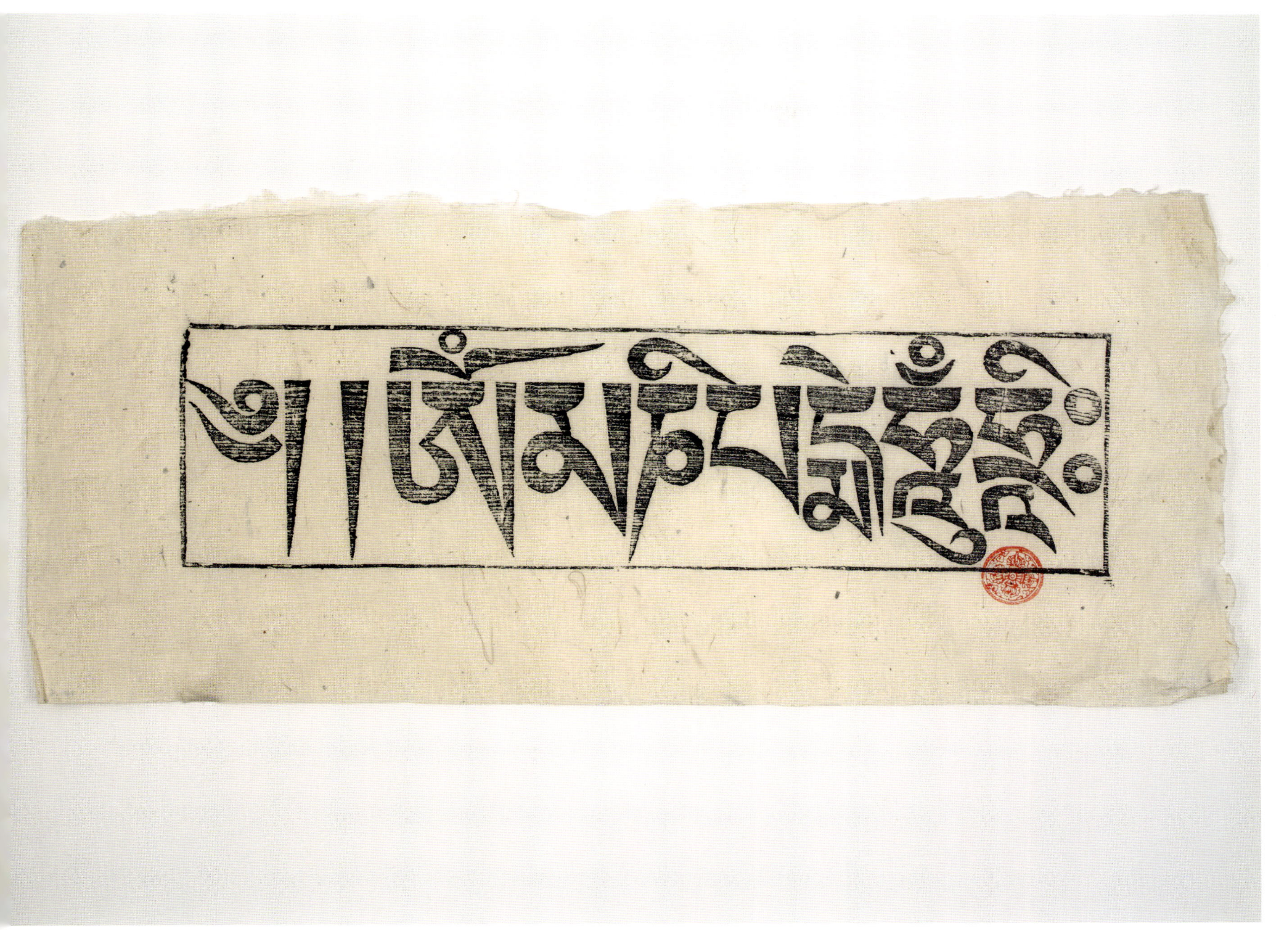

▲ **Woodblock print**
Nepal • n.d.
Woodcut print
25.2 × 57.1 cm
MOA COLLECTION, N4.4

This woodblock print bears a Tibetan calligraphic inscription of the mantra *|| Oṃ maṇipadme hūṃ hrīḥ, *which includes the six sacred syllables of the mantra followed by a seventh tantric syllable at the end. A red circular seal on the bottom shows the* vajra *(thunderbolt or diamond) emblem of Vajrayana Buddhism. This print was likely produced by hand from a hand-carved woodblock, as one can see the patterned wood grain coming through the pressed ink. The calligraphic text is written in the "headed" or* uchen *(also transliterated as* dbu can*) Tibetan script, which is characterized by upright block letters and short horizontal lines (heads) along the tops of many letters. Historically, this type of crisp and angular calligraphy would have been written with a stylus bamboo pen rather than a brush. The bold and graphic script was suitable for formal text and mass printing. The sharp lines are also easily transferred into wood or stone, as is the case here and for many other stone carvings of the same mantra. Such printed images were displayed inside temples and homes, or as framed tourist souvenirs.*

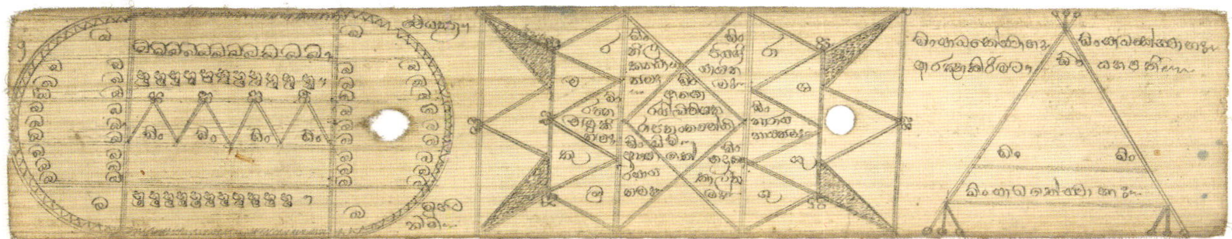

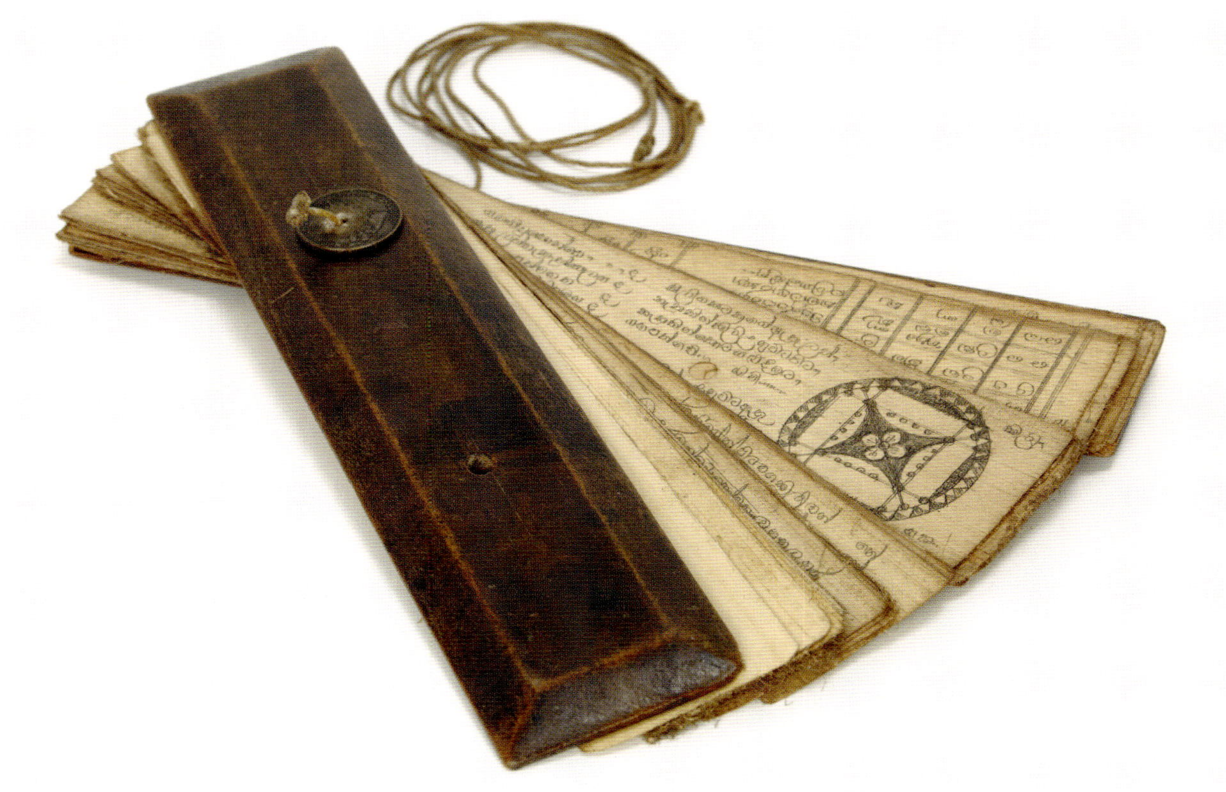

▲ **Palm leaf manuscript in Sinhala script**
Sri Lanka • n.d.
Ink on palm leaf, and wood, metal, and fibre
2.0 × 25.5 × 5.3 cm
MOA COLLECTION, 812/7

Many manuscripts from Sri Lanka, like this one, contain astrological texts or horoscopes, illustrated with symbols, diagrams, and charts. Until the early nineteenth century, palm leaf was the main medium for writing in Sri Lanka and was used to produce many Buddhist texts.

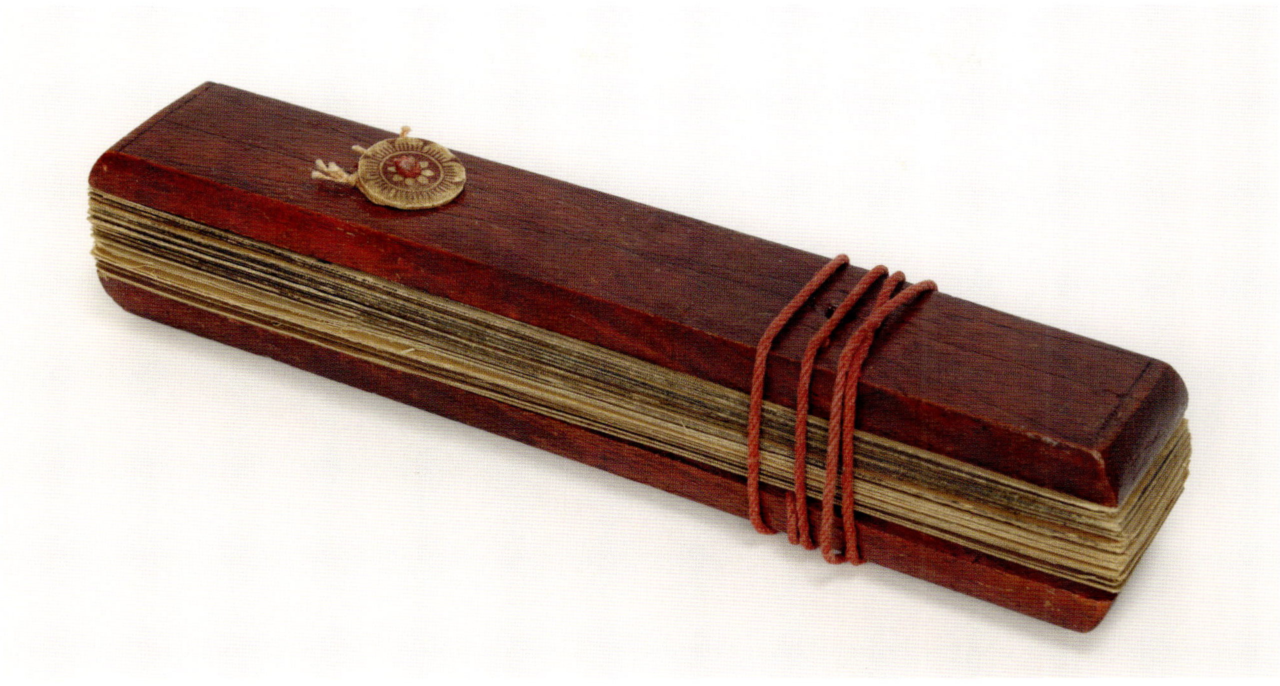

Palm leaf manuscript in Malayalam script
Kerala, India • n.d.
Ink on palm leaf, and wood, fibre, and ivory
3.9 × 21.3 × 3.8 cm
MOA COLLECTION: B557

This manuscript is in Malayalam script. Malayalam is a Brahmic script used to write Sanskrit, Prakrit, Pali, or Malayalam, a South Indian vernacular language spoken in Kerala, India.

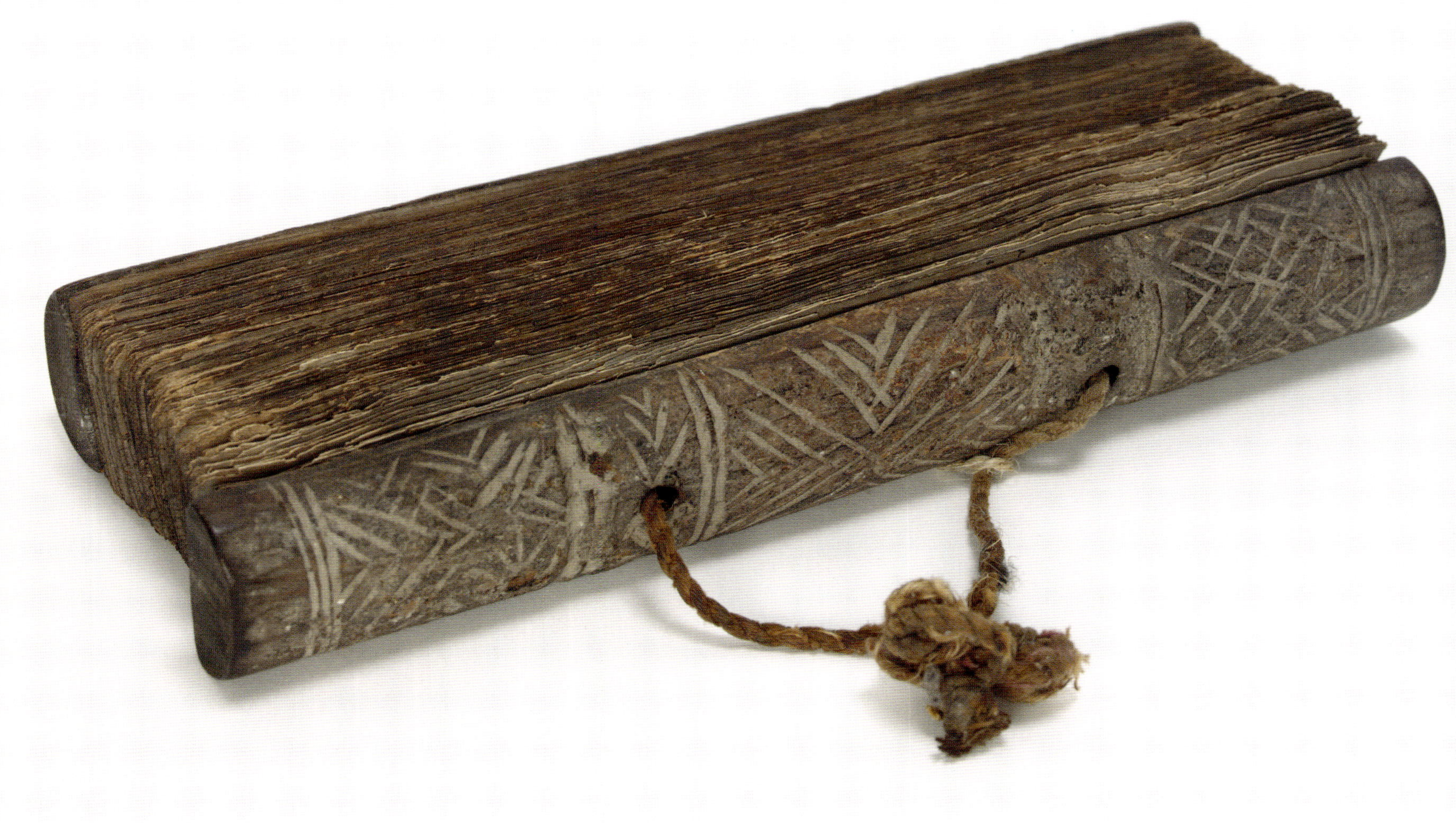

▲ ▶ **Palm leaf manuscript in Tham script**
Thailand • n.d.
Ink on palm leaf, and wood and plant fibre
10.3 × 23 × 3.8 cm
MOA COLLECTION, 2902/23

Palm leaf manuscripts are an important cultural heritage of Southeast Asia and were traditionally considered not only as the medium of knowledge transmission but also as sacred objects. Palm leaf manuscripts from Thailand contain writings that are mostly religious and sacred but also cover other subjects, including medicine, astrology, history, and folktales. This manuscript contains a Buddhist scripture. The unusually rough medium of this manuscript suggests that it may not have been made for professional use at a temple, monastery, or other public setting, but rather for private or domestic purposes. *(See page 56 for another view of this manuscript.)*

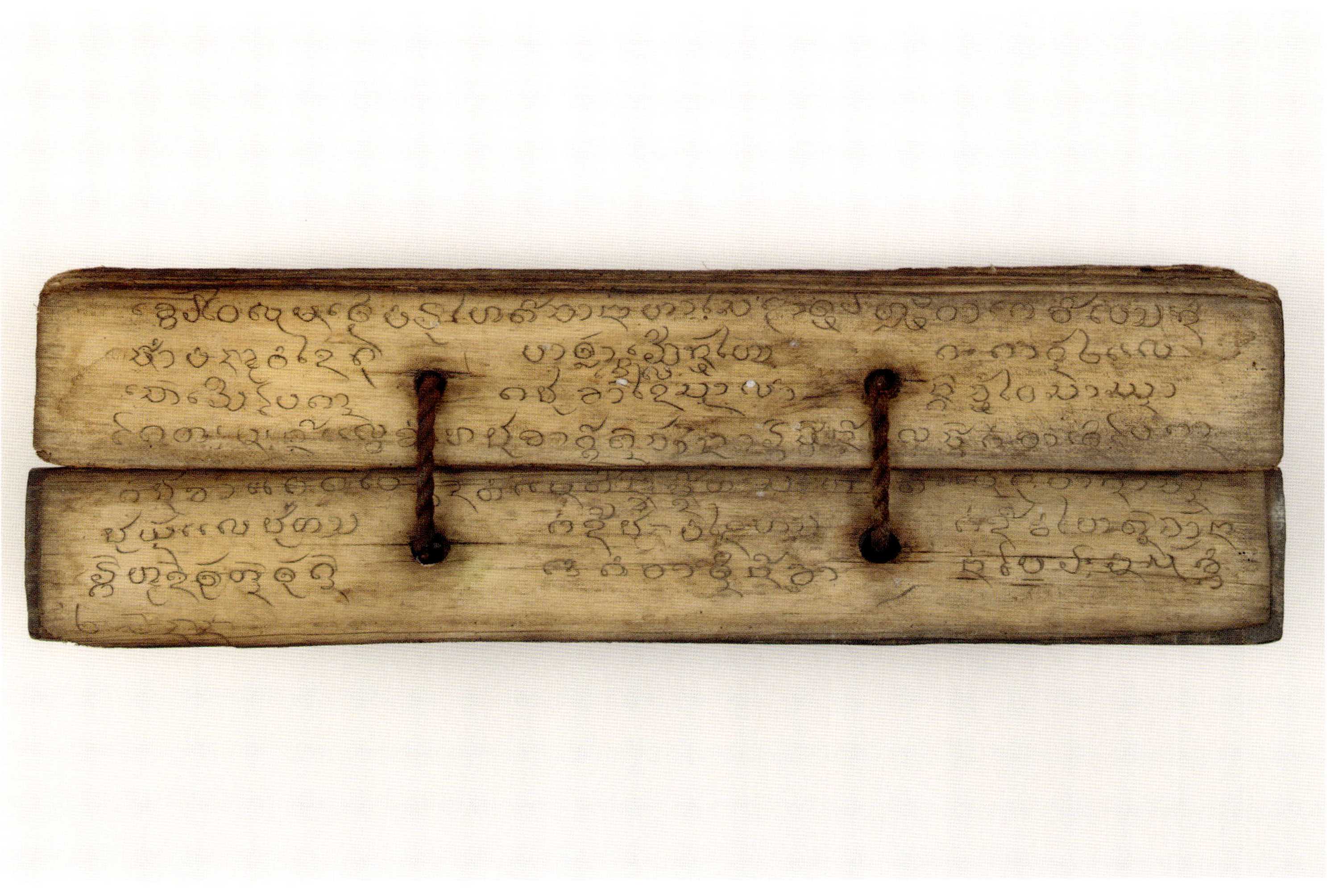

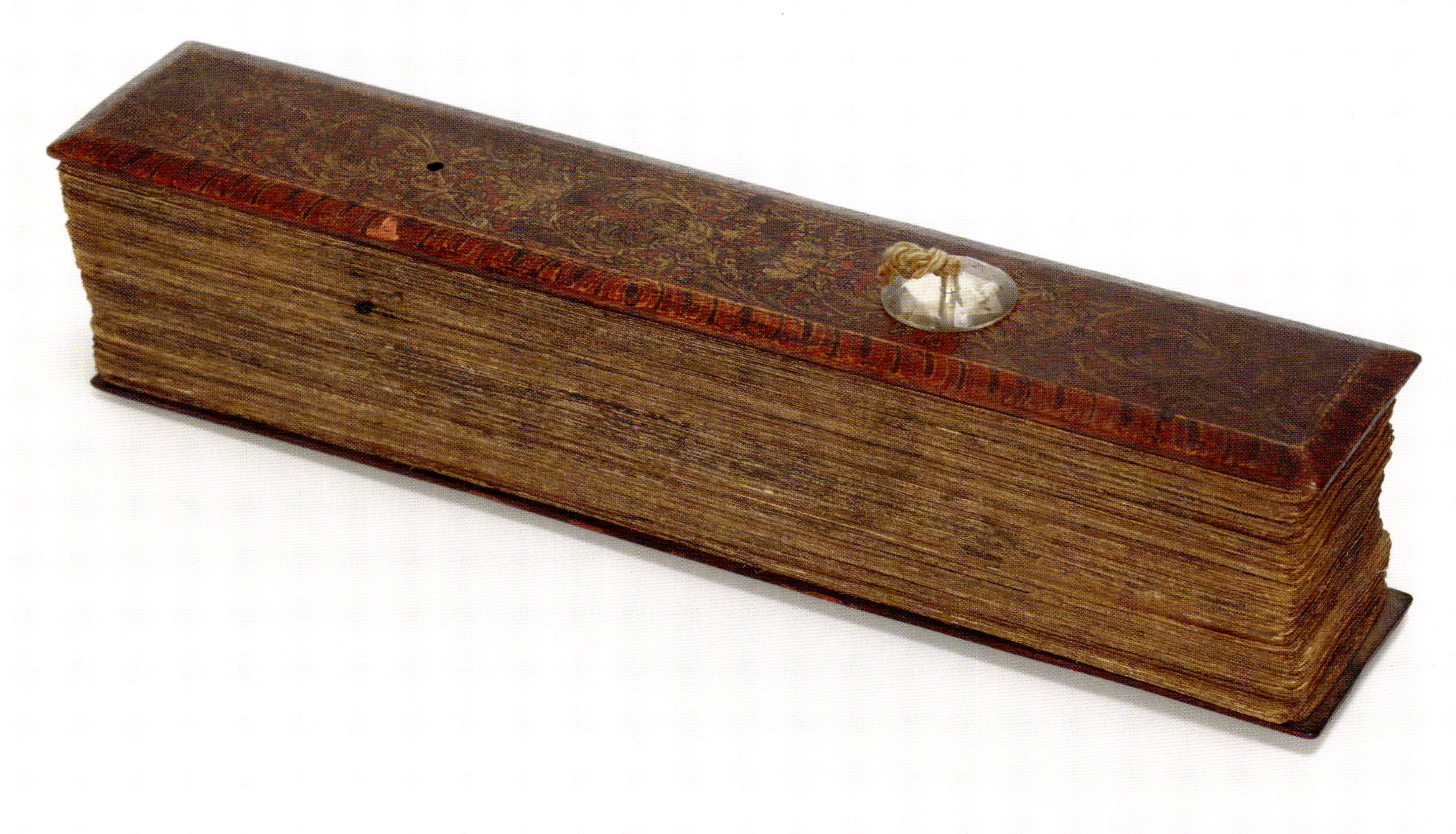

▲ ▶ **Palm leaf manuscript in Sinhala script**
Sri Lanka • early 19th century
Ink on palm leaf, paint on wood, and glass and fibre
7.7 × 34.0 × 5.9 cm
MOA COLLECTION, 2569/15

Palm leaf manuscripts from Sri Lanka were often produced by Buddhist monks or scribes to record the Theravada Buddhist scriptures, like this one. They were also made for various other kinds of texts, from medicine to astrology.

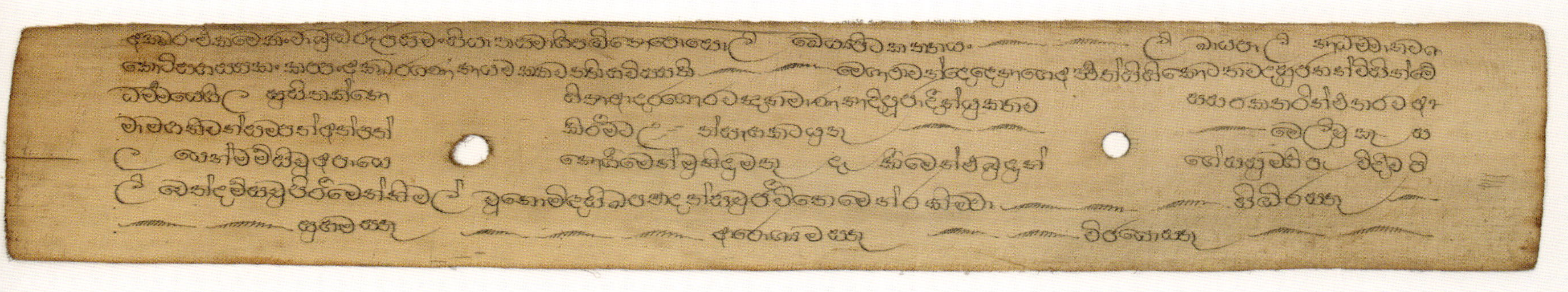

Asian Materials from the UBC Library Collections

HANA KIM

THE UNIVERSITY OF BRITISH COLUMBIA (UBC) LIBRARY holds one of the few major collections of pre-modern Asian books and manuscripts outside of Asia. The collection includes a vast number of unique items of high literary, historical, and artistic importance. The Council on East Asian Libraries consistently ranks UBC's Asian Library among the best in the world: the Asian Library has the highest number of Asian materials in Canada and is number twelve across North America in terms of the size of its collection (as of 2016). The Asian Library's crown jewels are its rare Chinese and Japanese books and materials, making UBC a top-tier research library.

In 1959, the UBC Library acquired one of the most prominent Chinese special collections in North America—the outstanding Puban Collection 蒲坂書樓, which includes forty-five thousand stitch-bound volumes. This collection marked the beginning of the Asian collection at UBC, providing an excellent source of traditional Chinese works published prior to 1912. UBC Library also holds one of the world's largest collections of maps and guidebooks of the Japanese Edo, also known as the Tokugawa, period (1603–1867). The Asian Library started out as an Asian Studies division and became a discrete branch of the UBC Library in 1960. It moved into the Asian Centre in 1981 (the first UBC campus building to be devoted to Asia-related study); prior to that, it was housed in the old Main Library, now the Irving K. Barber Learning Centre.

While a number of the university's earliest collections were acquired through purchase, many private collections were donated by the local community. The Asian Library's collection currently totals six hundred and fifty thousand volumes in eleven languages: Chinese, Japanese, Korean, Hindi, Urdu, Punjabi, Sanskrit, Tibetan, Indonesian, Persian, and most recently, Vietnamese. This is unique in that many Asian libraries across the world are focused only on East Asia (China, Japan, and Korea).

The items featured in the publication are highlights of the Asian Library and the Rare Book and Special Collections, and are part of the satellite exhibition at the Irving K. Barber Learning Centre at UBC (May 1–31, 2017). They demonstrate a diverse range of Asian scripts with varying visual and material expression.

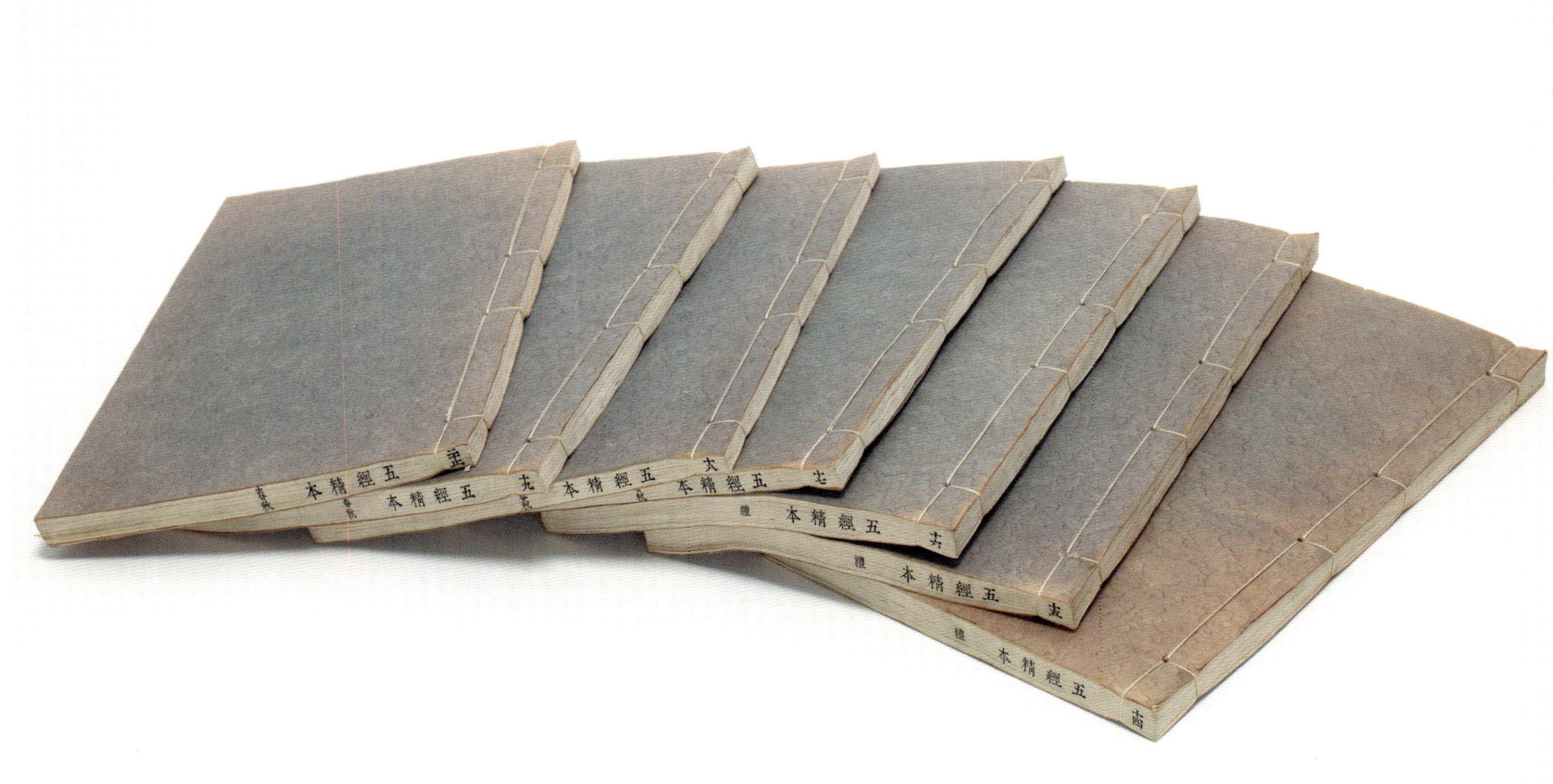

▲ ▶ *Wujing jingben* 五經精本
(Essence of the five classics)
China • 1821–50
Manuscript with double leaves;
traditional stitched binding
20 volumes in 3 cases, each volume
27.8 × 17.5 cm (various thickness)
UBC LIBRARY COLLECTION
THE PUBAN COLLECTION, ASIAN RARE-1
NO.2 (RBSC)

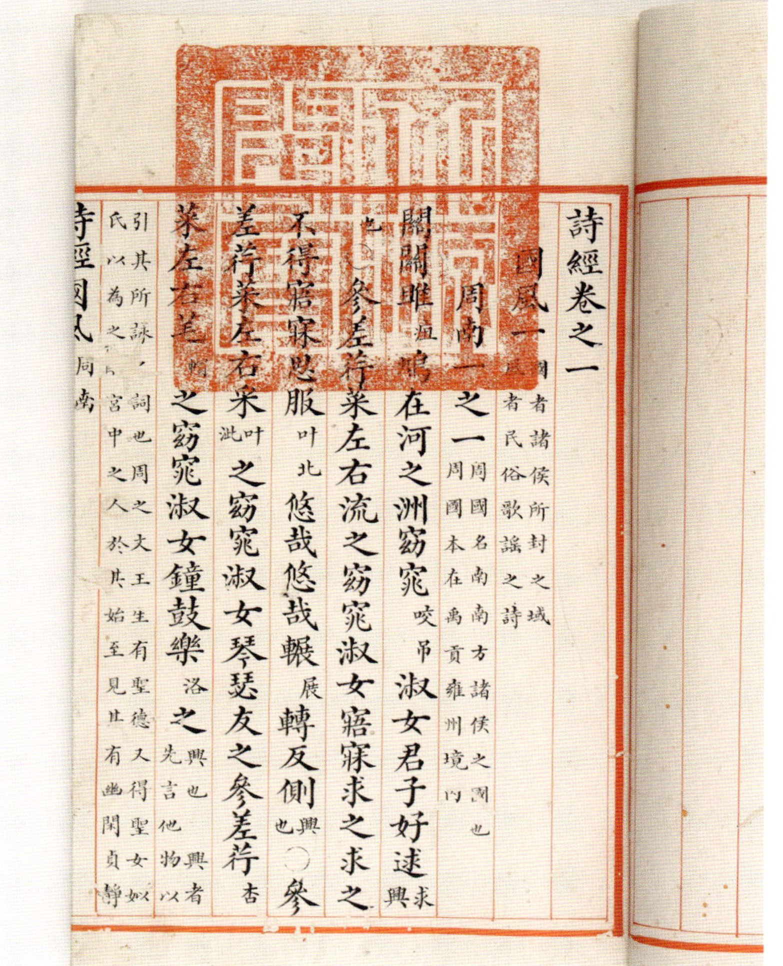

詩經卷之一
國風一 國者諸侯所封之域 風者民俗歌謠之詩
周南一之一 周國名南南方諸侯之國也 周國本在禹貢雍州境內
關關雎鳩在河之洲窈窕 咬吊 淑女君子好逑 求 興
也 ○ 參差荇菜左右流之窈窕淑女寤寐求之求之
不得寤寐思服 叶北 悠哉悠哉輾 展 轉反側 興也 ○ 參
差荇菜左右采 叶泚 之窈窕淑女琴瑟友之參差荇 杏
菜左右芼 帽 之窈窕淑女鐘鼓樂 洛 之 興也 興者先言他物以
引起所詠之詞也周之文王生有聖德又得聖女姒
氏以為之配宮中之人於其始至見其有幽閒貞靜
詩經國風 周南

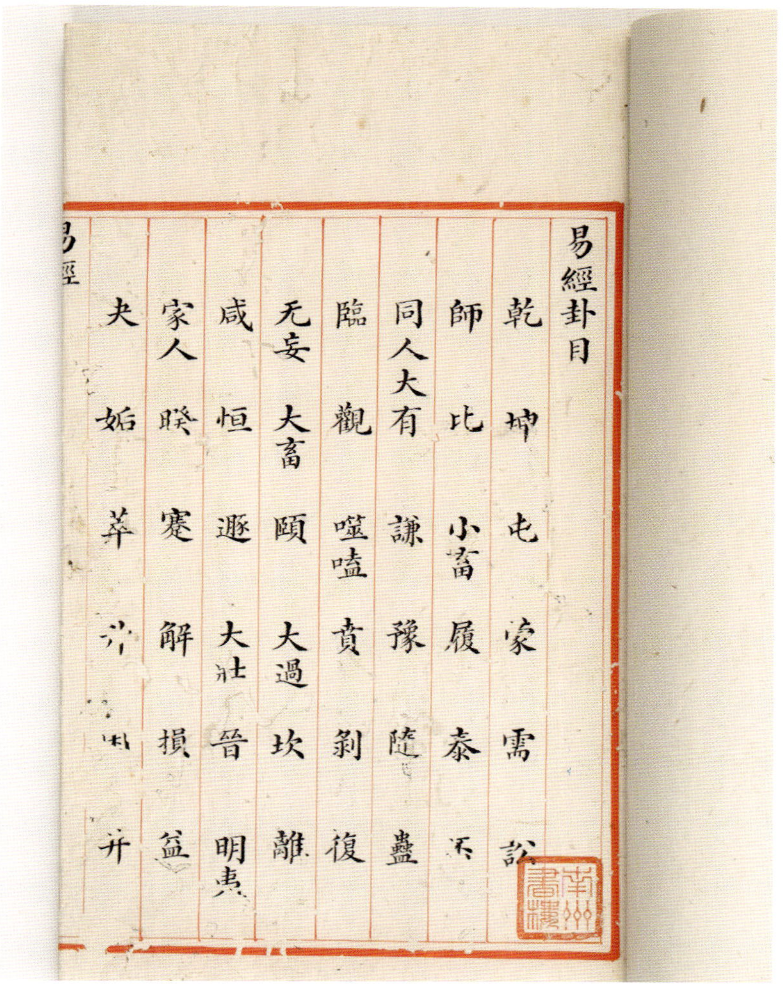

易經卦目
乾 坤 屯 蒙 需 訟
師 比 小畜 履 泰 否
同人 大有 謙 豫 隨 蠱
臨 觀 噬嗑 賁 剝 復
无妄 大畜 頤 大過 坎 離
咸 恒 遯 大壯 晉 明夷
家人 睽 蹇 解 損 益
夬 姤 萃 升 困 井
易經

Wujing jingben, or Essence of the Five Classics, *consists of five core Confucian texts with selected commentaries. The Five Classics contain a wide variety of material on ancient history, ethics, ritual, music, divination, and related topics, some of it dating as far back as the Western Zhou period (1046–771 BCE). These five books* (Poetry Classic, Documents Classic, Record of Rites, Classic of Changes [*the* I Ching], *and* Spring and Autumn Annals) *were authoritative sources for Confucian scholars and the subject of a vast commentarial tradition. This copy contains the full text of the classics and (in half-size characters in double columns) selections from standard commentaries. It was produced by government scribes during the Daoguang period (1821–50), in the latter part of the Qing dynasty (1644–1911), and kept in the Wenyuan ge (Pavilion of literary profundity), an imperial library in Beijing that was destroyed during the Second Opium War (1856–60).*

服以日視朝於內朝朝辨色始入君日出而視之退
適路寢聽政使人視大夫大夫退然後適小寢釋服
又朝服以食特牲三俎祭肺夕深衣祭牢肉朔月少
牢五俎四簋子卯稷食 嗣 菜羹夫人與君同庖君無
故不殺牛大夫無故不殺羊士無故不殺犬豕君子
遠庖廚凡有血氣之類弗身踐 翦 也至于八月不雨
君不舉年不順成君衣布搢 薦 本關梁不租山澤列
而不賦土功不興大夫不得造車馬卜人定龜史定

豆葅醢禮相助奠十有五年而笄二十而嫁有故二十三年而嫁聘則為妻奔則為妾凡女拜尚右手

玉藻第十三（此記天子諸侯冕笏佩諸侯及行禮之節）

天子玉藻十有二旒前後邃（粹）延龍卷（衮）以祭元端（冕）而朝（潮）日於東門之外聽朔於南門之外閏月則闔門左扉立于其中皮弁以日視朝遂以食日中而餕奏而食日少牢朔月大牢五飲上水漿酒醴酏（移）卒食元端而居動則左史書之言則右史書之御瞽幾聲之上下年不順成則天子素服乘素車食無樂

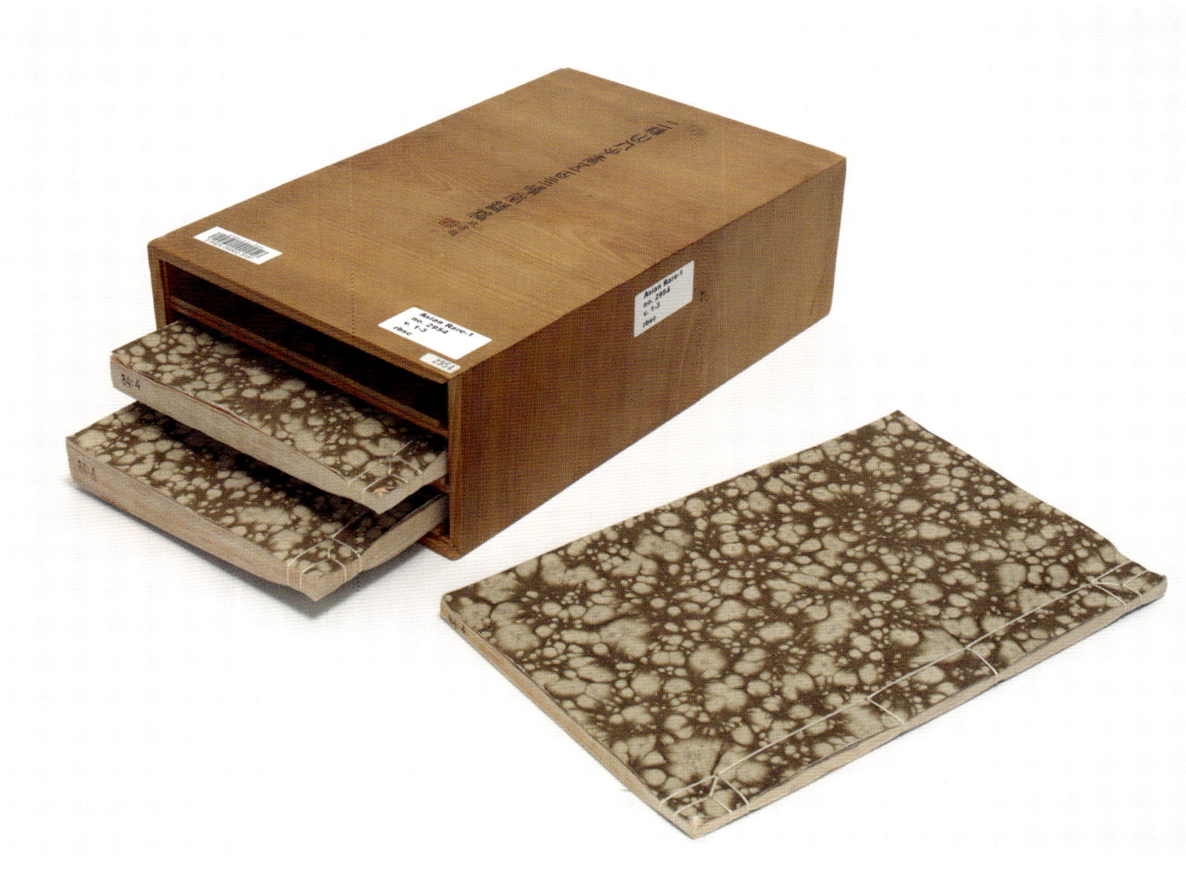

▲ ▶ ***Wubaisi feng caotang shigao* 五百四峰草堂詩稿 (Draft of poems from the thatched hall of five hundred and four peaks)**
China • 1785–97
Manuscript with printed gridlines and running title; double leaves; traditional stitched binding
3 volumes in a wooden box, each volume 29.2 × 18.4 cm (various thickness)
UBC LIBRARY COLLECTION
THE PUBAN COLLECTION, ASIAN RARE-1 NO.2954 (RBSC)

Wubaisi feng caotang shigao *is an original manuscript of poems by Li Jian* 黎簡 *(1747–99). Like many elite men in pre-modern China, Li Jian gave various poetic names to his homes and studios; Thatched Hall of Five Hundred and Four Peaks was one of these. Li Jian was a leading painter, calligrapher, poet, and seal carver active in southern China during the late eighteenth century. His landscape painting lay the foundation for the distinctive Lingnan school of painting, associated with his native province of Guangdong, that would flourish for generations to come. Li revitalized the literati landscape-painting conventions of his time by experimenting with uninhibited brushwork and by introducing vibrant elements of his local environment. This manuscript is in imperfect condition and shows signs of having been rebound many times. It includes seals by the poet Li Jian and its subsequent owners Deng Rongjing, Liang Ruhong, and Yao Junshi.*

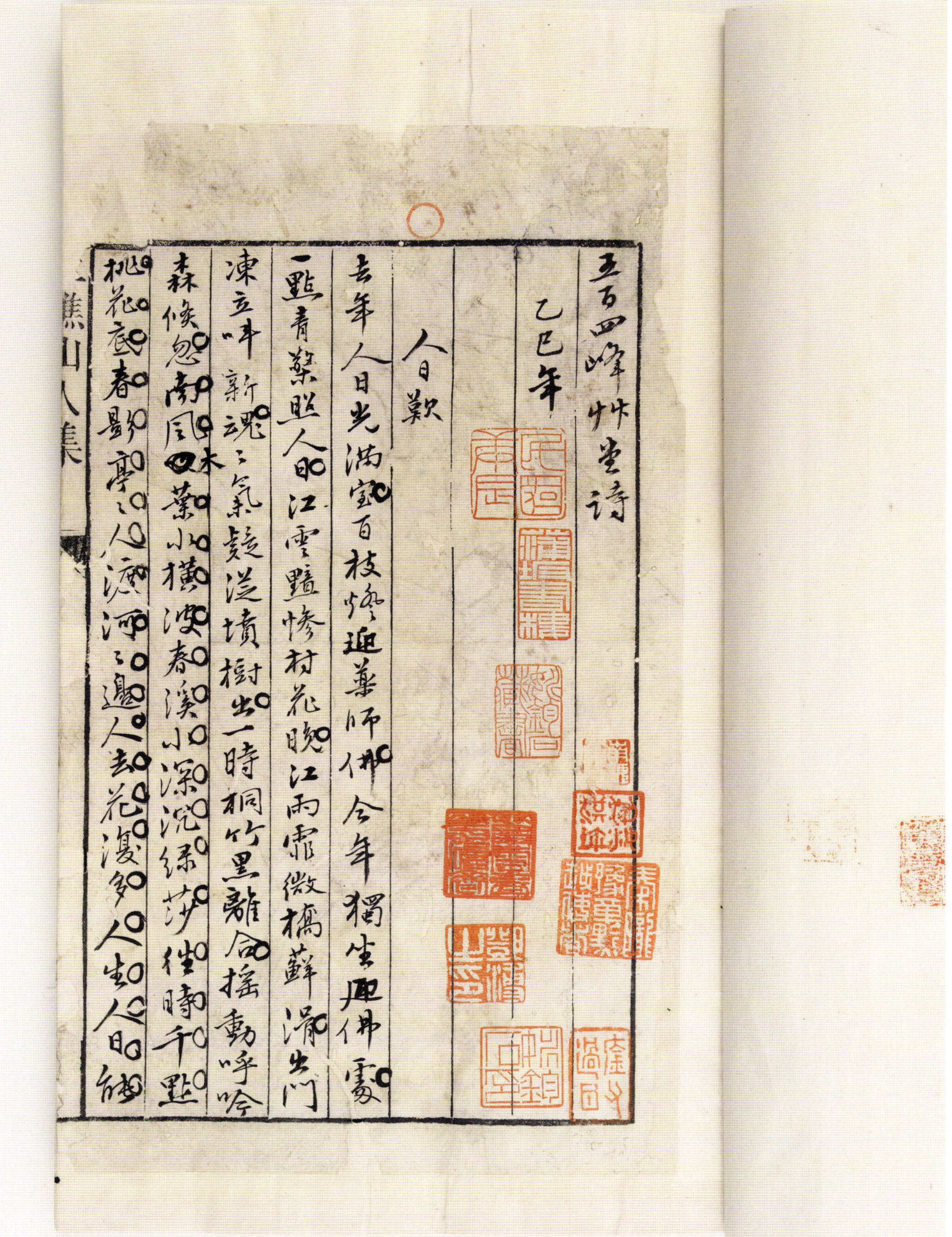

五百四峰艸堂詩

乙巳年

人日歎

去年人日光滿窗百枝燈迎藥師佛今年獨坐迎佛處一點青燈照人眠江雲黯慘村花晚江雨霏微橋蘚濕出門凍立半新魂々氣旋從墳樹出一時桐竹黑離合搖動呼吟森倏忽南風木葉小橫波春溪小深流綠莎徑晴千點桃花底春影亭々人渡河々邊人去花復多人出人日緣

樵山人集

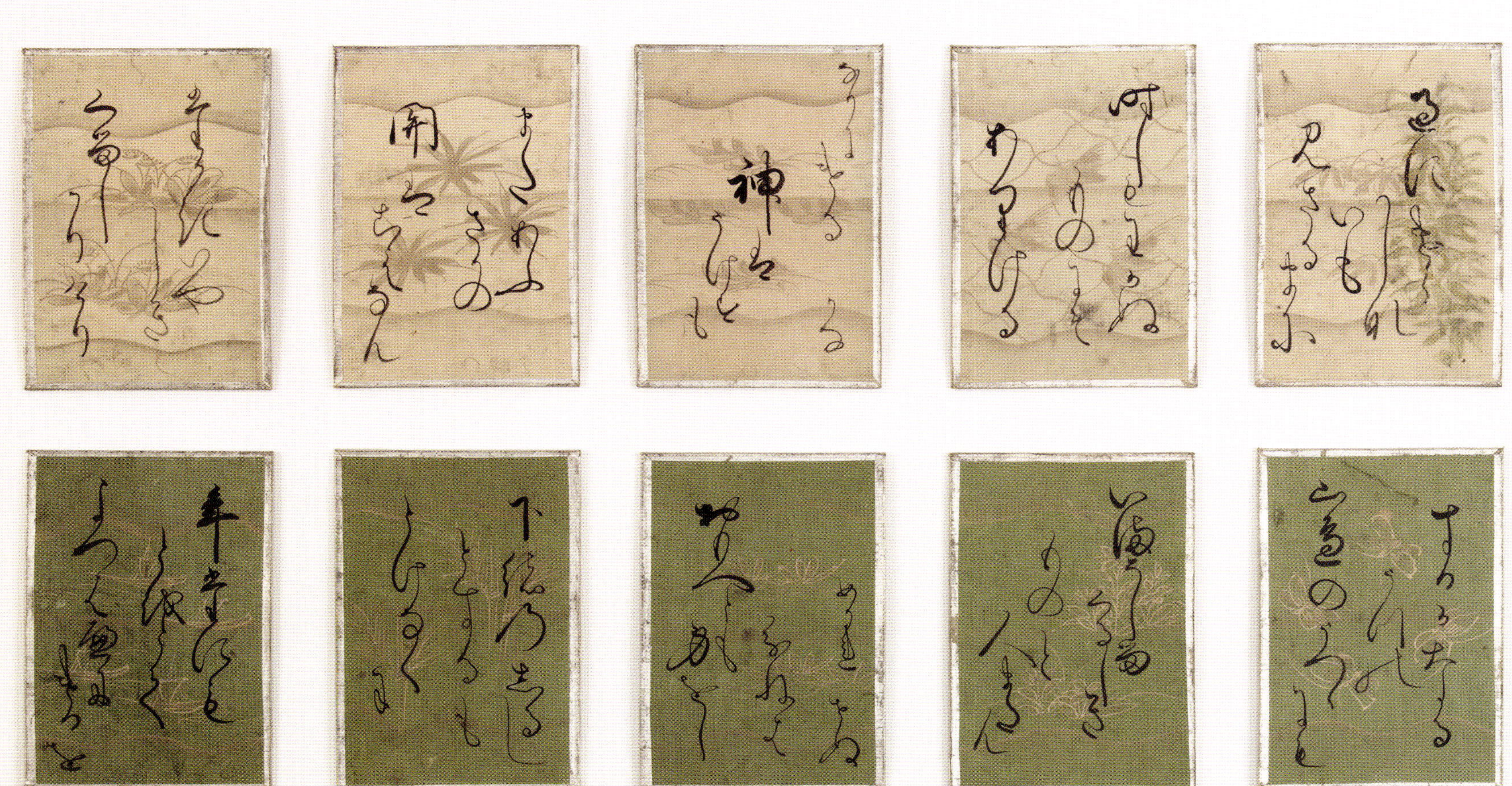

▲ ▶ ***Ise monogatari uta karuta***
伊勢物語うたかるた
(*The Tales of Ise* poem cards)
Japan • mid-17th century
418 cards in a wooden box
[card] 8 × 5 cm (each)
[box] 14 × 15 × 19 cm
UBC LIBRARY COLLECTION, PL787. I82 1700Z (RBSC)

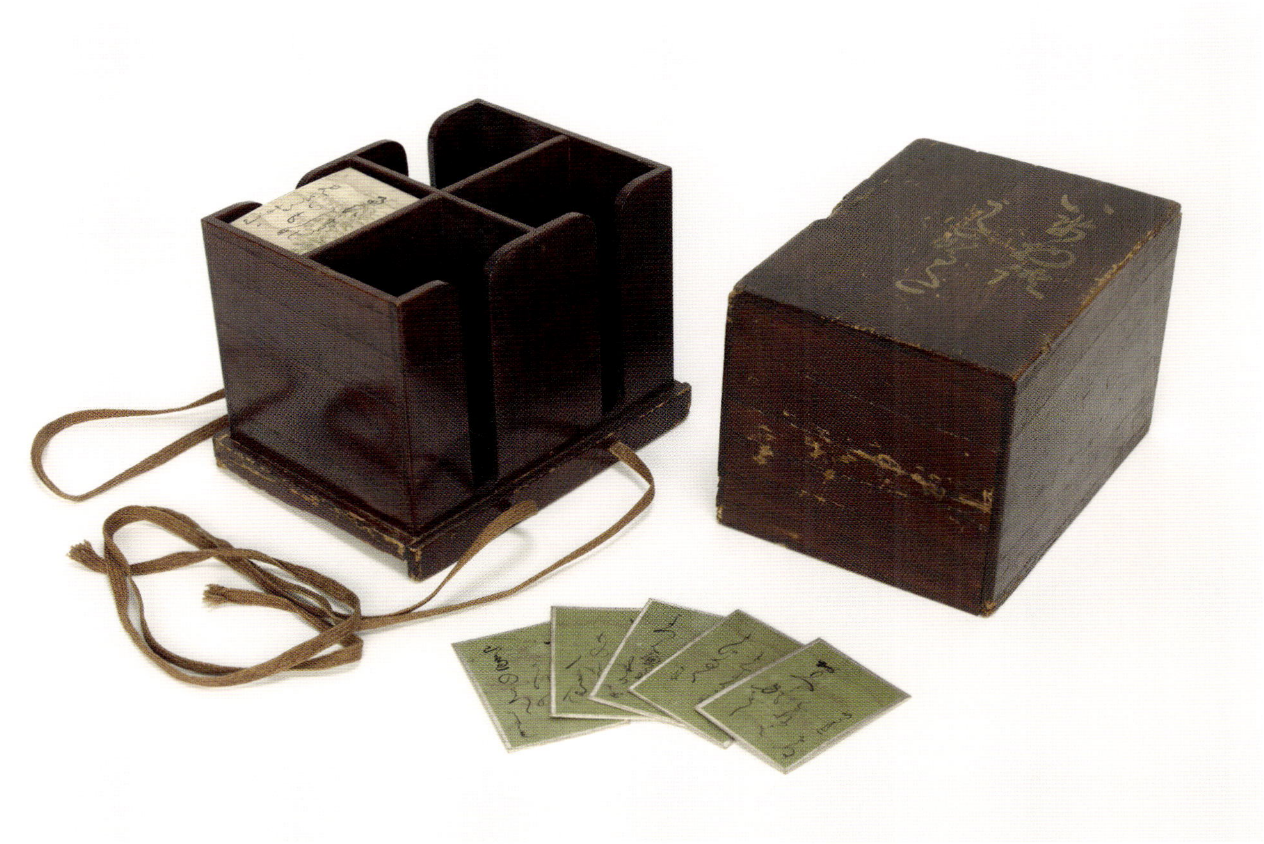

Uta karuta (*poem cards*) *are a form of play that was popular in the Edo period (1603–1868). "Pairing games" such as shell matching* (kaiawase *or* kaiooi) *were common beginning in the Heian period (794–1185* CE). *In shell matching, players tested their ability to match up clamshells based on poems on their colourful painted interiors. Playing cards were brought to Japan in the mid-sixteenth century by the Portuguese. Known as* karuta (*from the Portuguese word* carta), *the game combined tenets of pre-existing Japanese pairing games with European playing cards.* Uta karuta *use playing cards and get players to recall verses from classical Japanese poetry* (waka). *This set of* uta karuta *features the 209 poems in* Ise monogatari (The Tales of Ise, *circa 905*) *in cursive script on decorated paper.* Ise monogatari *is a series of loosely linked episodes thought to depict the amorous exploits of the courtier Ariwara no Narihira (825–80) and an essential work for the aristocratic reader.* (*See page 30 for a detailed view of one of the cards.*)

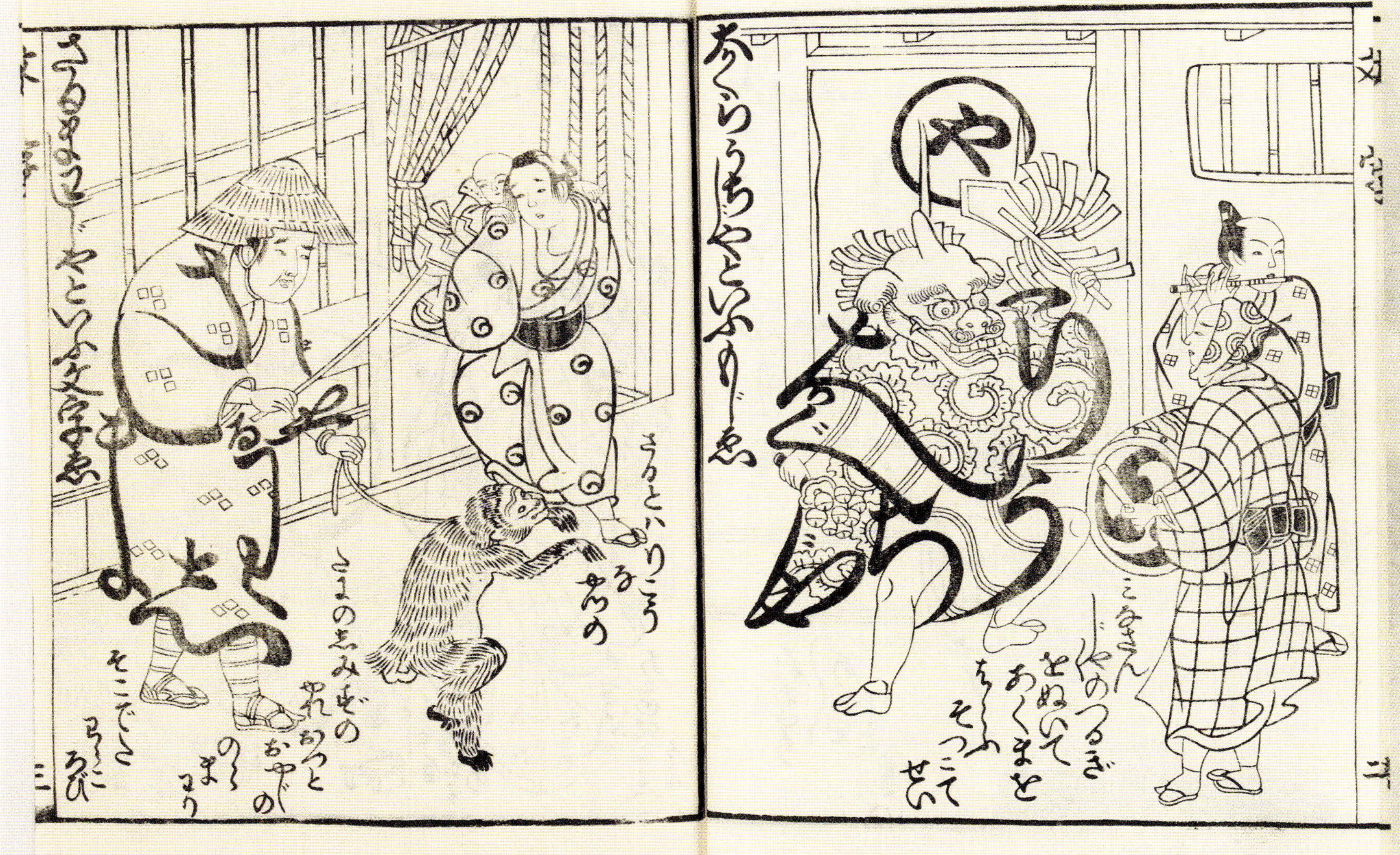

▲ ▶ ***Shin moji-e zukushi* 新文字ゑづくし**
(New compilation of script pictures)
Japan • 1766 reprinted in 1930
Book of illustrated woodblock prints, double leaves; traditional stitched binding
Vol. 23, no. 6, of the *Kisho fukuseikai sōsho* 稀書複製会叢書 [Collection of reprints of important texts] series, edited by Seisaku Yamada, limited edition no. 14/500 (Tokyo: Yoneyamadō, 1930).
18.8 × 13.5 × 0.3 cm
UBC LIBRARY COLLECTION, PL752. K585 SER.6 V.23 (RBSC)

This work is a compilation of moji-e *(文字絵), or "script pictures," a form of text-play that merges Japanese script (including* kanji, *i.e., Chinese characters) with illustrations to create a unified image.* Shin moji-e zukushi, *originally published in 1766, is a remodelled version of the original 1685* Moji-e zukushi, *both of which are considered representative of the* moji-e *genre.* Moji-e *that indicated the names or the professions of those portrayed were often integrated into folds and lines of clothing. The woodblock for this edition was carved by Yūji Otsuka.*

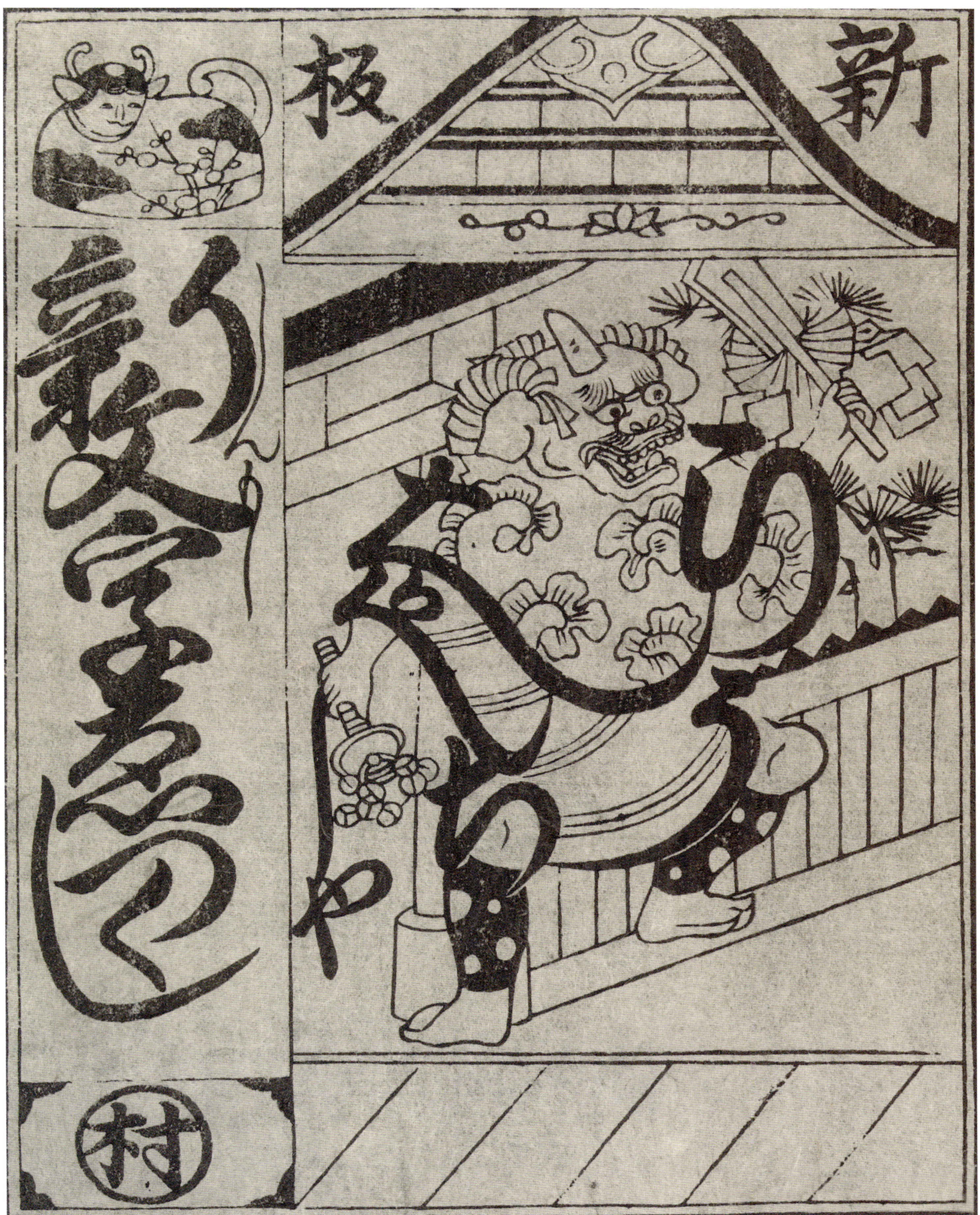
新板
村

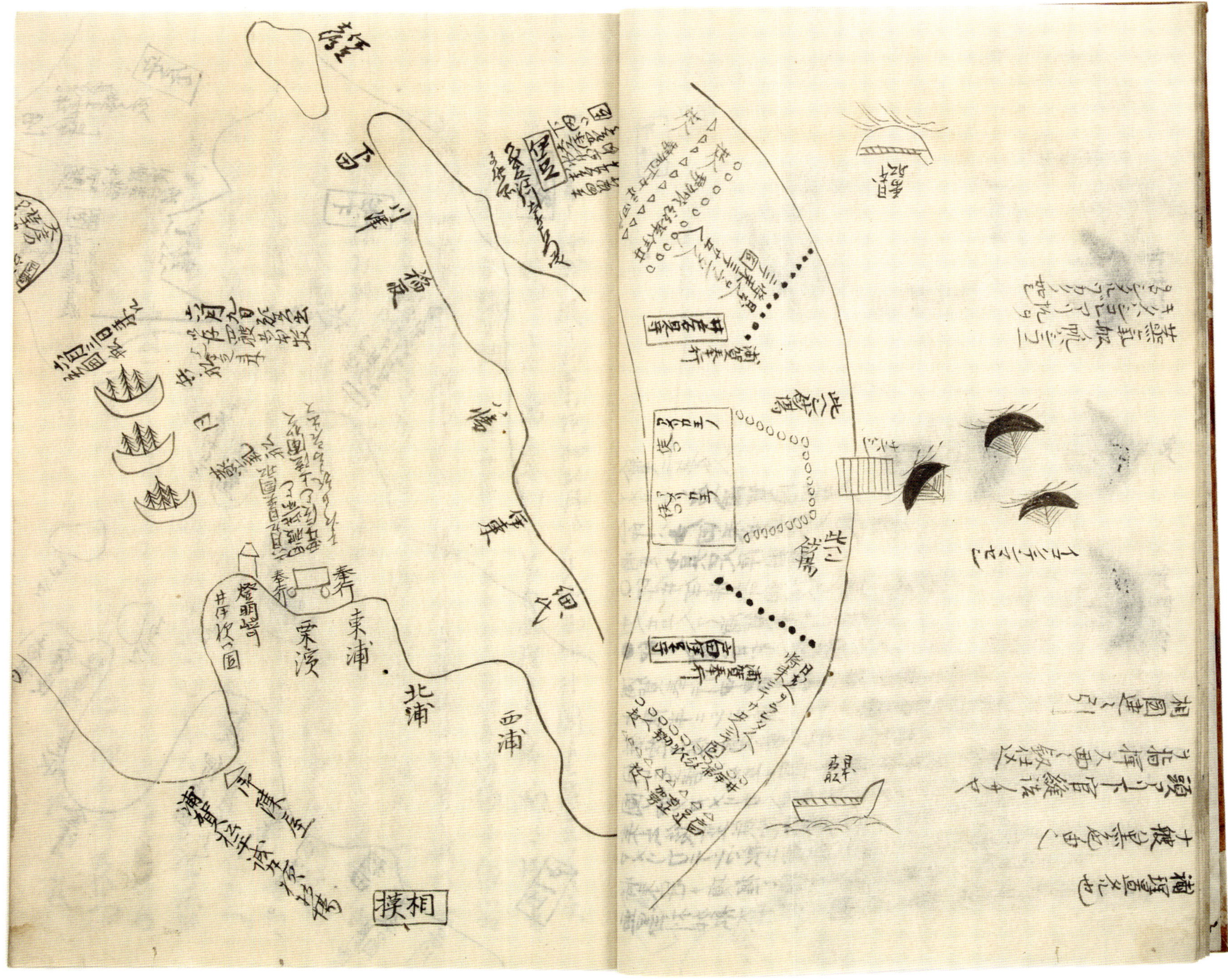

▲ ▶ ***Ihakuki*** **異船記**
Japan • 1854
Illustrated manuscript, double leaves: traditional stitched binding
[book] 26.2 × 17.9 × 0.9 cm
[case] 26.5 × 19.2 × 1.8 cm
UBC LIBRARY COLLECTION, DS881.8 I383 1854 (RBSC)

This manuscript describes the Perry Expedition of 1853, an expedition sent from the United States to demand that Japan open up diplomatic and trade relations with foreign powers, and to reverse its policy of seclusion. The success of this expedition ended two centuries of closed trade relations and resulted in the opening of Japan's ports to foreign traffic in 1859. This book details the arrival of the delegation at the Tokyo harbour and depicts, through illustrations and maps, the types and number of vessels that dotted Japan's shoreline, particularly around Tokyo and Yokohama.

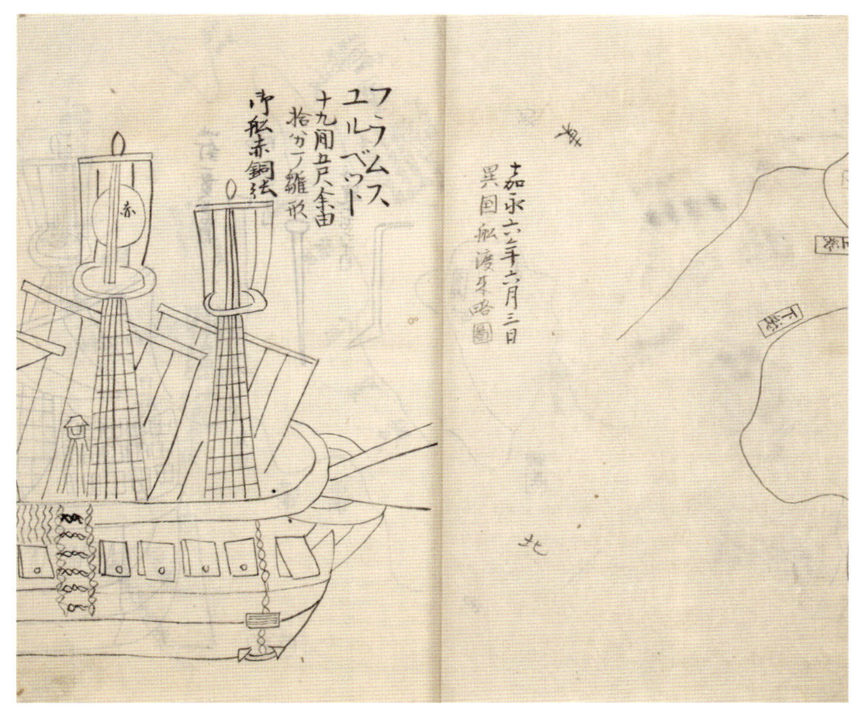
フラウムス、
ユルベウト
十九間五尺余
嘉永六年六月三日
異国船渡来略圖

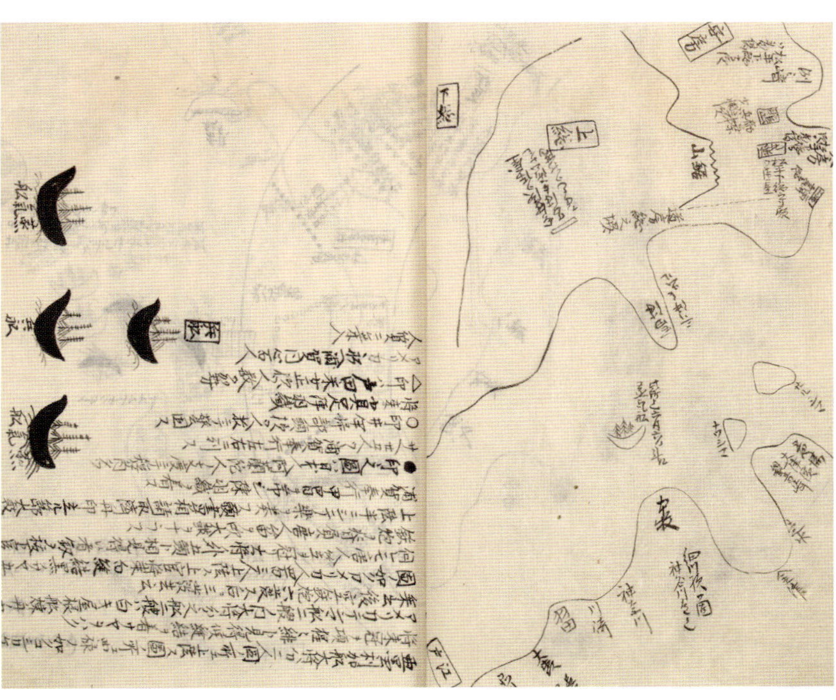

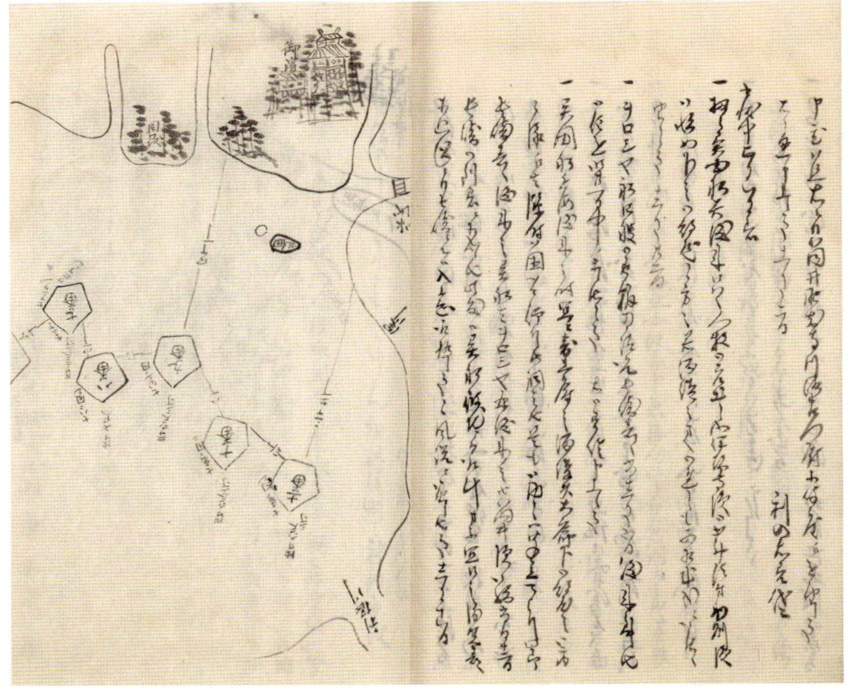

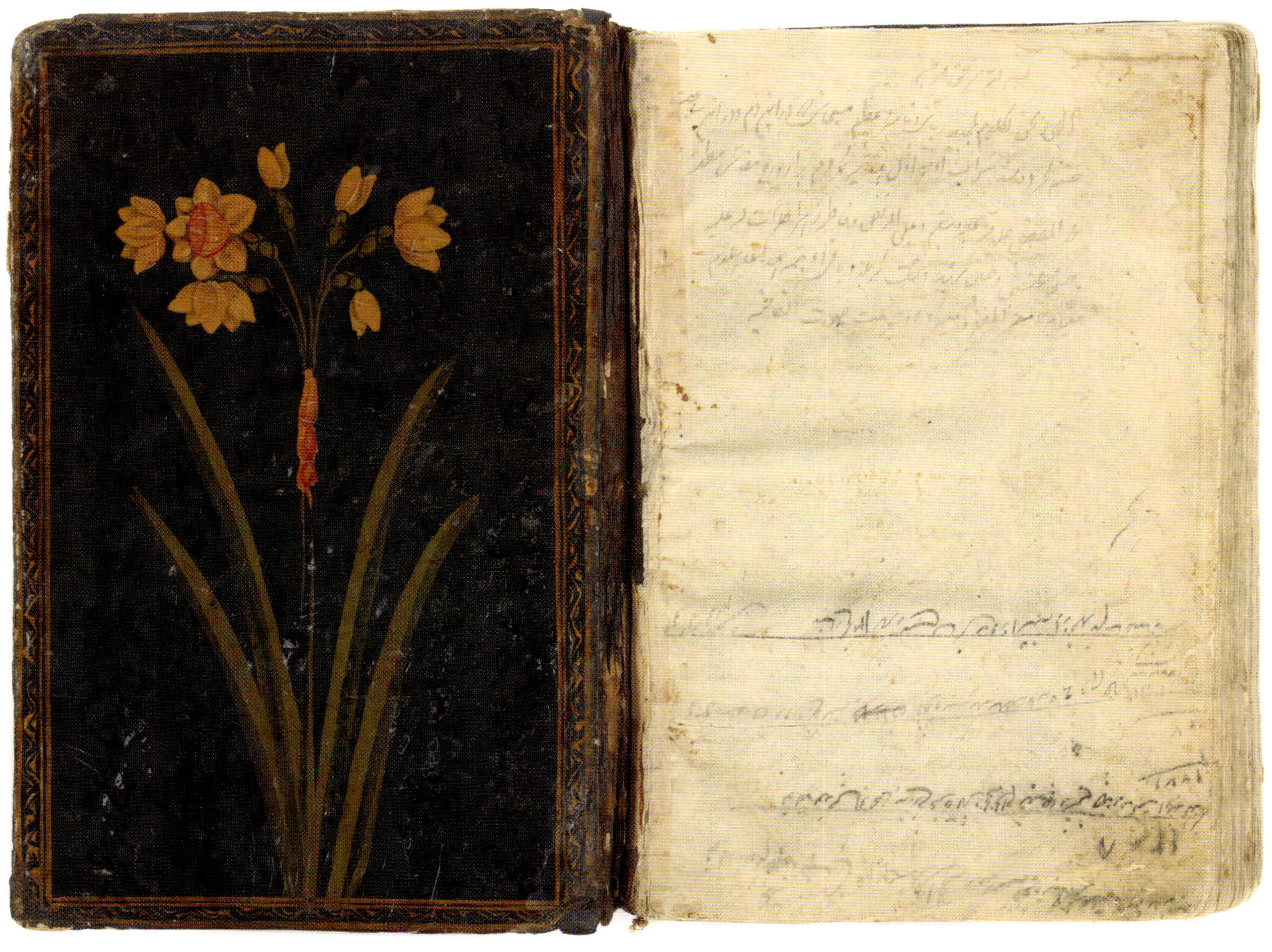

▲ ▶ **Qur'an القرآن**
Iran • 1842–43
Illuminated book, lacquered leather binding, approx. 350 unnumbered pages
19.7 × 13.4 × 3.2 cm
UBC LIBRARY COLLECTION, BP100 1842 (RBSC)

This illuminated Qur'an in classical Arabic text was likely created in Tabriz, Iran. The calligrapher, Muhammad al-Tabrīzī, intentionally left space for an illuminator to add colour embellishments, illuminated sūra *(chapter) headings, and Persian annotations by hand. Illumination was commonly used within the Qur'an to demarcate the beginning of* sūra *and verses. The calligraphy is dated 1258AH (1842–43 CE) in the colophon.*

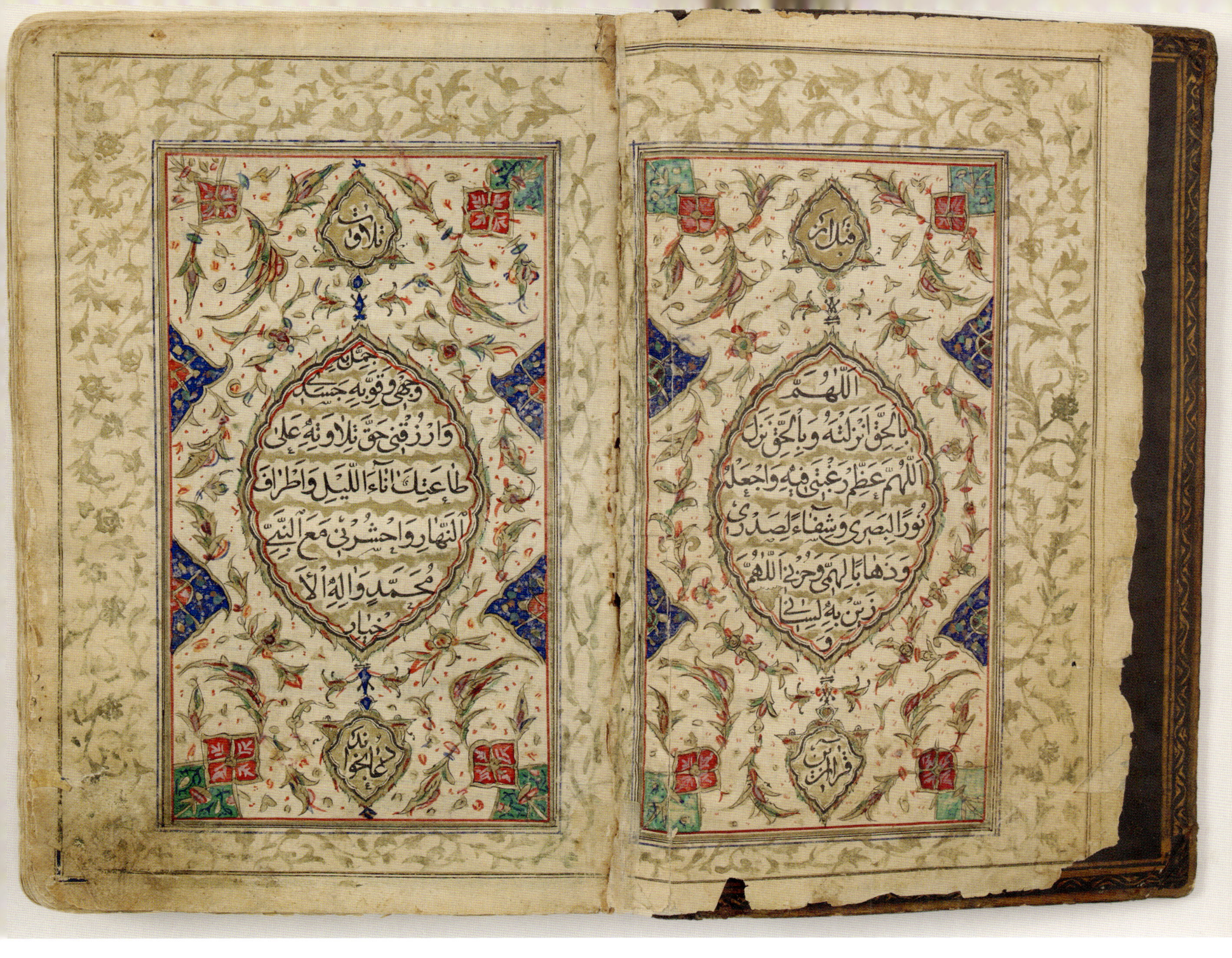

اللّٰهمّ
بالحقّ انزلته وبالحقّ نزل
اللّٰهمّ عظّم رغبتي فيه واجعله
نوراً لبصري وشفاءً لصدري
وذهاباً لهمّي وحزني اللّٰهمّ
زيّن به لساني
و
جمّل به
وجهي وقوّ به جسدي
وارزقني حقّ تلاوته على
طاعتك آناء الليل واطراف
النهار واحشرني مع النبيّ
محمّد واله الاخيار

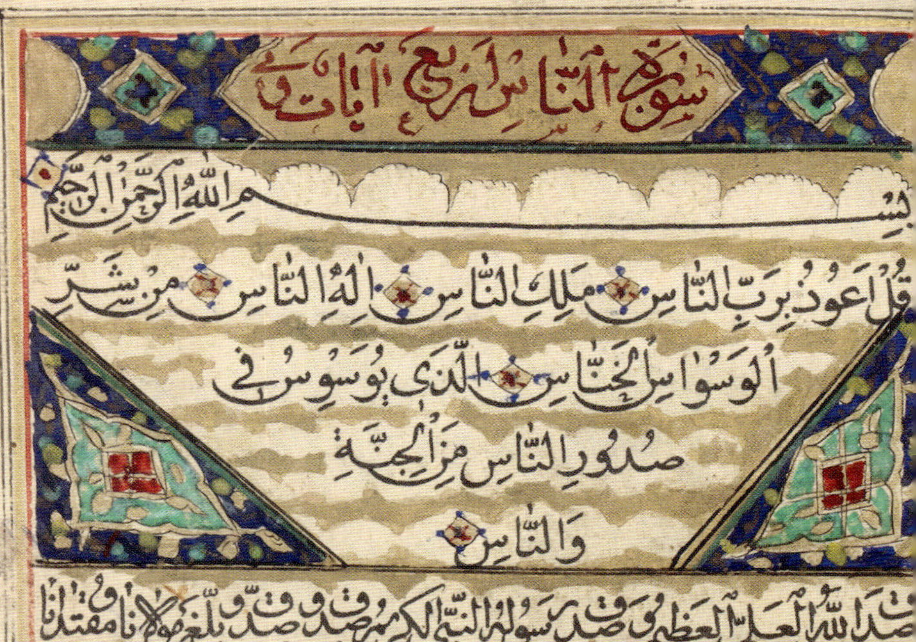

صدق الله العلي العظيم وصدق رسوله النبي الكريم وصدق وبلغ مولانا ومقتدانا
وسيدنا وامامنا بالحق امير المؤمنين وقائد الغر المحجلين ويعسوب الدين ووصي رسول رب
العالمين والحاكم يوم الدين علي بن ابي طالب والائمة المعصومين المنقوبين المصطفين المكرمين
صلوات الله عليه وعليهم السلام ونحن على ذلك من الشاهدين والشاكرين والحمد لله رب العالمين
وفقني الله الناصر المعين لاتمام كتابة كتابه المبين في عهد اعدل السلاطين واكرم الخواقين
ناصر الشريعة القويمة سالك الطريقة المستقيمة ظل الله على الانام ماحي بلاد الايمان واهل
لواء الولاية في الافاق مالك سرير الخلافة بالاستحقاق السلطان بن السلطان
السلطان محمد شاه الغازي لازال التاج واعاظم السلاطين خاضعة على بابه وجباه افاخم
نحو افق معفرة بتراب اعتابه وذلك باستدعاء عمدة التجار حضرتهما الزكي فطرتهما المخاديم العظام
الحاج ... وكتابته بحسن طباعة باهتمام عمدة التجار كربلائي ... الفخار المباهر
طباعة الموصوف فيها بالتفوق والبراعة الاستاد آقا جبار الحاج غفار التبريزي لازال
هذا فيتوفيق الله وتأييده وانا الخاطي الاثيم الجاني العبد احمد بن محمد التبريزي وتلميذ ...
نظر فيه يذكرنا بخير الدعاء وكان تحرير ذلك في حول الثامن والخمسين بعد المائتين والالف من الهجرة
١٢٥٨

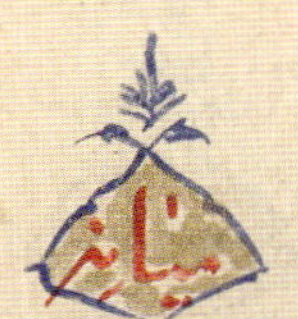

سورة الكافرون ست آيات

بسم الله الرحمن الرحيم

قل يا ايها الكافرون لا اعبد ما تعبدون ولا انتم عابدون ما
اعبد ولا انا عابد ما عبدتم ولا انتم عابدون ما اعبد لكم دينكم ولي دين

سورة النصر ثلث آيات

بسم الله الرحمن الرحيم

اذا جاء نصر الله والفتح ورايت الناس يدخلون في دين الله
افواجا فسبح بحمد ربك واستغفره انه كان توابا

سورة ابي لهب خمس آيات

بسم الله الرحمن الرحيم

تبت يدا ابي لهب وتب ما اغنى عنه ماله وما كسب سيصلى
نارا ذات لهب وامراته حمالة الحطب في جيدها حبل من مسد

سورة التوحيد اربع آيات

بسم الله الرحمن الرحيم

قل هو الله احد الله الصمد لم يلد ولم يولد ولم يكن له كفوا احد

سورة الفلق خمس آيات

بسم الله الرحمن الرحيم

قل اعوذ برب الفلق من شر ما خلق ومن شر غاسق اذا وقب
ومن شر النفاثات في العقد ومن شر حاسد اذا حسد

بسم ا

Notes

Note: For this book, Chinese and Japanese names follow the order indigenous to these countries, whereby the family name is given first followed by the given name, unless an individual (such as the contributors to this book) has deliberately adopted the alternative way, in which case we have honoured that preference.

Foreword

1 Stanley Tambiah, "The Magical Power of Words," *Man* (New Series) 3, no. 2 (1968): 181.
2 Jean-Jacques Rousseau, *Essai sur l'origine des langues*, ed. Charles Porset (1781; repr., Bordeaux: Ducros, 1970).
3 Jacques Derrida, *Of Grammatology*, trans. Gayatri Chakravorty Spivak (Baltimore: Johns Hopkins University Press, 1997), 87.
4 Ibid., 26.
5 Ibid., 90.
6 Ibid., 17.

Introduction

Part of this introduction is based on essays that originally appeared in the catalogues for the exhibitions I have previously curated: Ephemeral but Eternal Words: Traces of Asia *(Canberra: Australian National University, 2010) and* Trazos del tiempo, trazos de palabras: obras de artistas japoneses (Traces of Time, Traces of Words: Artworks by Japanese Artists) *(Buenos Aires: National Museum of Oriental Art, 2011). The exhibition* Traces of Words: Art and Calligraphy from Asia *has been developed from these two exhibitions.*

1 Roger Chartier, *Forms and Meanings: Texts, Performance, and Audiences from Codex to Computer* (Philadelphia: University of Pennsylvania Press, 1995), 2; cf. Marshall McLuhan, *Understanding Media: The Extensions of Man* (London: Routledge and K. Paul, 1964).
2 Robert E. Harrist Jr. and Wen C. Fong, *The Embodied Image: Chinese Calligraphy from the John B. Elliott Collection* (Princeton, NJ: Art Museum, Princeton University, with Harry N. Abrams, 1999).
3 Yu-kung Kao, "Chinese Lyric Aesthetics," in *Words and Images: Chinese Poetry, Calligraphy, and Painting,* ed. Alfreda Murck and Wen C. Fong (New York: Metropolitan Museum of Art, with Princeton, NJ: Princeton University Press, 1991); see also chapter 1 in this book.
4 Johanna Drucker, *The Visible Word: Experimental Typography and Modern Art,* 1909–1923 (Chicago: University of Chicago Press, 1994), 33.
5 Webb Keane, "Signs Are Not the Garb of Meaning: On the Social Analysis of Material Things," in *Materiality*, ed. Daniel Miller (Durham, NC: Duke University Press, 2005), 184.
6 Ibid., 183.
7 Phaptawan Suwannakudt, *Phaptawan Suwannakudt: Three Worlds*, media release for the exhibit (Melbourne: Arc One Gallery, 2009), arc-one.squarespace.com/s/phaptawan-suwannakudt-media-09.pdf.
8 Clare Harris, "In and Out of Place: Tibetan Artists' Travels in the Contemporary Art World," in *Asia through Art and Anthropology: Cultural Translation across Borders*, ed. Fuyubi Nakamura, Morgan Perkins, and Olivier Krischer (London and New York: Bloomsbury Academic, 2013), 43.
9 Yukio Lippit, "teamLab: Past, Present, and Future," teamLab website, accessed June 19, 2016, exhibition.team-lab.net/siliconvalley/review.
10 Fuyubi Nakamura, Morgan Perkins, and Olivier Krischer, "Introduction: Images of Asia across Borders," in *Asia through Art and Anthropology*, ed. Nakamura, Perkins, and Krischer, 4.

Chapter 1

A section of this chapter originally appeared in "Between Text and Image: the Ambiguity of Chinese Written Characters" in Glimpse | the art + science of seeing *2, no. 1 (Spring 2009).*

1 Yuehping Yen, *Calligraphy and Power in Contemporary Chinese Societies* (Abingdon, UK, and New York: RoutledgeCurzon, 2005), 52.
2 Ibid.
3 Ibid.
4 "Fashi" is an honorific used to address an ordained Buddhist monk in modern China.
5 Special thanks to Yixin Fashi for his help with selecting the works by Hongyi Fashi. I am also grateful to a couple of friends (who wish to remain anonymous) for their help in getting the images print-ready.
6 「於當人所注意之字畫、筆法、筆力、結構、神韻，乃至某碑、某帖、某派，皆一致摒除，絕不用心揣摩。」(He pays no attention to the standard elements for calligraphic appreciation emphasized by most people—including the strokes, the techniques, the force of execution, the character structure and composition, and the aura of the work, and down to the stylistic lineage or artistic school. None of these is on his mind when he writes. [My translation.]) From "Letter to Ma Donghan" (dated 1938) in Lin Ziqing, *Hongyi dashi xinpu* [New chronicle of Hongyi Dashi's life] (Taipei: Dongda Tushu Gongsi, 1993), 402.
7 「聚精會神，落筆遲遲，一點一劃，均全力赴之。五尺整幅，需二小時左右方成。」Quoted in Jinman Liang, "Shufa bu bieyu fofa" [Calligraphy is not unlike Dharma], *Rensheng zazhi* [Humanity], no. 364 (December 2013), 46.

Chapter 2

Some parts of this chapter originally appeared in some of my previous publications: Nakamura, ed., Ephemeral but Eternal Words: Traces of Asia *(Canberra: Australian National University, 2010); and Nakamura, ed.,* Trazos del tiempo, trazos de palabras: obra de artistas Japoneses (Traces of Time, Traces of Words: Artworks by Japanese Artists) *(Buenos Aires: National Museum of Oriental Art, 2011).*

1 W.J.T. Mitchell, *Iconology: Image, Text, Ideology* (Chicago: University of Chicago Press, 1986), 43.
2 Michael Sullivan, *The Three Perfections: Chinese Painting, Poetry and Calligraphy* (London: Thames and Hudson, 1974).
3 Ryan Holmberg, "The Pseudography of Hidai Nankoku," in *Yale University Art Gallery Bulletin* 2008*: Recent Acquisitions* (New Haven, CT: Yale University, 2008), 111.
4 Takahashi Toshirō, *Kindai Nihon ni okeru sho eno manazashi* [Looking at calligraphy in modern Japan] (Kyoto: Shibunkaku, 2011); and Kasashima Tadayuki, *Nihon bijutsuni okeru "sho" no zōkeishi* (The history of modelling theory of calligraphy in Japanese art [sic]) (Tokyo: Kasama shoin, 2013).
5 I have adopted the modified Hepburn romanization system in this chapter. There are some cases where the normal romanized spelling does not use macrons (which indicate long vowels), usually place names; for example, Tokyo rather than Tōkyō.
6 Kyūyō Ishikawa, *Kindai shoshi* 近代書史 [The history of modern Japanese calligraphy] (Nagoya: University of Nagoya Press, 2009); and Nagoya Akira, ed., *Ketteiban Nihon shodō-shi* 決定版 日本書道史 [The history of Japanese calligraphy: The definitive edition] (Tokyo: Geijutsu Shinbunsha, 2009).
7 There are two main theories on how to read and interpret this engraving: *Kan no Wa no Na no kokuō* (漢倭奴国王) is the dominant theory. It is believed that the seal was given to the sovereign of the Wa kingdom—which had flourished in northern Kyūshū in southern Japan in the mid-first century—by the emperor of the Eastern Han dynasty of China (25–220 CE). The seal was presented as a symbol of authority. Another theory presents a different reading, *Kan no Ito no kokuō* (漢李委奴(伊都)国王), arguing that the seal was given to the kingdom of Ito (around Fukuoka city).
8 The earliest extant example of Japanese calligraphy executed on paper is a work by Prince Shōtoku (574–622 CE) made in 615 CE known as *Hokke gisho* (Commentaries on the Lotus Sutra).
9 *Routledge Encyclopedia of Modernism*, s.v. "Calligraphy in Japan," by Fuyubi Nakamura, May 9, 2016, www.rem.routledge.com, doi: 10.4324/9781135000356-REM411-1.

10 Ichirō Hariu, "Sengo Nihon no zen'eisho: Kaiga tono mitsuduki jidai wo koete" [Avant-garde calligraphy in postwar Japan: Beyond the honeymoon period with paintings], in O Bijutsukan (O Art Museum), *Sho to kaiga no atsuki jidai,* 1945–1969 [Calligraphy and painting, the passionate age: 1945–1969] (Tokyo: O Bijutsukan [O Art Museum], 1992), 2–5; and Alexandra Munroe, "Circle: Modernism and Tradition," in *Japanese Art after 1945: Scream against the Sky*, ed. Alexandra Munroe (New York: Harry N. Abrams, 1994), 125–47.

11 Alfred Gell, *Art and Agency: An Anthropological Theory* (Oxford: Oxford University Press / Clarendon Press, 1998), 18.

12 Louise Boudonnat and Harumi Kushizaki, *Traces of the Brush: The Art of Japanese Calligraphy* (San Francisco: Chronicle Books, 2003), 170.

13 Sōfū Okabe, "Hidai and His Work" (chapter translated by Audie Bock), in *Hidai Nankoku sakuhinshu*, ed. Hidai Nankoku (Yokohama: Shogaku-in Shuppan-bu [Shogakuin Publications], 1987), 231.

14 Fuyubi Nakamura, "Creating or Performing Words?: Observations on Contemporary Japanese Calligraphy," in *Creativity and Cultural Improvisation*, ed. Tim Ingold and Elizabeth Hallam (Oxford: Berg, 2007).

15 Tim Ingold, "Notes Toward an Anthropology of the Line," *Dwelling* no. 2 (2003).

16 Nakamura, "Creating or Performing Words?"

17 Christine Flint Sato, "Tsubasa Kimura," *Letter Arts Review* 23, no. 3 (Summer 2009); Fuyubi Nakamura, "Creating New Forms of 'Visualised' Words: An Anthropological Study of Contemporary Japanese Calligraphy" (DPhil thesis, University of Oxford, 2006); Nakamura, "Creating or Performing Words?"; Nakamura, "Tsubasa Kimura: The Infinite Possibility of Words," in *Ephemeral but Eternal Traces of Words*, ed. Nakamura, 31–33; and Nakamura, "A Brief Introduction to Japanese Calligraphy," in *Trazos del tiempo, trazos de palabras*, ed. Nakamura, 4–6.

18 Kimura held a series of three exhibitions entitled, originally in English, *Crowd*; *After the Crowd*; and *and crowd lost* in 2005, and then a series of four exhibitions called *Crowded* 1/3, *Crowded* 1/3 *high*, *Crowded* 2/3, and *Crowded* 3/3 in 2006. See Nakamura, "Creating New Forms"; and Christine Flint Sato, "Tsubasa Kimura," 34–36.

19 *Iroha uta* is often attributed to the Buddhist monk Kūkai (774–835 CE), but the use of certain syllables suggests it was composed after 950. See Christopher Seeley, *A History of Writing in Japan* (Leiden, the Netherlands: E.J. Brill, 1991), 106.

20 Kimura majored in Buddhist studies for her bachelor of arts at Ryūkoku University in Kyoto and studied *bokuseki*, or the calligraphy of Buddhist monks, during her postgraduate years at Kyoto University of Education. While her practice at private schools did not necessarily focus on Buddhism-inspired calligraphy, her calligraphy teacher of many years was a Buddhist monk.

21 Norman Bryson, "The Gaze in the Expanded Field," in *Vision and Visuality*, ed. Hall Foster (Seattle: Bay Press, 1988), 103.

22 Kimura, email message to author, February 2, 2010.

23 Ingold, "Notes Toward an Anthropology of the Line."

Chapter 3

1 Mohamed Zakariya, *Music for the Eyes: An Introduction to Islamic and Ottoman Calligraphy* (Los Angeles: Los Angeles County Museum of Art, 1998), pamphlet published in conjunction with the exhibition *Letters in Gold*.

Chapter 4

I offer my gratitude to Stefan Baums, Dominik Wujastyk, Fuyubi Nakamura, and Grace Yaginuma, whose detailed and thoughtful comments on earlier drafts of this essay have greatly enriched its revision; all remaining flaws, however, are my own.

1 Most of the Southeast Asian manuscripts held by MOA are not in Sanskrit, but in either the closely related Pali—the language of the Southern Buddhist canon—or hybrid registers that synthesize Sanskrit and Pali with local languages (Burmese, Thai, Sinhala, etc.). For the purposes of this essay, however, I am treating them as falling within a larger historical formation that we may call "Sanskrit manuscript culture."

2 On Sanskrit manuscriptology, see Dominik Wujastyk, "Indian Manuscripts," in *Manuscript Cultures: Mapping*

the Field, ed. Jörg B. Quenzer, Dmitry Bondarev, and Jan-Ulrich Sobisch, Studies in Manuscript Cultures no. 1 (Berlin: De Gruyter, 2014), 159–82. On Sanskrit literary culture and the "Cosmopolis," see Sheldon Pollock, *The Language of the Gods in the World of Men: Sanskrit, Culture, and Power in Premodern India* (Berkeley: University of California Press, 2006). For key overviews of Sanskrit manuscript studies, see S.M. Katre, *Introduction to Indian Textual Criticism* (Bombay: Karnatak, 1941); and Jayant P. Thaker, *Manuscriptology and Textual Criticism* (Vadodara, India: Oriental Institute, 2002).

3 On the marginalization of Sanskrit studies, see Sheldon Pollock, "Future Philology? The Fate of a Soft Science in a Hard World," *Critical Inquiry* 35: 931–61.

4 On Gāndhārī birch bark manuscripts, see Stefan Baums, "Gandhāran Scrolls: Rediscovering an Ancient Manuscript Type," in *Manuscript Cultures*, ed. Quenzer, Bondarev, and Sobisch, 183–226.

5 On the early history of writing in South Asia, see Richard Salomon, *Indian Epigraphy: A Guide to the Study of Inscriptions in Sanskrit, Prakrit, and the Other Indo-Aryan Languages* (New York: Oxford University Press, 1998); Harry Falk, *Schrift im alten Indien: ein Forschungsbericht mit Anmerkungen*, ScriptOralia, no. 56 (Tübingen: Gunter Narr Verlag, 1993); and Oskar von Hinüber, *Der Beginn der Schrift und frühe Schriftlichkeit in Indien*, Abhandlungen der Geistes- und Sozialwissenschaftlichen Klasse (1989), no. 11 (Mainz: Akademie der Wissenschaften und der Literatur / Stuttgart: Franz Steiner Verlag, 1990).

6 *World Checklist of Selected Plant Families*, Royal Botanic Gardens, Kew, accessed June 13, 2016, apps.kew.org/wcsp.

7 On the technical details of manuscript production see Katre, *Introduction to Indian Textual Criticism*; Thaker, *Manuscriptology and Textual Criticism*; and P. Perumal, "The Sanskrit Manuscripts in Tamilnadu," in *Aspects of Manuscript Culture in South India*, ed. Saraju Rath (Leiden, the Netherlands: Brill, 2012), 157–72. Rath's collection of essays offers an invaluable and up-to-date resource for South Indian manuscriptology.

8 On the history of paper in South Asia, see Sita Ramaseshan, "The History of Paper in India up to 1948," *Indian Journal of History of Science* 24 (1989): 103–21; and Jeremiah P. Losty, *The Art of the Book in India* (London: British Library, 1982).

9 The primary sources I consulted were *The Mahābhārata* (Critical Edition), ed. Vishnu S. Sukthankar et al., 19 vols. (Poona [Pune]: Bhandarkar Oriental Research Institute, 1927–66); *Kāvyamīmāṃsā* of Rājaśekhara, ed. C.D. Dalal and R.A. Shastry, 3rd ed. (Baroda [Vadodara]: Oriental Institute, 1934); and *Dānasāgara* of Ballālasena, ed. Bhabatosh Bhattacharya (Calcutta [Kolkata]: Asiatic Society, 1956).

10 "śrutvaitat prāha vighneśo yadi me lekhanī kṣaṇam |
likhito nāvatiṣṭheta tadā syāṃ lekhako hy aham |
vyāso 'py uvāca taṃ devam abuddhvā mā likha kvacit |
om ity uktvā gaṇeśo 'pi babhūva kila lekhakaḥ |
granthagranthiṃ tadā cakre munir gūḍhaṃ kutūhalāt |
yasmin pratijñayā prāha munir dvaipāyanas tv idam |"
Mahābhārata 1, appendix 1, note after 30, lines 10–14.

11 "sadaḥsaṃskāraviśuddhyarthaṃ sarvabhāṣākuśalaḥ śīghravāk cārvakṣara iṅgitākāravedī nānālipijñaḥ kaviḥ lākṣaṇikaś ca lekhakaḥ syāt | tadasannidhāv atirātrādiṣu pūrvoktanām anyatamaḥ | . . . tasya sampuṭikā saphalakakhaṭikā samudgakaḥ salekhanīkamaṣībhājanāni tāḍipatrāṇi bhūrjatvaco vā, salohakaṇṭakāni tāladalāni susammṛṣṭā bhittayaḥ satatasannihitāḥ syuḥ |"
Kāvyamīmāṃsā, 50, lines 7–10, 21–23.

12 I am indebted to James McHugh of the University of Southern California for providing me with an unpublished essay on the *Dānasāgara* that has motivated my thoughts in this section; his forthcoming study of this text will assuredly eclipse the cursory reflections I have presented here.

13 On Jürgen Habermas's public sphere, see Habermas, *The Structural Transformation of the Public Sphere: An Inquiry into a Category of Bourgeois Society*, trans. Thomas Burger with Frederick Lawrence (Cambridge, MA: MIT Press, 1989), originally published as *Strukturwandel der Öffentlichkeit* (Darmstadt and Neuwied: Hermann Luchterhand Verlag, 1962).

Chapter 5

1 Michael Sullivan, *The Three Perfections: Chinese Painting, Poetry, and Calligraphy* (London: Thames and Hudson, 1974).

2 Wai-kam Ho, "The Literary Concepts of 'Picture-Like' and 'Picture-Idea' in the Relationship between Poetry and Painting," in *Words and Images: Chinese Poetry, Calligraphy, and Painting*, ed. Alfreda Murck and Wen C. Fong (Princeton, NJ: Princeton University Press, with New York: Metropolitan Museum of Art, 1991), 359.

3 Xu Bing, "An Artist's View," in *Persistence/Transformation: Text as Image in the Art of Xu Bing*, ed. Dora C.Y. Ching and Jerome Silbergeld (Princeton, NJ: P.Y. and Kinmay W. Tang Center for East Asian Art, with Princeton University Press, 2006), 103.

4 Maxwell K. Hearn, "Past as Present in Contemporary Chinese Art," in *Ink Art: Past as Present in Contemporary Chinese Art* (New York: Metropolitan Museum of Art, 2013).

5 Wenda Gu, "face the new millennium: the divine comedy of our times—a thesis on the *united nations* art project and its time and environment," in *Wenda Gu: Art from Middle Kingdom to Biological Millennium,* ed. Mark H.C. Bessire (Cambridge, MA: MIT Press, 2003), 36–37.

6 Birgit Mersmann, "(Ideo-)Logical Alliances between Image and Script: Calligraphic Reconfigurations in Contemporary Chinese Art," in *Elective Affinities: Testing Word and Image Relationships*, ed. Catriona Macleod, Véronique Plesch, and Charlotte Schoell-Glass, Word and Image Interactions, vol. 6 (Amsterdam: Editions Rodopi, 2009), 387–99.

7 Gulbahar H. Beckett and Gerard A. Postiglione, "China's Language Policy for Indigenous and Minority Education," chap. 1 in *China's Assimilationist Language Policy: The Impact on Indigenous/Minority Literacy and Social Harmony*, ed. Gulbahar H. Beckett and Gerard A. Postiglione (Abingdon, UK, and New York: Routledge, 2012).

8 Trace Foundation, "Drawing the Gods: The Birth of Contemporary Tibetan Art," accessed June 10, 2015, www.trace.org/library/drawing-gods-birth-contemporary-tibetan-art.

9 Clare Harris, "In and Out of Place: Tibetan Artists' Travels in the Contemporary Art World," in *Asia through Art and Anthropology: Cultural Translation across Borders*, ed. Fuyubi Nakamura, Morgan Perkins, and Olivier Krischer (London and New York: Bloomsbury Academic, 2013), 42.

10 Woeser, "Those Giving Voice to 'Scorching Sun of Tibet,'" *High Peaks Pure Earth*, October 4, 2010, highpeakspureearth.com/2010.

11 Stephanie Ho, "Contemporary Tibetan Art on Display in Beijing," *Voice of America*, September 22, 2010, www.voanews.com/content/contemporary-tibetan-art-on-display-in-beijing-103625624/164781.html.

12 Harris, "In and Out of Place," 41.

13 Nortse, artist's statement, Rossi & Rossi website, 2014, accessed June 10, 2016, www.rossirossi.com/contemporary/artists/nortse/ashes.

14 Ben Meulenbeld, *Buddhist Symbolism in Tibetan Thangkas: The Story of Siddhartha and Other Buddhas Interpreted in Modern Nepalese Painting*, trans. Wanda Boeke (Havelte, the Netherlands: Binkey Kok, 2011), 80.

15 Shamsia Hassani interviewed by Emma Graham-Harrison, "Art in the Streets of Kabul," *The Guardian,* February 24, 2012.

Bibliography

Baums, Stefan. "A Gāndhārī Commentary on Early Buddhist Verses: British Library Kharoṣṭhī Fragments 7, 9, 13 and 18." PhD diss., University of Washington, 2009.

———. "Gandhāran Scrolls: Rediscovering an Ancient Manuscript Type." In *Manuscript Cultures*, edited by Jőrg Quenzer, Dmitry Bondarev, and Jan-Ulrich Sobisch, 183–226. De Gruyter.

Beckett, Gulbahar H., and Gerard A. Postiglione. "China's Language Policy for Indigenous and Minority Education." Chap. 1 in *China's Assimilationist Language Policy: The Impact on Indigenous/Minority Literacy and Social Harmony*, edited by Gulbahar H. Beckett and Gerard A. Postiglione. Abingdon, UK, and New York: Routledge, 2012.

Blair, Sheila. *Islamic Calligraphy*. Edinburgh: Edinburgh University Press, 2006.

Boudonnat, Louise, and Harumi Kushizaki. *Traces of the Brush: The Art of Japanese Calligraphy*. San Francisco: Chronicle Books, 2003.

Brac de la Perrière, Éloïse. "Manuscripts in Bihari Calligraphy: Preliminary Remarks on a Little-Known Corpus." *Muqarnas* 33 (2016).

Bryson, Norman. "The Gaze in the Expanded Field." In *Vision and Visuality*, edited by Hall Foster, 88–114. Seattle: Bay Press, 1988.

Chartier, Roger. *Forms and Meanings: Texts, Performance, and Audiences from Codex to Computer*. Philadelphia: University of Pennsylvania Press, 1995.

Dānasāgara of Ballālasena. Edited by Bhabatosh Bhattacharya. Calcutta (Kolkata): Asiatic Society, 1956.

Derman, M. Uğur. *Letters in Gold: Ottoman Calligraphy from the Sakip Sabanci Collection, Istanbul*. New York: Metropolitan Museum of Art, 1998. Exhibition catalogue.

Derrida, Jacques. *Of Grammatology*, translated by Gayatri Chakravorty Spivak. Baltimore: Johns Hopkins University Press, 1997.

Drucker, Johanna. *The Visible Word: Experimental Typography and Modern Art, 1909–1923*. Chicago: University of Chicago Press, 1994.

Ernst, Carl W. "The Spirit of Islamic Calligraphy: Bābā Shāh Iṣfahānī's Ādāb al-mashq." *Journal of the American Oriental Society* 112, no. 2 (April–June 1992): 279–86.

Ettinghausen, Richard. "Kufesque in Byzantine Greece, the Latin West and the Muslim World." In *Islamic Art and Archeology: Collected Papers*, by Richard Ettinghausen, 752–71. Prepared and edited by Myriam Rosen-Ayalon. Berlin: Gebr. Mann Verlag, 1984.

Falk, Harry. *Schrift im alten Indien: ein Forschungsbericht mit Anmerkungen*, ScriptOralia, no. 56 (Tübingen: Gunter Narr Verlag, 1993).

Flint Sato, Christine. "Tsubasa Kimura." *Letter Arts Review* 23, no. 3 (Summer 2009).

Gallop, Annabel Teh. "Islamic Manuscript Art of Southeast Asia." In *Crescent Moon: Islamic Art and Civilisation in Southeast Asia*. Also published as *Bulan Sabit: Seni dan Peradaban Islam di Asia Tenggara*. Edited by James Bennett, 158–83. Adelaide: Art Gallery of South Australia; Canberra, National Gallery of Australia, 2005. Exhibition catalogue.

Gell, Alfred. *Art and Agency: An Anthropological Theory*. Oxford: Oxford University Press / Clarendon Press, 1998.

George, Alain. *The Rise of Islamic Calligraphy*. London: Saqi Books, 2010.

Gu, Wenda. "face the new millennium: the divine comedy of our times—a thesis on the *united nations* art project and its time and environment." In *Wenda Gu: Art from Middle Kingdom to Biological Millennium*, edited by Mark H.C. Bessire, 36–37. Cambridge, MA: MIT Press, 2003.

Habermas, Jürgen. *The Structural Transformation of the Public Sphere: An Inquiry into a Category of Bourgeois Society*, translated by Thomas Burger with Frederick Lawrence (Cambridge, MA: MIT Press, 1989), originally published as *Strukturwandel der Öffentlichkeit* (Darmstadt and Neuwied: Hermann Luchterhand Verlag, 1962).

Hariu, Ichirō. "Sengo Nihon no zen'eisho: Kaiga tono mitsuduki jidai wo koete" [Avant-garde calligraphy in postwar Japan: Beyond the honeymoon period with paintings], in O Bijutsukan (O Art Museum), *Sho to kaiga no atsuki jidai*, 1945–1969 [Calligraphy and painting, the passionate age: 1945–1969]. Tokyo: O Bijutsukan [O Art Museum], 1992, 2–5.

Harris, Clare. "In and Out of Place: Tibetan Artists' Travels in the Contemporary Art World." Chap. 2 in *Asia through Art and Anthropology: Cultural Translation across Borders*, edited by Fuyubi Nakamura, Morgan Perkins, and Olivier Krischer. London and New York: Bloomsbury Academic, 2013.

Harrist, Robert E., Jr., and Wen C. Fong. *The Embodied Image: Chinese Calligraphy from the John B. Elliott Collection*. Princeton, NJ: Art Museum, Princeton University, with Harry N. Abrams, 1999.

Hearn, Maxwell K. "Past as Present in Contemporary Chinese Art." In *Ink Art: Past as Present in Contemporary Chinese Art*. New York: Metropolitan Museum of Art, 2013.

Ho, Stephanie. "Contemporary Tibetan Art on Display in Beijing." *Voice of America*, September 22, 2010, www.voanews.com/content/contemporary-tibetan-art-on-display-in-beijing-103625624/164781.html.

Ho, Wai-kam. "The Literary Concepts of 'Picture-Like' and 'Picture-Idea' in the Relationship between Poetry and Painting." In *Words and Images: Chinese Poetry, Calligraphy, and Painting*, edited by Alfreda Murck and Wen C. Fong. Princeton, NJ: Princeton University Press, with New York: Metropolitan Museum of Art, 1991.

Holmberg, Ryan. "The Pseudography of Hidai Nankoku." In *Yale University Art Gallery Bulletin* 2008*: Recent Acquisitions*, 111–18. New Haven, CT: Yale University, 2008.

Ingold, Tim. "Notes Toward an Anthropology of the Line." *Dwelling* no. 2 (2003).

Ishikawa, Kyūyō. *Kindai shoshi* 近代書史 [The history of modern Japanese calligraphy]. Nagoya: University of Nagoya Press, 2009.

Kao, Yu-kung. "Chinese Lyric Aesthetics." In *Words and Images: Chinese Poetry, Calligraphy, and Painting*, edited by Alfreda Murck and Wen C. Fong. New York: Metropolitan Museum of Art, with Princeton, NJ: Princeton University Press, 1991.

Kasashima, Tadayuki. *Nihon bijutsuni okeru "sho" no zōkeishi* (The history of modelling theory of calligraphy in Japanese art [sic]). Tokyo: Kasama shoin, 2013.

Katre, S.M. *Introduction to Indian Textual Criticism*. Bombay: Karnatak, 1941.

Kāvyamīmāṃsā of Rājaśekhara. Edited by C.D. Dalal and R.A. Shastry. 3rd ed. Baroda [Vadodara]: Oriental Institute, 1934.

Keane, Webb. "Signs Are Not the Garb of Meaning: On the Social Analysis of Material Things." In *Materiality*, edited by Daniel Miller. Durham, NC: Duke University Press, 2005.

Liang, Jinman. "Shufa bu bieyu fofa" [Calligraphy is not unlike dharma]. *Rensheng Zazhi* [Humanity], no. 364 (December 2013).

Lin, Ziqing. *Hongyi dashi xinpu* [New chronicle of Hongyi Dashi's life]. Taipei: Dongda Tushu Gongsi, 1993.

Lippit, Yukio. "teamLab: Past, Present, and Future." teamLab website, accessed June 19, 2016, exhibition.team-lab.net/siliconvalley/review.

Losty, Jeremiah P. *The Art of the Book in India*. London: British Library, 1982.

Mahābhārata (Critical Edition). Edited by Vishnu S. Sukthankar et al. 19 vols. Poona [Pune]: Bhandarkar Oriental Research Institute, 1927–66.

McLuhan, Marshall. *Understanding Media: The Extensions of Man*. London: Routledge and K. Paul, 1964.

Mersmann, Birgit. "(Ideo-)Logical Alliances between Image and Script: Calligraphic Reconfigurations in Contemporary Chinese Art." In *Elective Affinities: Testing Word and Image Relationships*, edited by Catriona Macleod, Véronique Plesch, and Charlotte Schoell-Glass, 387–99. Word and Image Interactions, vol. 6. Amsterdam: Editions Rodopi, 2009.

Meulenbeld, Ben. *Buddhist Symbolism in Tibetan Thangkas: The Story of Siddhartha and Other Buddhas Interpreted in Modern Nepalese Painting*, translated by Wanda Boeke. Havelte, the Netherlands: Binkey Kok, 2011.

Mitchell, W.J.T. *Iconology: Image, Text, Ideology*. Chicago: University of Chicago Press, 1986.

Moustafa, Ahmed, and Stefan Sperl. *The Cosmic Script: Sacred Geometry and the Science of Arabic Penmanship*. 2 vols. London: Thames and Hudson, 2014.

Munroe, Alexandra. "Circle: Modernism and Tradition." In *Japanese Art after 1945: Scream against the Sky*, edited by Alexandra Munroe, 125–47. New York: Harry N. Abrams, 1994.

Nagoya, Akira, ed. *Ketteiban Nihon shodō-shi* 決定版 日本書道史 [The history of Japanese calligraphy: The definitive edition]. Tokyo: Geijutsu Shinbunsha, 2009.

Nakamura, Fuyubi. "Creating New Forms of 'Visualised' Words: An Anthropological Study of Contemporary Japanese Calligraphy." DPhil thesis, University of Oxford, 2006.

———. "Creating or Performing Words?: Observations on Contemporary Japanese Calligraphy." Chap. 4 in *Creativity and Cultural Improvisation*, edited by Tim Ingold and Elizabeth Hallam. Oxford: Berg, 2007.

———, ed. *Ephemeral but Eternal Traces of Words: Traces of Asia*. Canberra: Australian National University, 2010.

———. "Tsubasa Kimura: The Infinite Possibility of Words." In *Ephemeral but Eternal Traces of Words*, edited by Nakamura, 2010, 31–33.

———, ed. *Trazos del tiempo, trazos de palabras: obras de artistas japoneses (Traces of Time, Traces of Words: Artworks by Japanese Artists)*. Buenos Aires: National Museum of Oriental Art, 2011.

———. "A Brief Introduction to Japanese Calligraphy." In *Trazos del tiempo, trazos de palabras*, ed. Nakamura, 2011, 4–6.

———. "Calligraphy in Japan." In *Routledge Encyclopedia of Modernism,* May 9, 2016, www.rem.routledge.com, doi: 10.4324/9781135000356-REM411-1.

Nakamura, Fuyubi, Morgan Perkins, and Olivier Krischer, eds. *Asia through Art and Anthropology: Translation across Borders*. London and New York: Bloomsbury Academic, 2013.

———. "Introduction: Images of Asia across Borders." In *Asia through Art and Anthropology*, edited by Nakamura, Perkins, and Krischer, 1–15.

Nortse. Artist's statement, Rossi & Rossi website, 2014, accessed June 10, 2016, www.rossirossi.com/contemporary/artists/nortse/ashes.

Okabe, Sōfū. "Hidai and His Work" (chapter translated by Audie Bock). In *Hidai Nankoku sakuhinshu*, edited by Hidai Nankoku. Yokohama: Shogaku-in Shuppan-bu [Shogakuin Publications], 1987.

Perumal, P. "The Sanskrit Manuscripts in Tamilnadu." In *Aspects of Manuscript Culture in South India*, edited by Saraju Rath, 157–72. Leiden, the Netherlands: Brill, 2012.

Pollock, Sheldon. "Future Philology? The Fate of a Soft Science in a Hard World." *Critical Inquiry* 35: 931–61.

———. *The Language of the Gods in the World of Men: Sanskrit, Culture, and Power in Premodern India*. Berkeley: University of California Press, 2006.

Quenzer, Jörg B., Dmitry Bondarev, and Jan-Ulrich Sobisch, eds. *Manuscript Cultures: Mapping the Field*, Studies in Manuscript Cultures no. 1. Berlin: De Gruyter, 2014.

Ramaseshan, Sita. "The History of Paper in India up to 1948." *Indian Journal of History of Science* 24 (1989): 103–21.

Rousseau, Jean-Jacques. *Essai sur l'origine des langues*, edited by Charles Porset. 1781; repr., Bordeaux: Ducros, 1970.

Safwat, Nabil F. *The Art of the Pen: Calligraphy of the 14th to 20th Centuries*. Vol. 5 of *The Nasser D. Khalili Collection of Islamic Art*. London: Nour Foundation with Azimuth Editions and Oxford University Press, 1996.

Salomon, Richard. *Indian Epigraphy: A Guide to the Study of Inscriptions in Sanskrit, Prakrit, and the Other Indo-Aryan Languages*. New York: Oxford University Press, 1998.

Schimmel, Annemarie. *Calligraphy and Islamic Culture*. London: I.B. Tauris, 1990.

Seeley, Christopher. *A History of Writing in Japan*. Leiden, the Netherlands: E.J. Brill, 1991.

Sullivan, Michael. *The Three Perfections: Chinese Painting, Poetry and Calligraphy*. London: Thames and Hudson, 1974.

Suwannakudt, Phaptawan. *Phaptawan Suwannakudt: Three Worlds*. Media release for the exhibit. Melbourne: Arc One Gallery, 2009, arc-one.squarespace.com/s/phaptawan-suwannakudt-media-09.pdf.

Takahashi, Toshirō. *Kindai Nihon ni okeru sho eno manazashi* [Looking at calligraphy in modern Japan]. Kyoto: Shibunkaku, 2011.

Tambiah, Stanley. "The Magical Power of Words." *Man* (New Series) 3, no. 2 (1968). 175–208.

Thaker, Jayant P. *Manuscriptology and Textual Criticism*. Vadodara, India: Oriental Institute, 2002.

Trace Foundation. "Drawing the Gods: The Birth of Contemporary Tibetan Art," accessed June 10, 2015, www.trace.org/library/drawing-gods-birth-contemporary-tibetan-art.

von Hinüber, Oskar. *Der Beginn der Schrift und frühe Schriftlichkeit in Indien*, Abhandlungen der Geistes- und Sozialwissenschaftlichen Klasse (1989), no. 11. Mainz: Akademie der Wissenschaften und der Literatur / Stuttgart: Franz Steiner Verlag, 1990.

Woeser. "Those Giving Voice to 'Scorching Sun of Tibet.'" *High Peaks Pure Earth*, October 4, 2010, highpeakspureearth.com/2010.

World Checklist of Selected Plant Families. Royal Botanic Gardens, Kew, accessed June 13, 2016, apps.kew.org/wcsp.

Wujastyk, Dominik. "Indian Manuscripts." In *Manuscript Cultures*, edited by Quenzer, Bondarev, and Sobisch, 159–82.

Xu, Bing. "An Artist's View." In *Persistence/Transformation: Text as Image in the Art of Xu Bing*, edited by Dora C.Y. Ching and Jerome Silbergeld. Princeton, NJ: P.Y. and Kinmay W. Tang Center for East Asian Art, with Princeton University Press, 2006.

Yen, Yuehping. "Between Text and Image: The Ambiguity of Chinese Written Characters." *Glimpse | the art + science of seeing* 2, no. 1 (Spring 2009): 11–15.

———. *Calligraphy and Power in Contemporary Chinese Societies*. Abingdon, UK, and New York: RoutledgeCurzon, 2005.

Zakariya, Mohamed. *Music for the Eyes: An Introduction to Islamic and Ottoman Calligraphy*. Los Angeles: Los Angeles County Museum of Art, 1998. Pamphlet published in conjunction with the exhibition *Letters in Gold*.

Acknowledgements

THIS BOOK AND THE *Traces of Words* exhibition are the results of the commitment, enthusiasm, and generosity of many people. Most especially, I would like to thank the artists—Shamsia Hassani, Kimura Tsubasa, Nortse, Phaptawan Suwannakudt, teamLab, and Yugami Hisao—for their passion and their trust in me to make these endeavours possible.

I am greatly indebted to the Andrew W. Mellon Foundation for their generous financial support of the exhibition and publication. I also acknowledge the Audrey Hawthorn Fund for Publications in Museum Anthropology at the Museum of Anthropology at UBC for its financial contribution. I gratefully acknowledge the artists and institutions for granting permission to use the images to make a fully illustrated book possible.

My deepest thanks to the contributors—Alain George, April Liu, Adheesh Sathaye, and Yuehping Yen—for their insightful essays, which explore the significance of written cultures in Asia. The following UBC colleagues generously offered their expertise by assisting me with researching the museum and library collections for this book: Lisa Cooper, Josephine Chiu-Duke, Yanlong Guo, Tom Hunter, Bruce Rusk, Yangyue Crystal Yin, and the Asian Library staff. The assistance from Pelma Dekyi, Behrang Nabavi Nejad, and Tsering Shakya to proofread some Asian texts was much appreciated. Thanks also go to Hana Kim, director of the Cheng Yu Tung East Asian Library at the University of Toronto and former head of the Asian Library at UBC, and Filiz Çakir Phillip and the staff at the Aga Khan Museum in Toronto.

The exhibition would not have been possible without the dedication of MOA's exhibition team and the support of all MOA staff members and volunteers. I especially thank Kyla Bailey, Skooker Broome, Teija Dedi, Gerald Lawson, April Liu, and Anna Pappalardo. A special note of thanks goes to MOA director Anthony Shelton for supporting this project and for his advice.

Finally, I wish to express my gratitude to the Figure 1 Publishing team, especially Chris Labonté, Natalie Olsen, Lara Smith, Jessica Sullivan, and Grace Yaginuma, for their support and patience in seeing this volume through to press.

Fuyubi Nakamura

Notes on Contributors

Fuyubi Nakamura is a sociocultural anthropologist. She joined the Museum of Anthropology (MOA) at the University of British Columbia (UBC) as its curator for Asia in 2014. Her investigation into the production and consumption of Japanese calligraphy has developed over multiple global locations. She has curated exhibitions, including *(In)visible: The Spiritual World of Taiwan through Contemporary Art* (Vancouver, 2015–16). She has taught at the Australian National University, the University of Tokyo, and the University of Oxford (where she obtained her doctorate in 2006). She is an associate member of the Departments of Anthropology and Asian Studies and Centre for Japanese Research at UBC. Her publications include *Asia through Art and Anthropology: Cultural Translation Across Borders* (Bloomsbury Academic, 2013).

Alain George is a senior lecturer in the History of Art at the University of Edinburgh, and specializes in the arts of the Islamic world. He studied at the University of Oxford, where he completed his DPhil in 2006. He has published extensively on early Qur'anic calligraphy, Arabic illustrated manuscripts, and Umayyad art. In 2010, he was awarded a Philip Leverhulme Prize for his research. His publications include *The Rise of Islamic Calligraphy* (Saqi Books, 2010).

April Liu received a PhD in Chinese art history from UBC in 2012, and joined the Museum of Anthropology at UBC as its Mellon Emerging Curatorial Postdoctoral Fellow (Asia) in 2015. Her doctoral project on Chinese print culture began with her research of MOA's collection of Chinese woodblock prints (*nianhua*), where she explored concepts of ritual agency, lineage identity, and symbolic capital. Her research interests include Chinese print culture, Cantonese opera, critical heritage studies, and contemporary art. She worked as an instructor in the Critical and Cultural Studies Department at the Emily Carr University of Art and Design (2011–15), and has published essays on Chinese art.

Adheesh Sathaye is an associate professor of Sanskrit literature and South Asian folklore in the Department of Asian Studies at UBC. He obtained his doctorate from the University of California, Berkeley, in 2005. He is the author of *Crossing the Lines of Caste: Viśvāmitra and the Construction of Brahmin Power in Hindu Mythology* (Oxford University Press, 2015). In his current research on Sanskrit narrative literature, he employs digital approaches to the textual and cultural history of the *Vetāla-pañcaviṃśati*, a popular medieval collection of Sanskrit riddle-tales. Broader research interests include Sanskrit theatre and aesthetics, mythological literature, and theories of textual production, performance, and folkloristics.

Yuehping Yen is a social anthropologist with a doctorate from the London School of Economics (2000). Her research interests include Chinese calligraphy; embodiment and art; Chinese contemporary art; and artistic practice as part of Buddhist practice. She is a freelance translator, a lifestyle columnist, and an art researcher and art-market analyst, advising collectors on art acquisition. She has managed a non-profit exhibition space in central London, and her current curatorial projects include an exhibition of a Chan/Zen master's calligraphic works rendered as a contemporary art event incorporating sound and video installations. Her published works include *Calligraphy and Power in Contemporary Chinese Society* (RoutledgeCurzon, 2005).

The contributors to the Aga Khan Museum item descriptions were the curator Filiz Çakir Phillip and the staff at the Aga Khan Museum in Toronto.

Contributors to the section on the MOA Asian Collections were Fuyubi Nakamura, April Liu and Yanlong Guo (N1.207); with assistance from the chapter authors Alain George, Adheesh Sathaye and Yuehping Yen; Tom Hunter (812/7, B557, 2902/23, 2569/15), Bruce Rusk (N1.572, N1.246, N1.266, N1.553, N1.554, N1.207, 2636/2, 2636/3) and Josephine Chiu-Duke (N1.246) of the Department of Asian Studies at UBC; and from Lisa Cooper of the Department of Classical, Near Eastern, and Religious Studies at UBC (M4.29).

Contributors to the section on the UBC Library Collections were Hana Kim, director of the Cheng Yu Tung East Asian Library at the University of Toronto, and former head of the Asian Library at UBC; the UBC Asian Library staff; Yangyue Crystal Yin, Fuyubi Nakamura and April Liu, with assistance from members of the Department of Asian Studies at UBC.

Credits

© The Aga Khan Museum: pages 48–51
© The British Library Board and Stefan Baums: page 55
Jessica Bushey: pages 14, 117
© eL Seed: page 47
Gu Wenda Studio: page 71
Shamsia Hassani: pages 10, 77, 87–93
Kimura Tsubasa: page 35
Kyla Bailey: pages vi, 2–4, 6, 7, 9, 13, 18, 30, 37, 41, 44, 56, 64, 109–11, 114–15, 118–31, 134–46, 148–49
Fuyubi Nakamura: front cover, pages 34, 99–101
Nortse: page 74
Rossi and Rossi: pages 95–97
Kryzsztof Osinski: pages x, 8, 83, 85
Song Dong: page 72
Derek Tan: pages 38, 43
© teamLab and Pace Gallery: pages 103–7
© Tenrai Shoin: page 31
Wellcome Library, London: pages 52, 57, 58–59, 60
Xu Bing Studio: pages 66, 68, 69
Yuehping Yen: pages 17, 21 (illustration)
Yugami Hisao: pages 26, 33